LEAD LIKE AN EDITOR

Praise for LEAD LIKE AN EDITOR

EDITOR'S PICK "An energetic, actionable leadership playbook. ... Maze's enthusiasm is persuasive and infectious. His advice will motivate anyone eager to grow professionally and provide them with tools to make a meaningful impact."
—**BOOKLIFE BY** *PUBLISHERS WEEKLY* **(Editor's Pick)**

"An intriguing, genre-jumping look at the basics of management. ... The book's main strength is Maze's upbeat, friendly presence on the page. He displays all the savvy of a magazine veteran, but none of the off-putting cynicism, which will make his advice more accessible to new entrepreneurs."
—*KIRKUS REVIEWS*

"*Lead Like an Editor* approaches leadership from your blind spot. It's the perspective you didn't know you needed. If you want an innovative and engaging lesson in leadership, you'll find it in this book."
—**DONALD MILLER**, bestselling author of *Building a StoryBrand 2.0*

"A masterful blend of storytelling and leadership advice, this book offers a road map to creating a business that not only succeeds but inspires."
—**JASON FEIFER**, editor in chief of *Entrepreneur* and author of *Build for Tomorrow*

"Maze's advice about curiosity and listening are integral to excelling in any career. His guidance is especially helpful to anyone trying to create better content and more authentic messaging, from startups to international brands."
—**SARAH Z. WEXLER**, founder of Flamingo Communications and a former editorial director at Nike

"Maze captures the essence of journalistic curiosity and integrity, and their application across almost every field of work imaginable. He keeps the reader's focus on what's important while guiding them effortlessly ... with writing that is engaging, concise, and even humorous."
—**CHRISTOPHER HARTMAN**, executive director of the Fairness Campaign

LEAD LIKE AN EDITOR

Hire Passionate Teams, Tell Stories That Inspire, and Build Brands People Love

VICTOR MAZE

BE AMAZED MEDIA

A DIVISION OF BE AMAZED GROUP, INC.

This book is dedicated to all the brilliant editors of the world, who bring order to chaos, shape good ideas into great ones, and leave every project they touch better than it was before.

Download your free workbook!

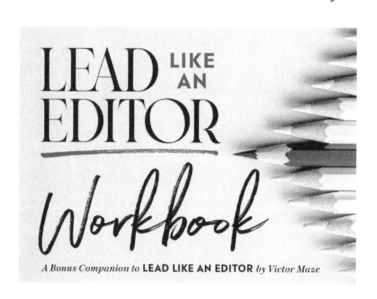

A Bonus Companion to **LEAD LIKE AN EDITOR** by *Victor Maze*

To download the 10 templates mentioned in this book for **FREE,** scan this code or visit **LeadLikeAnEditor.com**

CONTENTS

MY
—
Internal
Focus

STAMP
—
External
Focus

The Editor's Edge

n today's noisy marketplace, it is difficult to make your business stand out from the crowd. Consumers are bombarded countless times a day with choices about how to spend their money and time. Thanks to modern technology, advertisements and sales pitches come flying at us from every direction; oversized billboards, pinging emails and texts, slick TV commercials, and flashing web videos all compete for our constant attention.

It isn't enough to offer a quality product and rely on its merits to sell itself to the public. Today, all businesses, from small mom-and-pop operations to major corporations, must learn to tell stories and build relationships with their customers. Branding is no longer just about having a sharp logo or witty tagline; people want to support brands that make them feel good about themselves and the world. Whether that means choosing a product because it makes them look cool or because the company that produces it gives back to a particular charity, today's consumers use their dollars to make statements about themselves and their values.

As a business leader, this is a lot to live up to. And it doesn't stop there. Customers are not the only people you need to win over with compelling—but authentic!—marketing messages and a rock-solid brand story. Potential new hires must·be wooed as well, as millennial and Gen Z workers seek out employers who don't just look good on paper but rather do good in the world. For more than two decades, the communications firm Edelman has surveyed thousands of workers worldwide to gauge how much they trust the government, media, business, and nonprofit organizations. According to Edelman's yearly "Trust Barometer" report, distrust of the media and the government in recent years has made many people turn to their workplaces for a greater sense of stability and pride.[1] Collecting a paycheck is no longer the only goal; today, employees want to be both proud of where they work and "partners in change" with their employers—making money, of course, but also improving society along the way.[2]

At times, this level of pressure can feel overwhelming. But what if I told you there is a group of people who have been breaking through the noise to have their messages heard for decades? And that, taking it a step further, these marketing geniuses have created brands that people not only respect and trust but also develop relationships with? And finally, that despite long hours and low starting salaries, top-notch employees clamor to work there, often incorporating the brands' messages into their own lives and sense of identity?

If you think these visionaries sound like leadership unicorns who couldn't possibly exist in the real world, think again. They are real, alive, and walking among us. They are magazine editors.

WAIT A SECOND—AREN'T MAGAZINES DEAD?

When I first started talking about the idea for this book, some people wondered what business lessons they could possibly learn from the world of magazine editors. I heard the same question time and again: "But aren't magazines dead?"

I'll admit it: In the past decade, many of the world's most well-known magazine brands have stopped producing or reduced the frequency of their print editions. But others, including Hearst's luxury interior design magazine VERANDA, where I currently work, are thriving. In 2022, we expanded in both page count and trim size, making the magazine a half-inch wider to better showcase the beautiful photography that has become our hallmark, while also hiring new editors and designers to support this transition. And it paid off: The first issue in this new format had 68 percent more ads than the same issue the previous year. As I write this introduction, the issue currently on newsstands topped last year's version in ad sales by almost 10 percent, and saw several former advertisers come back after not buying print ads for months or years. By producing a larger magazine with glossy pages and thick paper stock that shows the elegant homes we feature in the most luxurious way, we are sending a message to the world that print isn't dead; rather, print is premium.

But even as we celebrate the enduring success of our print product, we also realize that it can't be our only source of earnings. In the last few years, we have significantly beefed up our website, while also publishing coffee-table books, launching a membership program, and hosting events for design enthusiasts. Although new income streams have helped bolster luxury publications like VERANDA, this kind of diversification has proven even more crucial for general interest magazines. While many legacy brands that focused solely on print have seen their demise, others that sought new sources of revenue continue to be profitable.

Let's look at *Good Housekeeping,* another Hearst brand that is much larger than VERANDA but has faced similar challenges in recent years. Despite the industry-wide contraction of print, its magazine remains one of the nation's largest, serving 13 million readers—but subscriptions and print advertising are definitely *not* its only source of income.[3] This venerable print brand is now rocking the digital landscape as well, building on a history of innovation that spans more than a century. Google almost any topic related to the home, and a *Good Housekeeping* article will be among the first results listed, driving significant digital advertising revenue.

At their hearts, magazines are brands that people trust, and few are as trusted as *Good Housekeeping.* As the proliferation of manufactured goods began to grow following the American Industrial Revolution, *Good Housekeeping* was one of the first media brands to realize that consumers would need a source they could trust to tell them which products were worth the hype. Only products that had passed a formal review and testing would earn the coveted Good Housekeeping Seal of Approval, which was introduced in 1909.[4]

Consumers quickly learned that the Seal stood for quality, and 125 years after it was founded, the Good Housekeeping Institute continues to employ scientists, editors, and other experts to test more than 15,000 items each year, making it a go-to source for discovering the best cleaning products, linens, appliances, and so much more.[5] The brand has even expanded the concept of the Seal by introducing several other seals and emblems, designating the best environmentally sound "green" products, as well as issuing awards to the top offerings in more than a dozen different categories, including fitness, beauty, travel, and toys.[6]

Finally, like many thriving magazine brands, *Good Housekeeping* is no longer only in the business of selling content and advertising. Today, their offerings include membership programs, books, in-person events and expos, and branded products ranging from cookware and bakeware to gadgets and small electronics. On GoodHousekeeping.com, they also link to products from a number of trusted partners, reasoning that if consumers are coming to their website for information *about* the best products, they might as well stay there to shop. In 2022, GoodHousekeeping.com was an e-commerce powerhouse, selling more than $407 million worth of products, making it the top-performing e-commerce site at Hearst.[7]

So are *all* magazines dead or just the ones who refused to adapt? It's easy to see why a multi-pronged media brand like *Good Housekeeping* or VERANDA might answer that question by borrowing a line often attributed to Mark Twain: "The report of my death has been grossly exaggerated."[8]

EDITORS ARE ALIVE—AND THRIVING

Whether or not you believe (as I do) that media brands originally founded as magazines will continue to play an influential role in society, there is one thing everyone can agree upon: The need for well-curated information and the overall feeling of trust that readers find in these publications is *not* dead, anymore than people's need for music died when we made the move from records to tapes to CDs, and, eventually, to digital downloads and then streaming services. More important than the physical magazines, it is the talented *people* behind them that I will focus on in this book. And what I am here to tell you is this: Their current and former editors are still very much alive—and flourishing.

But first, they were battered. Broadly speaking, declines in print advertising began during the Great Recession, which started at the end of 2007—the same year that Apple launched the iPhone. These two events and their aftermath created a double whammy for magazine publishing, as layoffs became more frequent and continued for the next decade and beyond.

But all those unemployed editors had to go somewhere. Instead of heading back into a media bubble that had fewer jobs to offer, many of them took their skills and infiltrated the halls of corporate America, finding new homes in the content and marketing departments of companies ranging from Netflix to Nike. Others went a different route, deciding they'd had enough of working for big corporations that could easily discard them when times got tough. Instead, these budding entrepreneurs hung shingles as brand consultants, travel advisors, and interior designers, among countless other professions.

One such editor, Chandra Turner, pivoted from executive-level positions at brands like *Parents, Cosmopolitan,* and Scholastic to a new role as a full-time career coach and talent recruiter through her agency, The Talent Fairy.

Serving as a literal fairy godmother to thousands of her peers who unexpectedly found themselves in career limbo, Chandra has stepped confidently into a successful second act, helping former magazine editors find new careers by connecting them with companies that are desperate for the skills these journalists bring to the table.

Along the way, she has also collected data about how these transitions have gone. According to The Talent Fairy's "2024 Editorial Hiring Report," the vast majority of editors who pivoted to non-media roles report being happy in their new jobs; more importantly, these editors find that the demand for their skills in non-media industries—ranging from healthcare to tech to entertainment to banking—will only continue to grow. "Each passing year gives non-media companies more understanding of how they can use all of us talented editors and writers the traditional media industry created but can no longer support," writes one of the survey's respondents.[9]

Many of these now-thriving former editors thought their careers were over when they were laid off or when the magazines they worked for shuttered. As trained journalists, they asked themselves what they would do if they could no longer write and edit publications. But the need for their skills never went away. If anything, the demand has only increased, as all brands—from shiny tech start-ups to centuries-old banking institutions—seek new and authentic ways to connect with consumers. It's not an easy thing to do, but for editors, it comes naturally. And with some real-life examples and practical advice, you can also learn how to develop these skills and put them to work in your own business.

WHY ME?

At this point, you might be wondering what makes me an expert on all of these things, so it may help if I explain a bit about my background, starting with my childhood. Like millions of American children, I would wait eagerly for the mail to arrive all month, knowing that my subscription to *Highlights* could appear any day. It's easy to guess how the publication got its title; finding that magazine in the mailbox was literally the highlight of my month. Among all the junk mail, bills, and other boring grown-up correspondence, there was finally a piece of mail with my name on it. What a treat!

As I pored over the puzzles, the comics, and the stories—which were stealthily educational while also entertaining—I felt as though each section was created just for me. Even if I didn't realize it at the time, I was learning an early lesson: People have a special relationship with magazines that is different from the relationships they have with most other types of brands. Although I thought that *Highlights* was my own little treat, each month it was inspiring two million other kids around the country to stake out their mailboxes as well (and has been doing so since 1946).[10]

My love for the printed word continued into high school, where I was co-editor of the monthly student newspaper, and into college, where I was a columnist at my university's award-winning daily. After graduating with two journalism degrees, including a master's degree from Northwestern University's Medill School of Journalism, I moved to New York City and dove headfirst into the world of publishing.

Although I loved writing, over the course of my education, I had become even more interested in visual storytelling and how information was packaged, particularly in magazine layouts. For the next decade-plus, I worked as an art director at a number of publications, starting in New York and moving across the map to California, Florida, Alabama, and even Sweden to take on new roles. Along the way, I continued to keep my writing skills sharp, contributing articles to many of the publications I worked for, while also collaborating with my editor colleagues on photo captions, article headlines, and cover lines (the blurbs that appear on the cover of a magazine).

Throughout my career, I have worked on staff at seven magazines (shown above) and have contributed to a dozen more.

In 2012, I landed my dream job as design director of *Coastal Living*, and for the next three years, I ran the art department at this national publication, owned by Time Inc. (Following two acquisitions, the brand is now owned by Dotdash Meredith.) Back then, Time Inc. was one of the largest magazine publishers in the world with a roster of iconic brands that included *Sports Illustrated*, *People*, *InStyle*, *Fortune*, and *Real Simple*—not to mention *Time* magazine, for which the company was named. During this period, I had a front-row seat to the evolution of an industry, as Time Inc. and its competitors faced some of the most difficult challenges print media had ever seen.

Though I loved my job, I also had an entrepreneurial itch and wondered what it would be like to work for myself. Inspired by friends and former coworkers who had made similar leaps, I left *Coastal Living* at the end of 2015 to start my own branding and consulting business, and went on to work with major corporations in the travel and retail industries, including Marriott, buybuy BABY, and Carnival Corporation (the giant parent company of Carnival, Princess, Holland America, Cunard, and several other cruise lines).

Having spent my entire career working in a medium that was very specific, I expected a bit of a learning curve as I applied my experience to other industries. But surprisingly, I found the opposite to be true. What I realized very quickly was that, although in my mind I had spent my career designing magazines, what I had *actually* been doing was creating brands that inspired loyalty in their consumers, while managing teams of people with diverse talents and personalities.

When it came to the nuts and bolts of running a business, I also had the skills to succeed. I knew how to set (and meet) deadlines, how to speak to my target customer in a voice that resonated, how to write copy that sells, and how to package it all in an appealing way. And when I didn't know how to do something, my journalism training kicked in, and I reached out to find an expert who could explain it to me—just as I had for every story I'd ever reported.

Twelve months later, my business was booming, and I was making more money than I had during my final year at Time Inc. But it wasn't just me who was thriving. Via social media, I watched while other editors and art directors started their second acts as leaders in new industries or as first-time entrepreneurs, meeting similar success. It was then that I began to realize that we editors had a secret sauce that could be used to shape—and launch—all sorts of businesses. Just because the magazine world was changing didn't mean that our careers were over or that our knowledge was useless. In fact, when it comes to storytelling and connecting with an audience in a crowded marketplace, I would argue that our skills may be more in demand now than ever.

IS THIS BOOK FOR YOU?

When I started writing this book, a friend suggested I tailor it specifically to new entrepreneurs; their needs, he reasoned, are much different than those of someone working within a large corporation. Though I see his point to some extent, I have to disagree. These days, the lines are much more blurry. I've seen one- and two-person start-ups compete with major companies, maximizing their nimbleness and ability to move quickly in a way that their mammoth competitors cannot.

On the flip side, many large corporations are trying to shake off the stifling bureaucracy of the "glory days," when it took weeks or months to make even the tiniest changes. Instead, these businesses are encouraging *all* employees (and especially leaders) to adopt an entrepreneurial mindset to create lucrative new revenue streams. The best ideas for new products or processes often come not from the C-suite but rather from the people on the ground doing the day-to-day work of running the business.

The trajectory of people's careers over the course of a lifetime has also changed. While we used to either run our own businesses or pledge our lives to one company for 40 years, today, many workers—including myself and several of my own friends—have gone back and forth from running solopreneur or freelance consulting businesses to holding jobs at major corporations. Many of the lessons I recount in this book were learned while I was working at some of the world's largest publishers; I then applied these tips to my own branding and design studio that I founded in 2015.

At that point, I honestly thought that I would never work for anyone else again, but life had some twists I didn't expect. At the end of 2018, I returned to magazine publishing, accepting an offer to oversee creative direction at Hearst's luxury interior design brand VERANDA. Today, I apply the same lessons through a different lens, while also learning some new ones—and continuing to run my own company on the side.

I have written this book for those just starting their own businesses with nothing more than an idea and a dream; for dutiful employees who have stepped into management roles and find themselves leading people and projects for the first time; and for leaders who have been running a business for years but are facing new challenges, making it a perfect time to shake things up and view their work with a fresh perspective.

While many of the stories I'll share focus on sales, marketing, branding, and content creation, I would argue that leaders in almost any area could benefit from these lessons. A human resources director, for example, might find a lesson in marketing that could improve the way that company culture is communicated to potential new hires. And for business owners and chief executives, who need to know about *everything* that goes into creating, branding, and selling their products, I hope you will find value in all of the techniques I share.

No matter where you fall in this spectrum, learning to lead like an editor can be an indispensable tool to propel your business, your team, and your career to the next level. But how?

PUTTING YOUR STAMP ON IT

In the world of publishing, whenever a new editor in chief is hired to run an existing magazine, other folks in the industry wait to see just how this person will put their stamp on the brand. Will there be a shift in the topics covered? Will this editor also bring on a new creative team, who will make their own mark on the visual direction? Such changes are not surprising but rather expected, as these superstar editors in chief are often hired *because* they have a vision for how the brand could evolve.

Similarly, when they are seeking out good writers, editors often look for someone who can put their own unique stamp on a story. Anyone with basic journalism training can report the facts, but the most highly sought-after writers also bring a distinct perspective and one-of-a-kind voice to their articles.

In the same way, don't be afraid to put your own spin on the process of starting or running a business. If you are stepping into a new role as a corporate leader, you don't need to model the same leadership style as the person who had that job before you, or the same style as the bosses you've had before, or even the same style as the boss you will have in your new role.

Putting your own stamp on your career is even more important as an entrepreneur. While you certainly can look to competitors for inspiration, be cautious of creating a business structure based solely on what others are doing, especially if it doesn't feel right in your gut. Conventional wisdom suggests bigger is better, but perhaps starting small and staying small feels right to you. You can use the work of others as a guide, but don't be afraid to mold the details to fit your vision for your company—and your life.

The MY STAMP Method

In this book, I will explain how you can take a page from the world of magazines (pun intended!) by focusing on seven pillars that will elevate your leadership skills and business acumen, while letting you put your own stamp on the results. We editors love an easy-to-remember acronym, so I call this process the **MY STAMP Method.**

Internally, you will focus on **MY** and learn to:

- Embody the editor's **Mindset**, including the five key traits all good editors possess.

- Develop **Yourself** as a leader who models integrity, inspires others, seeks out the truth in any situation, and makes tough decisions with ease.

Externally, you will focus on **STAMP** and learn to:

- Architect a vision- and mission-driven **Structure** that is designed to support the demands of your work throughout each day *and* each year.

- Hire and manage a **Team** of passionate people with diverse skill sets, who are excited about the work you do.

- Cultivate an **Audience** of dedicated fans, who have an instant affinity for everything you produce.

- Communicate a **Message** in a voice that resonates, empowering your customers to live better lives.

- Create a **Product** (or service) that offers both style and substance—and is delivered in an efficient, elegant way.

I encourage you to read the book from start to finish for one main reason: Before you dive into shaping a business, a team, or a product, you have to take a moment to reflect on yourself. In many ways, the **Mindset** section is the crux of the book and the basis of thinking like an editor. (Fair warning: This section deals with psychology and the way your thinking impacts your leadership style, making it a tad longer and more research-heavy than the others.)

That said, the book is not necessarily a sequential, step-by-step guide to building a business. I list **Product** as the last section, but obviously, it would be a good idea to have a product or service in mind *before* starting a business or hiring a team. Similarly, the lessons from the first two internally focused sections are great to look back on at *every* stage of planning your business or brand.

If you embrace these concepts and truly work at applying them to your own business, you will see results. To prove what kind of change is possible, I will include stories from my own career, along with thoughts from some of the most respected and seasoned editors out there, many of whom have gone on to apply their training to brilliant second acts. Like any good journalist, I have also sought knowledge from experts outside my industry. This book includes research and principles that I have learned from scientists, other authors, and leaders of both major corporations and scrappy start-ups, illustrating how these concepts can be applied to companies of any size.

ARE YOU READY?

It is easy to go along with the status quo, but true innovation requires looking at things from a new perspective and resolving to take action to make a good business great. I would be willing to bet that at some point you have had a positive interaction—or perhaps even a life-changing revelation—based on something an editor touched, whether that was a magazine, book, movie, online community, or other purpose-driven brand. Remember what that moment felt like, and know that you can create this kind of reaction with your business as well—but only if you discover the potential of learning to lead like an editor.

Editors and reporters and journalists, oh my!

———

In this book, I often use these three terms interchangeably, with the more general term *writer* thrown in as well. Essentially, these are all shorthand for a person who is trained in the principles of journalism: seeking out the truth and then using that information to craft compelling stories, which are written and edited to inform, educate, or entertain a particular audience.

PART ONE

M is for

MINDSET

"Mindset is the foundation on which we build our business, and you can't build a mansion on quicksand."

—Julia Pimsleur, founder and CEO of Million Dollar Women

I am a sucker for self-help books and the promise of reinvention. Personal finance books, weight-loss books, career books, organizing books—over the years, I've bought them all. In the name of personal development, I've dieted like the residents of South Beach, practiced the seven habits of highly effective people, and whispered the secret behind *The Secret* to anyone who would listen.

After decades of repeating affirmations, journaling about setbacks, tossing possessions that didn't spark joy, and even collaging a vision board or two, you know what I've learned? Almost all of these bestselling tomes have one thing in common: At some point, they preach the importance of creating change by starting with the right mindset. Thousands of pages (and dollars) later, that remains my biggest takeaway—and rightfully so. A winning mindset is perhaps the single largest predictor of success in any endeavor.

Developing a winning mindset at work comes from having a passion for what you do and genuine curiosity about your business and how it can continually improve. But developing a winning mindset isn't just a one-time, "set it and forget it" exercise; this quest for knowledge and positive evolution must continue every day, and must also be tempered with an ironclad work ethic and determination to succeed, even in the face of resistance.

But what does mindset mean exactly? The term was popularized by psychologist Carol S. Dweck to describe the underlying beliefs people have about learning and intelligence. (I'll share more about Dweck and her research later in this section.) Essentially, your mindset is a group of beliefs, attitudes, and assumptions that shape your thoughts and behaviors, and ultimately, how you respond to challenges, setbacks, and opportunities.

Studies have shown that mindset not only affects your worldview but can also impact your reality. A commonly cited medical example is the placebo effect, in which patients see positive results if they believe a medicine will help them. Nicole Serena Silver explains this unusual phenomenon in her *Forbes* article "Accessing the Power of Your Mind: Placebo Effect and Mindset." "This is not a fluke occurrence nor is it insignificant in what it means for humanity," she writes. "What happens with the placebo effect is that the brain anticipates an outcome. The mind then communicates to the body the anticipated outcome and prepares the body for healing."[11]

In an article published by Stanford University, psychiatrist and adjunct clinical instructor Jacob Towery notes that regardless of the ailment, "about 30 to 40 percent of people can have significant improvement in their symptoms even when taking a placebo (sugar) pill, if they believe that the pill is going to be helpful." This is the power of positive thinking—but the reverse is also true. Towery goes on to describe "the 'nocebo-effect,' a psychological response based on a person's expectations around side effects. When a physician emphasizes the potential side effects of a medicine, and the patient believes they will develop those symptoms, even if given a sugar pill, these patients can develop the adverse side effects, just based on what their mind expects."[12]

I would argue that these medical examples can be mapped onto other aspects of our lives. If we operate from a place of scarcity, thinking that we are not enough, don't have enough, and that we can't improve our situation, it is easy to stay stuck exactly where we are. But when we operate from a place of abundance, believing that we are capable of growth and improvement, it becomes easier for us to create positive change in our lives. Because you're reading this book, I would venture to guess that you are open to learning new methods to improve your leadership abilities. In this first section, we will learn how looking within yourself *before* making outward changes can be the key to achieving the most long-lasting results.

DEVELOPING THE EDITOR'S MINDSET

While the field of journalism attracts all types of people for different reasons, there are some core principles that go into learning to think like an editor—or at least, a good editor. In the following chapters, you will learn to embody:

- **Optimism** that you are capable of creating positive change—both in your own life and in the lives of others.

- **Curiosity,** tempered with objectivity and critical thinking.

- **Passion** for your subject and your craft.

- **Perseverance** in the face of internal and external challenges.

- **Adaptability** to ever-changing situations.

I believe these five attributes are key to developing a winning editor's mindset; as such, they are the foundation upon which the rest of the book is built. So let's start building!

CHAPTER 1

....

Choose Optimism

s there someone in your life who is relentlessly upbeat and cheerful—the type of person who seems to be endlessly energetic, usually has a smile to give, and almost always sees the glass as half full? Chances are, if you ask this person if they consider themselves to be "happy," the answer will be yes, regardless of what circumstances and challenges they face in life. Research has shown that positive people, even when faced with extreme hardships and losses—such as becoming paraplegic—come back to the same baseline level of happiness over time, often even seeing the silver lining in their tragedies and the opportunities in their challenges.[13]

Meaghan B Murphy, the editor in chief of *Woman's Day,* is one of those people—but that wasn't always the case. In her book *Your Fully Charged Life: A Radically Simple Approach to Having Endless Energy and Filling Every Day with Yay,* Murphy talks about a sulky childhood and angsty teen years during which she looked for the negative in any situation, earning her the nickname "Grumpy." (As a third grader, she even pooh-poohed a family trip to Disney World, citing long lines and hot weather as reasons to stay home.)[14]

Today, Murphy is a bubbly extrovert who hits the gym at 5 a.m. before spending her day exhorting millions of other women to live their best, most fully charged lives at home and at work. She wears bright colors, adopted a lighting bolt as her personal logo, was named Chief Spirit Officer by her town's mayor, and signs her emails with her favorite word: "Yay!"

So, what is her secret?

"Every day, every hour, sometimes moment to moment, you consciously choose to act in a positive way or look for the positive in situations," Murphy explains. "Making that choice then gives you the energy to make more positive and energizing choices, fueling a cycle that keeps your batteries charged."[15]

LEARN TO BE OPTIMISTIC

Humans are animals, and as such we are hard-wired to focus on the negative as a means of survival. Thousands of years of evolution have conditioned us to always have an eye peeled and an ear open so that we can quickly assess potential threats. But in this day and age, where most of us find ourselves in immediate physical danger far less often than our hunting and gathering ancestors, the instinct to look for the negative can easily make us prone to pessimism, hindering our ability to embrace change.

Similarly, prior to the mid-1990s, the field of psychology focused primarily on treating dangers to the human psyche: mental illness, emotional suffering, and trauma. But a shift began in 1996, when Martin E. P. Seligman was elected president of the American Psychological Association, thanks in part to the popularity of his book *Learned Optimism: How to Change Your Mind and Your Life* and the field of research that it spawned.

"At its best, psychology had only told us how to relieve misery, not how to find what is best in life and live it accordingly," Seligman writes. He boldly asserted that focusing only on the negative aspects of psychology was a "half-baked" approach, deciding that the main initiative of his tenure as president of the APA would focus on the unbaked half, which has come to be known as Positive Psychology.[16]

Seligman's research suggests that while some people are born naturally optimistic, this important character trait can also be learned. His conclusions largely focus on learning optimism—and improving our self-esteem along the way—by refining the messages we tell ourselves in the face of adversity. Whether we have had doors slammed in our faces as salespeople, or feel like we've "blown" a diet by indulging in nachos with friends after work, Seligman found that optimists focused more on how different actions or circumstances could change the outcome of these specific situations in the future, while pessimists were prone to sweeping statements that prompted them to eventually give up: "This is too hard," "I am weak," "I will never be good at this," etc.

Changing the messages we tell ourselves can improve not only our ability to bounce back in the face of adversity—both personal and work related—but also our overall happiness in life. "My subsequent research showed repeatedly that optimists do better in school, win more elections, and succeed more at work than pessimists do," Seligman writes. "They even seem to lead longer and healthier lives."[17]

ADOPT A GROWTH MINDSET

Before you can begin the process of choosing to live your life with more optimism, you must first believe that making such a change is possible. It is this belief—that we are all creatures capable of improvement and growth, despite whatever innate characteristics we were born with or circumstances we were born into—that is at the heart of a true mindset shift.

As mentioned in the introduction to this section, the concept of mindset was popularized by psychologist Carol S. Dweck in *Mindset: The New Psychology of Success*.[18] In her book, Dweck posits the idea that all people fall into two overarching mindsets: fixed and growth.

- **Fixed Mindset:** People with a fixed mindset believe that their abilities, intelligence, and qualities are unchangeable or fixed traits. They tend to avoid challenges because they fear failure might reveal their limitations. They might also avoid putting in effort, as they believe that if they were truly talented, things would come naturally. Criticism can be seen as a personal attack on their abilities.

- **Growth Mindset:** People with a growth mindset believe that their abilities and intelligence can be developed and improved over time through effort, learning, and perseverance. They embrace challenges as opportunities to learn and grow. They are more willing to put in the hard work required to improve because they understand that improvement is possible. Criticism is viewed as constructive feedback that can help them get better.

The concept for these mindsets first came about through Dweck's studies of children and how they approached puzzles, but she soon realized that her findings could be applied to how everyone approaches challenges in their lives—leaders included.

Leaders with a fixed mindset can fall victim to "CEO disease," she says.[19] Ruling from a pedestal, they like being the big fish in the pond and the smartest person in the room. Always concerned with their own reputations and egos, they surround themselves with sycophants, reacting warily to those who challenge them with new ideas they can't claim as their own.[20]

Leaders with a growth mindset, on the other hand, tend to lead with humility, seeking information and ideas from all levels of the organization, as they know that workers in the trenches may see day-to-day challenges and opportunities that they cannot. These leaders are willing to face their own failures and those of the company, confident that they can learn and grow from past mistakes. They are constantly trying to improve themselves and their businesses, and are not afraid to surround themselves with smart and resourceful people who can help them do so. In fact, they actually encourage others to step into leadership roles by promoting career development training and mentoring within the organization.

Growth-mindset leaders, Dweck concludes, "start with a belief in human potential and development—both their own and other people's. Instead of using the company as a vehicle for their greatness, they use it as an engine for growth—for themselves, the employees, and the company as a whole."[21]

HOW TO BRING OPTIMISM TO YOUR WORK

While the benefits of optimism are many, embodying an upbeat outlook can still be challenging in your everyday work, especially on days when it seems like everything is going wrong. To create a workplace culture of optimism that extends throughout your whole team and even on to the customers you serve, follow these three steps:

1. Start by embodying optimism yourself: Be a hero, not a victim.
Earlier in the chapter, I asked if you knew anyone in your life who was infectiously optimistic, spreading joy and good vibes wherever they go. These individuals likely have a growth mindset; they see the world as being full of endless possibilities and are excited to go out and achieve what they want, even if there will be challenges along the way.

Now, think about someone you know who exudes a different type of energy. They take a less active role in their own life, believing things happen *to* them and perhaps that they have been given a raw deal by the world or by others. When these people have failures, they are quick to place themselves in the role of the victim. It may feel good briefly, taking the blame off of them and any role that they played in the setback. And it is a surefire way to draw attention and coddling from others. But does it really serve their best interests in the long run?

In his book *Business Made Simple*, author and entrepreneur Donald Miller answers this question with a resounding "No." In fact, he takes it a step further, saying that the easiest way to predict whether someone will become a success is to ask one question: How often do they position themselves as a victim?[22]

We are all born into different circumstances that lead us to starting the game of life with advantages or disadvantages. Sadly, oppression related to race, gender, sexual orientation, socio-economic status, and disabilities exists in our world, and each of these issues—not to mention their inter-sectionality—may make it easy to feel like a victim at times. But when we look at those people in our culture who have achieved the most success and inspired others to do so, they all persisted and grew despite the fact that many started life with the deck stacked against them.

We can all point to examples of these unlikely superachievers, and I have been inspired by several from my own "work family" at Hearst. Oprah Winfrey, the namesake of Hearst brands Oprah Daily and *O, The Oprah Magazine*, has been quite forthcoming about her struggles as a Black woman from Mississippi who spent her early childhood in poverty,[23] while also experiencing molestation.[24] Though Oprah was literally a victim at times, she chose not to remain one in her life. Despite early setbacks, as well as sexism and racism throughout her career, she went on to become a news anchor, talk show host, and eventually a media tycoon with her own pro-duction company, magazine, and TV channel.

Michael Clinton, the former president and publishing director of Hearst Magazines, also achieved great success despite a humble beginning. Though he grew up with loving parents, he experienced a poor childhood, sharing a single bedroom with his five younger siblings. As a child, Michael began to suspect that education may be the key to a brighter future, although he had few role models to light the way; only one relative had finished college, and many had not completed high school either. Still, he worked hard, earning money through babysitting, chores, and a paper route; he went on to pay his way through college and grad school. Starting as a reporter, Michael eventu-ally rose the ranks to become a top magazine executive, while also trying his hand at other roles, including photographer, author, and marathon runner.[25] The only thing he *hasn't* done is play the victim.

"We think about our parents and our upbringing, and we sometimes slip into laying blame in places that may be misguided," he writes in his book *ROAR,* a how-to guide for anyone contemplating a midlife change. "I had an uncle who spent his whole life blaming my grandparents for his lack of direction and focus. Even at an early age, I wondered why he didn't take responsibility for his own life and stop blaming them."[26]

If you think of your life as a movie, does playing the role of the victim sound appealing? As author Donald Miller points out, the victim is essentially a bit part, whose only reason for existence is to make the villain look bad and hero look good. In movies, the victim doesn't grow or change by the end but rather is carted off in an ambulance while the hero who saved them is celebrated. "Victims do not lead the charge into the fight," Miller says. "Victims do not rescue others. Victims do not gain strength and overcome their captor. Only heroes do these things."[27]

As leaders, we must all choose to be the heroes in our stories, even on the days when it is easier to feel like a victim. When hardships befall us, we can take a moment to reset and bandage our wounds, but then we must pick up the pieces and carry on, reminding ourselves that heroes don't quit.

2. Transfer that heroic energy to your team: Lead with optimism and enthusiasm. Aside from the business advantage of having a growth mindset—typically, we want to believe that the reach and profits of our companies can *grow*—there is also a human reason that leaders should be optimistic: It inspires others to do the same.

In 2022, Bob Iger made history by returning to The Walt Disney Company for a second run as CEO, stepping out of retirement at the request of Disney's board of directors to replace Bob Chapek, who was ousted after just a few years in the role. Iger had previously held the position for 15 years (from 2005 to 2020), and for many, it was a joyful homecoming, as thrilled employees gave him a standing ovation at a town hall meeting held the week of his return.[28]

I live in Orlando, home of Walt Disney World, and my husband Craig has worked for the company for more than 20 years; this proximity made me privy to a number of anecdotal discussions that further illustrated what *The New York Times* called an "overjoyed" response to Iger's return by Disney employees.[29] Though some employees welcomed their former CEO back with open arms because they had disagreed with Chapek's decisions, for many, it was a more visceral response: What they had missed the most was Iger's energy and charisma as a leader.

In his 2019 book, *The Ride of a Lifetime*, Iger shares lessons learned from his first 15 years as CEO of Disney, as well as other positions he has held, including chairman of ABC. He starts the book by listing 10 essential principles for good leadership. At the top of the list is optimism, which he defines as "a pragmatic enthusiasm" for what can be accomplished. "Simply put, people are not motivated or energized by pessimists," Iger writes.[30] He goes on to explain:

> Pessimism leads to paranoia, which leads to defensiveness, which leads to risk aversion. Optimism sets a different machine in motion. Especially in difficult moments, the people you lead need to feel confident in your ability to focus on what matters, and not to operate from a place of defensiveness and self-preservation. This isn't about saying things are good when they're not, and it's not about conveying some innate faith that "things will work out." It's about believing you and the people around you can steer toward the best outcome, and not communicating the feeling that all is lost if things don't break your way. The tone you set as a leader has an enormous effect on the people around you. No one wants to follow a pessimist.[31]

In *Business Made Simple*, Miller adds another reason staying optimistic—and passing that energy on to your team—can make the difference between long-term success and failure in business. "By staying relentlessly optimistic, you dramatically increase the chances that at some point you will succeed," he writes. "The more optimistic you are, the more you will be willing to try—and the more you try, the more often you will actually experience success."[32]

3. Finally, pass the positivity on to your customers: Serve your audience with optimism. At this point, you may see the importance of having an optimistic attitude about your own personal growth, as well as the benefits that leading with positivity can have on your team. But there is still one more step that is needed to spread this optimism to all aspects of your business.

Have you ever been to a store where it looks like the staff is brimming with joy, so much so that they are laughing and joking among themselves, while ignoring the customers? You may have even seen employees cackling behind the counter, but then their laughs are silenced and their smiles turn to sour expressions when you approach them to pay or ask a question. I've experienced this on several occasions, and each time it perplexes me. It seems as though these workers are actually enjoying the camaraderie of their jobs but are not bringing that same joy to serving their customers.

For editors, the customer is never an interruption of the work but rather the reason for the work. Although I will dive into how to connect with your audience in Part Five of this book, it all starts with viewing your customer in a positive light and serving them with optimism. In the same way that we must have a growth mindset about ourselves, our work, and our team, that mindset must extend to our customers as well. We must believe that our work can help them improve their lives.

For editors, this is second nature. As Murphy writes in *Your Fully Charged Life*: "At every magazine, with every article, program or project, including this book, my goal has been to connect with and give people the tools to find a spark, improve their health and happiness and feel inspired to live their best lives."[33]

EDITOR'S TIP

How to stay optimistic in times of crisis

There are moments in business and in life when true tragedy strikes, and it becomes hard—if not impossible—to remain optimistic. At these times, *Woman's Day* editor in chief Meaghan B Murphy suggests following a three-step "Triple A" process: Acceptance, Acknowledgment, and Action.

First, practice **Acceptance** by admitting that it's okay *not* to be happy sometimes. People may try to cheer you up immediately, but you have permission to tune them out for a bit, Murphy says: "Don't try to manage your emotions or let anyone else before you've had a chance to sit with them." Once you've accepted your own feelings, you can progress to **Acknowledgment,** recognizing that the world isn't fair and that bad things happen to *everyone* at some time or another. "If you can try to redirect your brain from a 'why me?' to an 'okay, this happened' mentality, it may give you the clarity that can help you better figure out what to do next and how to cope," Murphy explains in her book.

Finally, resolve to take **Action.** Even if the situation is out of your control, what is a part of it that you *can* control? In the early days of the COVID-19 lockdown, Murphy recalls sitting at her kitchen table, feeling frustrated and helpless. She found that writing down her thoughts and adding them to a spot at her local church where people were pinning ribbons with their prayers was surprisingly cathartic. "In doing something that represented and expressed hope and positivity, I felt a charge of energy, and the tiniest bit of momentum that kept me moving," she says. "In your most trying times, think about what action might do that for you."[34]

THE TAKEAWAY

People with a **growth mindset** (as opposed to a **fixed mindset**) believe that they are capable of developing and improving themselves, through hard work, education, and perseverance. They see challenges as opportunities and criticism as constructive feedback. As leaders, we must have a growth mindset about ourselves, our teams, and our businesses.

Humans, like all animals, are wired to see the negative as a means of survival. We must make a conscious decision each day to think and act in a positive way. Even when it is easier to be pessimistic, **we must choose optimism** if we want to live our happiest lives at home and at work.

There are **three steps to spreading optimism** throughout your business. First, we must take responsibility for our own choices and actions, **casting ourselves as the heroes** and not the victims in our stories. Then, we must **spread this energy to our teams** by displaying enthusiasm for the work and optimism about what can be achieved, even in the face of challenges. Finally, we must **serve our customers with positivity,** viewing them as the reason for our work (and not as an interruption of it). We must extend our growth mindset to our customers as well, believing that our businesses can change their lives for the better.

Visit **LeadLikeAnEditor.com** to download a free workbook that includes **The Optimistic Leader Self-Evaluation,** as well as other templates and resources.

CHAPTER 2

Cultivate Curiosity

As a child, I had a lot of interests and tried my hand at a number of activities, which were often short-lived. Cub Scouts sounded fun, so I begged my dad to be our troop leader so that I would feel more comfortable joining. He spent several hours over multiple weekends getting his certification; but alas, a few months later, I was ready to try something new. (He never let me live it down.) Piano, swimming, and horseback riding lessons all met a similar fate. You could call me a quitter, but I always thought of myself more as a generalist, eager to learn a little about a lot of topics, try my hand at them, and move on.

This generalist's approach continued in high school, resulting in so many activities listed under my senior yearbook photo that there was barely room for anything else. Choir, drama club, debate team, literary magazine, student newspaper—the list went on and on. As a teen, unlike when I was a child, I kept up in most of these pursuits, while also filling my schedule with an array of electives, including creative writing, acting, and sculpture. This continued into college and beyond, as over the years, I tried my hand at a number of diverse roles, ranging from improv actor to radio DJ. Some hobbies lasted a few years; others a few months; and some just a few weeks.

It turns out I'm not the only one who goes through life this way. In her essay "In Defense of Dabbling," freelance writer and former magazine editor Liz Krieger tells a similar tale of a decade of short-lived forays into new hobbies that include "five guitar lessons, six tap-dancing classes, eight pottery-wheel classes, a two-day letterpress workshop, and two beginner ballet classes."[35]

"I loved those classes," Krieger writes. "I don't regret a dime spent or an hour filled. Each one scratched an itch I was having, taught me something, or filled time in a pleasant way. But I still can't help but feel a little sheepish whenever I look at my tap shoes. It's hard to shake the nagging suspicion that I've somehow failed."

Though, as Krieger points out, "the world doesn't look too kindly on a dabbler," she also makes the argument that maybe they should, citing David Epstein, author of *Range: Why Generalists Triumph in a Specialized World*. In the book, Epstein suggests that many of the top performers in elite fields such as sports, science, and the arts achieved success *because* they did so much dabbling before they found their calling.[36]

Although our competitive society can make it feel like pursuing an activity is a waste of time unless it can be quantified by an end goal or achievement, Krieger found the opposite to be true; her article notes that trying unfamiliar activities helps us maintain our openness to new experiences, one of the "big five" traits that psychologists use to assess personality, and one that often declines with age. Krieger concludes with advice from Kristin Neff, an associate professor of educational psychology at the University of Texas at Austin, who suggests that even a short-lived stint at a new activity can provide just what we needed in that moment. "If doing it satisfied your curiosity and if going back might not have been fun," Neff says, "then you did it just right."[37]

FIVE REASONS EDITORS ARE GREAT AT BEING CURIOUS

Journalism depends on curiosity, and no one knows this better than an editor. Here are five ways editors harness their natural curiosity to create a stronger story—and a better product.

1. Editors want to know more and never stop asking "How?" and "Why?" to find out. Stories that we read in newspapers and magazines don't come to the writers fully baked and ready to print. They usually start out as a nagging question, as a general thought about how things might be, or as a suspicion that there is more than meets the eye going on in business, politics, sports, the arts—you name it. The journalist's curiosity—and that of their editor—is what gives the story its initial premise, getting more fleshed out as the journalist starts down a trail, talking to people, following up on leads, and repeatedly, over and over, asking the same two questions: "How?" and "Why?"

Childlike curiosity about everything in life can lead to great discoveries, both in journalism and in business. In her *Harvard Business Review* article, "The Business Case for Curiosity," Francesca Gino gives the example of Edwin Land, who invented the Polaroid camera after his young daughter was impatient to see a photo he had just snapped. When he explained that the film had to be processed, she wondered aloud, "*Why* do we have to wait for the picture?" Gino says that we shouldn't be surprised that this invention was inspired by the question of a three-year-old:

> As every parent knows, *Why?* is ubiquitous in the vocabulary of young children, who have an insatiable need to understand the world around them. They aren't afraid to ask questions, and they don't worry about whether others believe they should already know the answers. But as children grow older, self-consciousness creeps in, along with the desire to appear confident and demonstrate expertise. By the time we're adults, we often suppress our curiosity.[38]

Unfortunately, this suppression is frequently encouraged in the workplace. Although leaders might say they value inquisitive minds, in reality, most stifle curiosity, fearing it will increase risk and inefficiency. But Gino says that smart leaders take the opposite approach, citing Toyota's "Five Whys" method. Developed by the company's founder, this method invites employees to explore the cause-and-effect relationship of any problem by asking "Why?" After coming up with an answer, they are then to ask why *that's* the case, and so on until they have asked the question five times, eventually getting to the root of the problem.[39] In business, going "Five Whys deep" into a problem may be the fastest way to get to the underlying cause, but it is also a natural response for the best reporters and editors, who always strive to answer readers' questions before they have them.

2. Editors know how to listen. Sometimes in conversations—and often in business meetings—many of us "half listen," while using the other half of our attention to think about the next point we want to make or how we will respond. As a result, it's easy to miss a key piece of information, which may lead to errors down the road. Even in the moment, this inattention could result in a missed opportunity, either to ask a clarifying question or to formulate a next-level idea that sprouts from a seed someone else planted.

Talking to other people to find out more is the lifeblood of good reporting, but finding sources, scheduling interviews, prepping questions, deciphering notes, and transcribing taped interviews is also time-consuming work. Why go to all of that trouble just to half listen to the person?

Good journalists know there is no point asking a question if you aren't going to listen to the response. In some ways, they are like therapists, asking open-ended questions and not being afraid to sit through a stretch of silence as the other person takes a moment to respond. When you give your subject a chance to elaborate on a topic in their own way, at their own pace, unexpected answers will often surface, taking the story in a new direction. Leaders in any industry can also be well served by following this approach, whether with their current customers, their target customers, or even their employees.

As dean of Medill since 2019, my grad school professor Charles Whitaker told me he uses the power of listening—a skill he honed as a newspaper reporter and later as an editor at *Ebony*—to lead more than 60 faculty members and 1,100 students. "One of the things that makes a good reporter—and a good manager—is someone who listens more than they talk," says Whitaker, who strives to show Medill faculty and staff that he cares as much about their development as about student development. "Listening to people, hearing them out, trying to get a feel for what makes them tick: That's what I loved about magazine writing and that is the way I have attempted to manage."[40]

To see what this looks like in practice, take former director general of the BBC Greg Dyke. After being named to that role, he spent five months visiting the BBC's major locations, where he assembled the staff to ask employees two simple questions: "What is the one thing I should do to make things better for you?" and "What is the one thing I should do to make things better for our viewers and listeners?" Displaying the characteristics of a growth mindset leader, Dyke created a win-win situation: He gained the respect of his employees early on *and* was able to use their responses to create a road map for how the company should move forward. Just as important, by taking time to listen as a means of filling in his own knowledge gaps, Dyke suggested to employees that they might benefit from the same information-gathering technique.[41]

Though asking questions and listening to the answers likely felt intuitive to Dyke, who worked for years as a newspaper and broadcast journalist, many high-level leaders would rather talk than listen. When one study asked executives what they would do to solve an organizational crisis stemming from both financial and cultural issues, most leaders said they would take immediate action to stop financial bleeding, while introducing initiatives to refresh the culture; only a handful suggested they would ask questions first, before imposing their ideas on others. In her *Harvard Business Review* article, Francesca Gino notes: "Management books commonly encourage leaders assuming new positions to communicate their vision from the start rather than ask employees how they can be most helpful. It's bad advice."[42]

3. Editors don't take things at face value. While having childlike curiosity when approaching a new subject can be advantageous, having childlike naivete is not. We can't always take people's answers at face value and assume that they are fact. Asking questions and listening to responses is important; however, the job of the reporter and editor is not to regurgitate what their sources said but rather to question it, poke holes in it, and draw their own conclusions.

For many years, there was an assumption that what you read in a reputable newspaper or magazine was the unvarnished truth, unless you were reading an editorialized article, which was clearly labeled as an opinion piece. Although the rise of the internet and social media has brought about many positive changes, with the proliferation of millions of new voices, it can now be harder to separate truth from unsubstantiated "facts" or opinion.

That's where skepticism comes into play. Reporters have long been the watchdogs of society, and being somewhat skeptical of any "facts" presented to them is ultimately the best way to ensure accuracy and avoid their own implicit bias, while also holding those in power accountable for the statements that they make.

As leaders, we should apply the same skepticism to both new ideas and to our industries' "sacred cows"—ideas and beliefs so commonly held that they almost seem above criticism. But we should do so while still remaining optimistic. Does this sound like an impossible task?

In his *Forbes* article "How to Use Skepticism to Lead More Innovatively (Without Being a Jerk)," writer and entrepreneur Shane Snow says that the best leaders tend to be "Skeptical Optimists," who question all information and assumptions that are presented to them, while still assuming that the best is possible. The people who model this counterintuitive blend of two seemingly opposite personality traits often doubt the status quo and ask the paradigm-shifting questions needed to make monumental changes. In this group, Snow puts a number of professionals, including the world's top innovators, inventors, and—not surprisingly—journalists.[43]

But what does this look like on a daily basis? Snow says the key to making your skepticism productive and not demoralizing is to make sure that when you question the ideas of others, they know that it is not a personal attack but genuine curiosity about why they think or how they know that something is true. And those who truly master this approach will also turn the skepticism onto themselves, internally interrogating their own assumptions and arguments with two questions: *Where did this come from?* and *Is it really true?*

4. Editors are always looking to improve. By definition, the job of an editor is to improve writing and storytelling at every phase of the process. When a writer pitches the idea for a story, an experienced editor will often "Yes, and …" the original pitch, accepting the writer's premise and next-leveling it with a new angle or twist—and for good reason. Though some stories are truly unique, many have been told before or are variations on a common type of storytelling. Think about the stories you see all the time about the new spring fashion collections and the latest health research, or the ubiquitous "New Year, New You!" articles that grace magazine covers each January.

A good editor will help shape the narrative, homing in on the angle that makes the story unique both to their particular audience *and* this particular time. When we hear pitches at VERANDA, even if the idea sounds interesting, we have to ask ourselves, "What would make this topic interesting to a VERANDA reader?" and "Why now?" This narrowing of scope makes sure that going into interviews and the writing process, a writer knows which questions to ask to make the story both timely and appropriate for the intended audience.

But the fine-tuning doesn't end there. When the copy comes in, a good editor puts on the hat of a reader and becomes super curious. Almost all novice writers, as well as many seasoned ones, have had the experience of slaving over a story for weeks, self-editing it for days, and then turning in the perfect, polished draft to their editor—only to have it come back with a million notes.

Good editors try to anticipate any questions, concerns, or objections a reader may have and address them head-on. The status quo is not good enough; copy can always be improved by asking a few more questions or clarifying certain points. To have an editor read a 500-word story and ask a writer to answer 10 new questions—but still keep the story at that word count—requires further writing and editing gymnastics to trim the fat. It isn't easy, but this process of adding more pertinent info while removing the unnecessary bits usually makes for the most satisfying (and efficient) storytelling.

The concept of taking someone's pitch and asking questions to improve on it can lead to a much better final product, no matter the industry. At Pixar, writers and directors are trained to do this through a variation on the "Yes, and …" technique that they call "plussing," which allows these creatives to build on one another's ideas in a positive way that doesn't completely discount the original concept. Instead of rejecting a sketch of the *Toy Story* character Woody, a director might soften a critique by saying, "I like Woody's eyes, and what if we …?" This line of creative inquiry invites someone else to jump in with another "plus," encouraging active listening and respect for others' ideas, while fostering creativity.[44]

5. Editors' curiosity helps them spot and capitalize on trends others might miss. Good writers and editors aren't just listening when they ask someone a question in an interview; they are always listening, reading, and watching to see what people are talking about. At the same time, frequent contact with a wide range of experts on the topics they cover allows editors to see what common threads keep coming up, which could lead to spotting the next big trend.

When I started at VERANDA in 2018, my editor in chief and I began rethinking the magazine's cover imagery, which had often shown interiors decorated in clean whites and calming neutrals. The rooms were beautiful, but they didn't represent the influx of vintage patterns and mismatched antiques we were beginning to see in the houses that decorators submitted for publication. Although we recognized that tastes were shifting to a new aesthetic that combined maximalism, traditionalism, and even 1980s decorating styles, we didn't really name that change in any specific way.

But then someone else did. In September 2019, Emma Bazilian, an editor at our sister publication *House Beautiful*, wrote an article called "The Rise of Grandmillennial Style." Using quotes from designers and examples from social media, she explained how grandmillennials—a portmanteau of *grandmother* and *millennials*—range in age from mid-20s to late-30s and can be identified by their love for design styles considered stuffy or outdated by mainstream culture; think "Laura Ashley prints, ruffles, and embroidered linens."[45]

As an editor at the nation's oldest decorating magazine, Bazilian's recognition of this new trend was fueled in part by her own tastes, as well as her daily interaction with design experts. But she also noticed it simply by remaining curious about what people engaged with on social media. "I would post an old *House Beautiful* article on Instagram from the '80s or a

Laura Ashley ad, and all these people would comment at how much they loved the images," she recalls. "So I started to realize it's not just me."[46]

The term went viral in the decorating community overnight, earning *House Beautiful* tons of attention. Then in Spring 2020, when everyone was stuck at home during the early days of the COVID lockdown, the trend picked up speed as consumers moved away from the sleek mid-century modern style that had dominated the past decade to looks that felt more cozy. With new furniture on backorder because of pandemic-related supply chain issues, antiques became an in-demand resource for home renovations.

Soon, even mainstream news outlets had begun covering the rise of grandmillennial style, crediting Bazilian as the editor who first recognized the trend, but more importantly, who had made it real by coining a new term. Though Bazilian left *House Beautiful* in 2021 to take on a new role as content director at the textile company Schumacher, her legacy as the original grand-millennial maven lives on. As a *Washington Post* article asserts: "By giving these like-minded traditionalists a name, Bazilian legitimized a movement."[47]

EDITOR'S TIP

———

Own the trend by naming it.

The funny thing about trends is that, once they are pointed out, they become obvious, something anyone might have noticed all along. For that reason, successful trendspotting is not just about seeing the trend but about what you do with that realization. Good editors are skilled at recognizing patterns in the world around them and writing about how these patterns may constitute a broader movement in society. The best editors go one step further, *naming* the resulting trend with a unique but catchy moniker.

In his memoir *Dilettante: True Tales of Excess, Triumph, and Disaster*, former *Vanity Fair* deputy editor Dana Brown explains how spotting, naming, and owning trends helped the magazine skyrocket in the 1990s, as it coined terms like the "New Establishment" to describe the transfer of power from industrial giants to media moguls as we entered the Information Age. Successful editors "recognize the cultural shifts, create a narrative, package it, and sell it at a premium," Brown writes. They "give the people what they didn't know they wanted."[48]

THE TAKEAWAY

Editors and journalists are great at being curious—it is practically a requisite for the job.

Leaders in any industry can follow their example by **keeping an open mind** and embracing a **sense of curiosity**, which can lead to both personal and professional discoveries.

When reporting a story, a good editor channels their inner child, always wanting to know more and **asking "Why?"** to find out. When they are gathering information, they **take time to listen** and seek input from stakeholders at all levels.

Editors don't take things at face value but instead maintain a **skeptical optimism** about information they receive and assumptions they hold. They are constantly looking to improve, next-leveling their own ideas and those of others.

Finally, **editors look for patterns** in the fields they cover and in our culture at large, using both data and empirical evidence to **spot—and even name— trends** that others might miss.

CHAPTER 3

....

Let Passion Guide You

When Walt Disney started his company in 1923, making money was not the primary reason for his efforts; if it were, he certainly could have found a more profitable business than animation. Like many entrepreneurs, Disney started his company because of his dual passions: delighting audiences with his charming animations and creating forms of entertainment that had never been seen before. The same is true of his first theme park, Disneyland. A family man at heart, Disney hatched the initial concept for Disneyland not in a boardroom but rather while watching from the sidelines as his daughters rode the merry-go-round at Griffith Park in Los Angeles, leading him to dream about a place where adults and their children could go and have fun *together*.[49]

Having a passion for your work is helpful in any endeavor, and it is the primary reason many people begin or stay in careers that are known for paying lower salaries. This would include artists (like the young Walt Disney) as well as many other occupations. Take teaching, for example: While there are certainly some educators who fell into their profession by happenstance, the ones who stick with it for decades often do so not for the money but because they love both their chosen subject matter and the process of helping others learn. These teachers may view their work as a calling rather than a job; not surprisingly, they are often the educators who make the biggest impact, the ones we remember as being our favorites years after we graduate.

The same goes for nonprofits, which are often led and staffed by workers who harbor a burning passion for the cause. Someone who doesn't like animals certainly *could* take a position at a dog and cat shelter, but if they aren't enthusiastic about their work, why not go somewhere else that pays more? And would they enjoy the work as much as the person who loves animals and is excited to go into the shelter and work with them and on their behalf every day?

Similarly, salary size has never been the primary motivation for writers and editors. Though top-level editors can earn respectable salaries, starting pay in the field of journalism is notoriously low. "We certainly don't do this for the money" is a phrase uttered throughout newsrooms every day, and one that I have heard many times in my career. But this begs the question: If we don't do it for the money, why *do* we do it? Often, the answer is passion.

IT'S JUST WORK, SO WHY DOES PASSION MATTER?

During my late 20s and early 30s, I worked for almost five years at a special-interest magazine publisher called Bonnier Corporation. The company's tagline at the time was "Connecting People with Their Passions." Although a few of its titles were household names (*Popular Science*, *Parenting*, and *Field & Stream*), the majority of its publications were smaller niche brands, often focused on outdoor and water-based pursuits: *Sailing World, Salt Water Sportsman, Scuba Diving, Wakeboarding,* and so forth.

Bonnier stocked issues of its magazines in the lobby and break rooms. Often, I would flip through some of these titles and think: *Wow! I never even realized this sport existed!* I loved that people who were interested in such specific activities had a magazine that spoke just to them. It was also amazing that writers, editors, graphic designers, and photographers who were passionate about that activity had a magazine they could work for.

Our parent company was based in Sweden, but we had offices across the U.S., from California to New England to Florida. On the rare occasions when a large group of us was together, it was interesting to hear people talk about their publications with a fervor that was obviously fueled by a passion for their sport. Our tattooed teammates from Southern California waxed poetic about what went into capturing the most gnarly photos for *Surf* and *Skateboarding*, while the preppy *Yachting* and *Sailing World* folks from New England extolled the virtues of the world's fastest and most luxurious watercraft.

Sure, I could have learned to design or write for any of these magazines, but would I have been as good as someone who truly loved the sport? And would I have been excited about covering weekend competitions or finding a photographer who could capture breathtaking action shots? Probably not.

The same holds true in business. When we have true passion for the product we create or the service we provide, authenticity shows through in our words, in our actions, and on our faces. Running a business—either as an entrepreneur or as a high-level executive—is exhausting work that can often seem to take over all of our waking hours. For a happy life, you should try your hardest to make that business something you have a personal passion for. Working in a subject area that you are passionate about unlocks two life-changing secrets that editors know well:

Secret 1: First, your work will get better—and easier.

A piece of advice all beginning writers hear is the ubiquitous: "Write what you know." To that, I would add a caveat: "Write what you know—and are passionate about." While a great writer can cover a variety of topics and may even discover a new passion by exploring an unknown subject, it generally holds true that our best work comes when we write about—or, in the case of business, focus on—that which we are passionate about. When you have a passion for something, it allows you to:

- **Naturally seek out and connect with other people** who share your passion. Cold-calling a stranger suddenly becomes easy when you have a common interest that unites you, despite any differences in age, location, beliefs, or income.

- **Communicate genuinely** with people who share your passion. In journalism, this means finding and getting to know your audience, and then speaking authentically to them as a guide. In business, this manifests in your brand messaging: in written form, in the visuals you use, and even verbally when you are out in the marketplace meeting potential customers face-to-face.

- **Dive deep into the minutiae of the subject,** maintaining interest and curiosity about new information, without getting bored. When you have a true passion for a topic, you are legitimately curious and never tire of learning more about it.

My last semester of college, I decided to write a thesis through the university's honors program. Thesis writing was considered an optional independent study that you could take for anywhere from three to 15 credit hours; it was suggested that for each credit hour you took, you should add 10 pages to the thesis. I had already completed all of my required classes, so after much consideration, I took a deep breath and elected to sign up for the maximum credit hours, making the thesis my only course for the semester. And just like that, I had a deadline for a 150-page book that was due in 16 weeks.

Some writers spend years working on a book, and most doctorate programs recommend spending one to three years on a graduate thesis; I had just over four months to finish mine. As a journalism major with a gender studies field of concentration, I could have written on a variety of topics, but I knew that choosing something I was deeply interested in—to the point of obsession—was the only way that I could research, write, and edit an entire book between mid-January and early May.

For me, that topic was Madonna. Although I had known about the star for most of my life, during high school and college, I had truly progressed into being a superfan. I found her music to be positively electric—but what I *really* loved was her confidence, her unrelenting self-love, and her refusal to care what anyone thought of her. To me, she was a living incarnation of fabulousness, fearlessness, and above all else, power. The way that she embodied all of these traits—while also celebrating her sexuality and experimenting with gender-bending attire—was positively inspirational for an awkward gay teen who had spent so many years hating himself, afraid of who he was, and terrified of what his family and friends would think if they knew the feelings he was having.

Discovering Madonna changed the way I looked at myself. As my fandom grew, I slowly came out of my shell and into my own: coming out in my hometown newspaper, standing up to high school bullies, and exploring my sexuality and gender in ways I'd never dared to before. In college, she even led me into a new field of study, as I signed up for a women's studies course—called "Roles of Women in Twentieth Century America: From Eleanor Roosevelt to Madonna"—simply because her name was in the title. In my high school love of Madonna, I had come for the music but stayed for the empowerment; similarly, in my exploration of gender studies, I came for Madonna but stayed for the academic and personal revelations it provided.

Knowing that I wanted to explore Madonna and feminism for my thesis, I dove into feminist essays, magazine critiques, and biographies about the Material Girl, while also poring over each of her "texts"—albums, videos, concert tours, and even the *Sex* book—with abandon, often working late into the night on the project. I interviewed other Madonna fans as well as feminists who both loved and hated her, summarizing popular critiques of her work, while also positing a few new ideas of my own. Conducting this amount of research and then writing about it was certainly no easy task; it required saying no to other commitments and spending many days (and nights) glued to my desk. But the topic was endlessly fascinating to me, so it never really felt like work. By the end of the semester, at the age of 21, I had finished my first book: *Madonna, Like a Feminist: The Ideology and the Icon.*

While good writers and editors can expound on a variety of topics, for long-term success and career satisfaction, most narrow in on a specific area of coverage. Often this "beat" aligns with their personal interests—and that's no coincidence. For almost every article of a few hundred words that you read in a magazine, a writer spent hours pitching the idea, finding and interviewing sources, crafting a first draft, sending it to their editor, receiving a marked-up version, rewriting, sending it back to their editor, eventually looking at it in several more rounds of layout, making more changes, and so on. As one can imagine, if you are doing this on a daily basis for years on end, the process will be a lot less painful—and actually quite enjoyable!—if you are passionate about the topics you are covering.

Secret 2: Then, the rest of your life will also get better.

There is an old adage that if you choose a job you love, you will never work a day in your life. As hokey as it may sound, this has largely been the case throughout my career. If you truly love what you do for a living, it doesn't feel like work. Having this type of professional passion makes it easier to get out of bed and go to the office each day, and much less annoying when you have to work late or put in a few extra hours on the weekend. The fact is, this level of happiness at work not only improves the work itself but also creates a spillover effect, improving the rest of your life. It does this by allowing you to do three important things:

1. Get into the flow. There are the necessary annoyances and tasks of any job—answering emails, returning phone calls, submitting expense reports, etc.—but then there is the actual work, the thing that you do best that keeps the business running. For writers and editors, the crux of their work is really diving into the text, getting their thoughts out on paper (or on screen), moving words around, and refining ideas into sentences and sentences into paragraphs, ultimately crafting a story that will engage readers.

If you don't like writing and editing, this may sound like drudgery, and even for the best editors, the process isn't always easy. But when we are doing this type of "in the weeds" work that we actually love, even when it is challenging, we get into the flow, and magic happens. For journalists, this means that where once there was a blank screen with a blinking cursor, there is now a fully formed series of ideas, laid out in an article. If you are passionate about what you are writing and enjoy the process of writing (even if it can be difficult at times), you can sit down to work on a story at 9 a.m. and suddenly feel your stomach growling, only to look up and see that it is noon and you have been lost in the work for the last three hours.

Although I enjoy writing, the work that *really* gets me in the flow is graphic design, especially designing magazine pages. There is a huge sense of accomplishment involved in visual storytelling; I start with a blank screen, eventually turning some text and a collection of images or illustrations into a multi page feature that, like any good story, is thoughtful and well paced, leading the reader on a journey. It sounds nerdy to say, but there are some days—usually when I know I am going to be working on a layout that has a fun challenge or really beautiful photography—that I literally pop out of bed at 6 a.m. and head straight to my desk to get started.

This has happened more times than I can count, even on the weekends and even when I am out of town visiting friends and family. My loved ones have stared at me in disbelief, wondering if I am in fact a workaholic, but the simple truth is that I enjoy the process so much that it doesn't *feel* like work, which we often associate with draining our energy. Quite the opposite, the hours I spend in the flow actually energize me, while also allowing me to feel calm, relaxed, and accomplished when I come up for air a few hours later.

2. Make time to go deeper. In his book *Deep Work: Rules for Focused Success in a Distracted World*, Georgetown University computer science professor Cal Newport argues that this type of work is essential for high achievers in business: "To build your working life around the experience of flow produced by deep work is a proven path to deep satisfaction," he writes.[50] And although deep work has always been around, it may matter now more than ever; Newport hypothesizes that because our modern society is filled with constant notifications, noise, and distractions, "the ability to perform deep work is becoming increasingly rare at exactly the same time as it is becoming increasingly valuable in our economy. As a consequence, the few who cultivate this skill, and then make it the core of their working time, will thrive."[51]

Newport expounds on this by introducing his four philosophies of deep work; one of these is actually called the Journalistic Philosophy, which involves scheduling deep work whenever you can fit it into your schedule. He provides an interesting example of this concept in action using the famed writer Walter Isaacson as an example. You've likely seen Isaacson's work in some capacity, on a newsstand or bookstore shelf. He is the former editor in chief of *Time* magazine and also wrote several epically long and in-depth books, including what many consider to be the definitive biographies of Benjamin Franklin, Albert Einstein, Steve Jobs, and Elon Musk. In *Deep Work,* Newport recounts a story from his uncle, who shared a summer beach rental with Isaacson and noticed something interesting about the prolific writer:

> It was always amazing … he could retreat up to the bedroom for a while, when the rest of us were chilling on the patio or whatever, to work on his book … he'd go up for twenty minutes or an hour, we'd hear the typewriter pounding, then he'd come down as relaxed as the rest of us … the work never seemed to faze him, he just happily went up to work when he had the spare time.[52]

If the most important part of your job does not align with your passions and what you are good at, it can start to feel like spending hours on your deep work is torture, rather than bliss. But if, like Walter Isaacson, the deep work required of your job is something that comes naturally to you and that you enjoy, tackling a massive project—like writing an 800-page book—becomes a lot less daunting, and even exciting. This leads to greater job satisfaction, and allows you to …

3. Achieve "Work/Life Brilliance." These days, work and personal life end up bleeding together for most of us. This has really been true since the advent of modern technology, when email and cell phones allowed us to respond to people at any time of day, without being tethered to our desks. During the pandemic, the concept of work/life balance was brought to center stage as even the most office-centric professions went remote, with people working from their living rooms, dining rooms, and even bedrooms while juggling childcare and family responsibilities.

On our deathbeds, few of us will wish we had spent more time working. When all is said and done, work is work, and we should carve away some time exclusively for our friends and family, as well as for other interests and pursuits. But when your career involves a subject you are passionate about, it is easy to blend work and the rest of your life together more seamlessly. Novelist and former *Cosmopolitan* editor in chief Kate White calls this "Work/Life Brilliance"—and to editors covering a topic they love, it is second nature.

For example, many editors at Hearst's *Runner's World* magazine have an interest in running. While long Sunday runs with friends may not technically be part of their work, such runs could easily spawn several new story ideas, from the science behind a new shoe one friend is loving to a different friend's running injury to a pretty route they hadn't considered before. This is true in other professions as well; even when they are technically off the clock and on vacation, many interior designers will make antique shops their first stop when they hit a new town, while real estate professionals will often check out local listings or attend an open house to see what another market is like.

The people who strive to create a line-in-the-sand separation between their work and their personal lives usually have one thing in common: They simply are not passionate about the work they're doing. In her book *Grit*, psychologist Angela Duckworth maintains that the secret to outstanding achievement is mixing passion with perseverance, a trait that I will talk more about in the next chapter. She explains that top performers in any field are almost *always* working, putting in well over 40 or even 50 hours a week at their jobs. Duckworth admits that the trade-offs involved in this time commitment may not be for everyone but also maintains that for her and many high achievers, it is their passion for the work that makes these long hours not just tolerable but actually enjoyable:

> Must you work seventy hours per week to be gritty? No. But when you really love what you do, you might find that you *want* to. You might feel, as I do, that nearly everything you see, hear, read, or experience is in some way relevant to your work. You might find that you don't want to take a vacation from your calling.[53]

WHAT IF YOU AREN'T PASSIONATE ABOUT YOUR BUSINESS?

So what happens if you find yourself having to work on a project or in a business that you have no passion for? Ironically, this actually happened to me while I was working at Bonnier, the same publishing company that, if you recall, was committed to "Connecting People with Their Passions." I have always loved travel and interior design, and in 2011, I was happily working on the magazine *Caribbean Travel + Life*, designing stories about some of the most gorgeous beaches and beautifully decorated resorts in the world. Then, unexpectedly, the company underwent a restructuring and layoffs ensued. Thankfully, I was spared, but a new editor and art director were assigned to that brand, while I floated between a few different magazines in an interim "special projects" role for the next few months. Then, when the dust settled, I was asked to take a permanent position as the art director of *Parenting* magazine.

My gut reaction was one of resistance—well, actually, sheer terror. I had no children of my own and never intended to. Simply put, I never really "clicked" with kids. I'm an only child, and even as a kid, I preferred hanging out with adults to playing with people my own age. In this new job, I would not only be designing stories about kids but also art directing photoshoots with pint-sized models, who (spoiler alert!) are notoriously unpredictable.

There were some positives: *Parenting* had a circulation of more than two million, making it one of the top 25 magazines in the U.S. and the largest in Bonnier's portfolio. With that came larger budgets, a bigger staff, and even the opportunity to work on something brand new: a digital edition that would be sold on Apple's recently debuted iPad.

Harnessing my optimism, I jumped into the role and tried to find my passions where I could. At the time, I was one of two art directors and later four, plus a junior designer, all reporting to a creative director. I quickly found that some of my colleagues loved kids, and their passion showed through on set, putting the child models at ease, which in turn made them more photogenic. Although I definitely faced my share of tense moments as I tried to cajole a shrieking toddler into smiling, I largely left this to the staff members who excelled at it.

Instead, I played to my strengths and passions by overseeing parts of the magazine that better fit my interests: the entertainment section, which meant designing articles about books, movies, and celebrities; the activities section, with stories on family-friendly hobbies and vacation destinations; and the cooking section, for which I spent hours in kitchenware stores, finding the perfect plate to use as a prop in a cookie recipe photoshoot, or creating a DIY hot chocolate bar with kid-friendly gourmet toppings. Unlike many creatives, I have always been as much right brain as left brain, which came in handy when, for a period of time, the magazine was without an on-site managing editor. During this period, I again let my colleagues handle some of the day-to-day interactions with families and children, while I focused on scheduling layout due dates and getting the finished pages to the printer on time.

I also found my passion elsewhere in the benefits provided by Bonnier, applying for the company's Global Exchange Program. When I was selected to leave my role at *Parenting* for three months to work as an art director at two interior design magazines in Sweden, I jumped at the chance and packed my bags. That summer in Stockholm reinforced what I already knew: that my passion definitely lied in the interior design and travel realm. Trying to avoid children while working on travel stories at *Parenting* was like putting a Band-Aid on the problem and wasn't a long-term solution. I knew that I would never truly be happy working there because parenting wasn't my passion.

During my first few weeks in Stockholm, I took advantage of the long summer evenings by exploring new neighborhoods after work, crossing places off in my guidebook as I visited the recommended museums, parks, and shops along the way (a further reminder of my travel bug). But by the end of my time there, I had stopped playing tourist and instead began heading back to my charming studio apartment each evening, where I polished my résumé and built a portfolio website so that I could start looking for a new position as soon as I returned to the U.S.

Exactly two weeks after I returned, I applied for my dream job as design director of *Coastal Living*, a magazine that covered interior design, travel, and food through the lens of a laid-back lifestyle, lived by the water. And I got it. I went from being unhappy as one of five designers on a brand I didn't love to leading the art department at my dream magazine.

EDITOR'S TIP

—

Channel your passion into a new venture.

Sometimes an unexpected plot twist can prompt us to look at our passions in a new way. For 15 years, Susan Moynihan worked happily as a travel editor, serving as editor in chief of Bonnier's *Destination Weddings & Honeymoons* for the better part of a decade. When the magazine closed in 2013, she was laid off and forced to consider what came next. "I had been working in my mind on a post-publishing plan to be a travel agent," she says, "but it was still shocking when it happened."

Moynihan researched the market and found that many people use a travel agent for the first time on their honeymoon. Armed with this info and her brand-building expertise, she parlayed her knowledge of the world's most luxurious and romantic destinations into a second act as The Honeymoonist, a boutique travel agency focused on honeymoons, destination weddings, and other special-occasion travel. Though she continues to write and edit on the side, even authoring a travel book, Moynihan has resisted returning to a full-time corporate role. "It was scary," she says, "but I knew that starting my own business sooner rather than later was going to benefit me. So I took a leap of faith."[54]

THE TAKEAWAY

When we love what we do, our work feels less like a job and more like a calling.

When we have true passion for the products we create or the services we provide, **authenticity shows through** in our words, in our actions, and on our faces.

Having a passion for the deep work our jobs require allows us to **get into the flow,** so that hours pass by quickly as we are absorbed in producing our best, most valuable work.

If you are passionate about the work you do, this passion may spill over into other aspects of your life—and that's okay. Finding work/life balance becomes less of a concern, and in some cases, you may even actively try to integrate the two to achieve **Work/Life Brilliance.**

If you find yourself unhappy in a job you aren't passionate about, **explore aspects of the work that** *do* **appeal to you,** and try to find meaning in those. If this does not improve your job satisfaction in the long run, you may want to consider looking for a new job or career path.

CHAPTER 4

Practice Perseverance

We've all heard the maxim, "Showing up is half the battle." This quote is most often attributed to Stephen Hawking, though Woody Allen takes his estimation even further, saying that "80 percent of success in life is showing up."[55]

As mentioned in the last chapter, one of the most recognized experts on the art of showing up is pioneering psychologist Angela Duckworth. (Fun fact: Martin Seligman, the father of Positive Psychology mentioned in Chapter 1, was Duckworth's graduate school advisor.) Over the course of many years, Duckworth has studied a wide variety of high achievers, from cadets at West Point to competitors in the National Spelling Bee. What she found is that talent and intelligence are only a part of the reason for people's success.

Finalists at the National Spelling Bee were not necessarily more intelligent than those who were eliminated in earlier rounds, but they did practice more. Likewise, the likelihood of new West Point cadets making it through the intensive seven-week "Beast Barracks" boot camp without dropping out had less to do with their natural aptitude or athletic prowess than their ability to fail and keep coming back the next day anyway, exhibiting a "never give up attitude." Duckworth theorizes that passion (as covered in the last chapter) tempered with this type of perseverance is the true determination of whether or not an individual will succeed in any pursuit. The combination of these two traits is what she defines as *grit*.[56]

In her book *Grit: The Power of Passion and Perseverance,* Duckworth describes a test Harvard University researchers created in the 1940s to measure the characteristics of healthy young men in order to help people live happier, more successful lives. The researchers asked 130 sophomores to run on a treadmill for five minutes; however, the treadmill was set at such a steep incline and cranked up to such a high speed that most could only last four minutes or less, with some losing steam after just 90 seconds. Researchers followed up with these men every two years into their 60s, asking them about income, career advancement, satisfaction in their personal lives and marriages, and whether they had faced mental health challenges or substance abuse. Decades later, the study concluded that those who had stayed on the treadmill the longest, exerting the most effort regardless of their overall physical fitness, were the same subjects who earned the highest marks for psychological adjustment throughout adulthood.

Duckworth notes that if she were running the test today, she would make one small adjustment: allowing the young men to come back the next day, if they wanted, to try the test again and see if they could improve their time. "Staying on the treadmill is one thing, and I do think it's related to staying true to our commitments even when we're not comfortable," Duckworth writes. "But getting back on the treadmill the next day, eager to try again, is in my view even more reflective of grit."[57]

GOING PRO

In his book *The War of Art: Break Through the Blocks and Win Your Inner Creative Battles,* author and former Marine Steven Pressfield offers advice on how to overcome the internal obstacles to success, particularly in creative pursuits. Though he is a writer and his examples are often related to the work of writers and artists, I would argue that building a business is as creative an endeavor as any.

According to Pressfield, what makes the difference between a novelist or screenwriter versus an *aspiring* novelist or screenwriter is simply making the decision to "go pro." Though we usually categorize professionals as earning money from their pursuits, for Pressfield, this really has little to do with it; making a decision to go pro is more about choosing to commit to your goals in the way that a professional does. When you treat creative pursuits like a hobby versus a profession, he says, you will get the ho-hum results of a hobbyist. He goes on to list 10 traits of being a professional, and the first three all revolve around showing up:

- We show up every day.
- We show up no matter what.
- We stay on the job all day.[58]

Pressfield considered these qualities so important that he later expanded the list to 20-plus traits in a second book called *Turning Pro*; not surprisingly, "showing up consistently"—even in times of crisis—was a recurring theme in that book as well:

> The amateur believes that she must have all her ducks in a row before she can launch her start-up or compose her symphony or design her iPhone app. The professional knows better. Has your husband just walked out on you? Has your El Dorado been repossessed? Keep writing. Keep composing. Keep shooting film. Athletes play hurt. Warriors fight scared. The professional takes two aspirin and keeps on truckin'.[59]

When the going gets tough—during times of illness, crisis, and failure—a lot can be learned from editors, who are experts at showing up, no matter what.

SHOW UP IN TIMES OF ILLNESS

My first role out of grad school was at *Home Channel News*, a biweekly trade magazine focused on the building materials industry. We covered lumber companies as well as retailers like Home Depot, Lowe's, and Ace Hardware—most definitely not my passion, but a first job is a first job! The staff was fairly small with just a handful of editors, and I was not only the lone art director but also the copy editor for every article in the magazine.

I had been working there less than a month when, one freezing February day, I woke up with what felt like the worst cold I had ever had, just a step short of the flu. Now, my boss at the time was understanding, and on any other day, I could have called in sick. But this was a Friday that we were closing a big issue. As the designer *and* copy editor of the entire issue, it was essential that I be there, and probably work late as well, not going home until the pages were out the door and sent to the printer. Really, there was no other option: I took a shower, popped a double dose of DayQuil, and set off to work with a 100-degree fever.

Since then, I have seen magazine editors and art directors show up with the flu, broken bones, and sick children in tow—all under the pressure of an impending deadline. I've definitely gone to work when I shouldn't have, quarantining myself in my office and using hand sanitizer constantly so as not to infect anyone else—all because deadlines wait for no one. (It's worth noting: The pandemic and the rise of remote work have changed whether or not people physically show up to work when sick, but many still do their work virtually.)

There is a mindset that takes over when you have a love for your craft, a sense of responsibility to your team, and fierce pride about your work as a writer, editor, or designer. For better or worse, magazines often run pretty lean, especially in recent years, and when there is a deadline looming and no one to cover for you, your only option is to *show up.*

I can almost hear your protests now: *You really want me to show up when I'm sick? Isn't that irresponsible? And what about self-care?* In the world of publishing, if you have just finished closing a big issue and are at a slow point in your work cycle, sure—call in sick when the fever strikes. But if an issue is shipping to the printer, and you still have a part to play, then there is one rule to remember: Unless you are in the hospital, if you are well enough to get out of bed and call in sick, then you are well enough to go to work—or at least work from home—and get your part finished. You can be sick and rest tomorrow; the deadline is today, and it waits for no one.

SHOW UP IN TIMES OF CRISIS

One of the cardinal rules of working in live entertainment is that "the show must go on"—except when it doesn't. In October 2012, Hurricane Sandy rocked New York, devastating Staten Island and leaving much of Lower Manhattan without power. President Obama declared a state of emergency, and the city suspended subway, bus, and commuter rail service for several days. Broadway theaters also closed completely for four days, while the New York Stock Exchange saw its first unscheduled market-wide shutdown since the days following September 11, 2001, and its first two-day weather-related shutdown since the Great Blizzard of 1888!

The morning after the hurricane, many New Yorkers stayed home with their families, as schools and workplaces remained shuttered throughout the city. But while most people hunkered down, the news cycle kept right on spinning at a hyper pace. In many ways, reporters function like first responders, running toward, rather than away from, danger. During these literally dark days in New York, the city's media outlets—including radio and TV stations, newspapers, and magazines—were working around the clock to provide coverage, telling the stories that people around the city and around the world were desperate to hear.

Here is a personal account, from the editors of *New York* magazine, which at that time, was a weekly publication located in a part of the city that was without power:

> The first order of business Tuesday morning was locating staffers, several of whom had woken up in what were now cell-phone and e-mail dead zones. That afternoon, a group of editors met … to begin plotting our coverage of the storm and to deal with an even more urgent question: Who would volunteer to go down to One Hudson Square bright and early Wednesday morning to retrieve the computers?
>
> An improvised newsroom was soon up and running, with 32 editors, photo editors, designers, and production specialists squeezed around a conference-room table, down the length of which snaked a tangle of power strips, extension cords, and chargers resembling similar arrays sprouting across the city. At this point, proofs were due to go to press in 72 hours. Staffers spent them scrambling to secure writers and photographers as well as exchanging personal e-mail addresses to make it possible to transfer files (our servers were still down), arranging car pools, finding rooms at three different hotels for colleagues from darkened neighborhoods, and draining our hosts of coffee and soda. The easiest part of a harried three days came Friday around noon, when we met to settle on the cover. A photograph taken by Iwan Baan on Wednesday night, showing the Island of Manhattan, half aglow and half in dark, was the clear choice, for the way it fit with the bigger story we have tried to tell here about a powerful city rendered powerless. We crammed back into the conference room, raced to finish our pages, and hoped, like other New Yorkers, that everyone would find the lights on when they got home.[60]

Overhead photo of a half-darkened Manhattan on October 31, 2012, shown on the cover of the November 12 issue. Photograph by Iwan Baan for New York *magazine.*

Of course, this adrenaline-pumping determination could also be seen during other New York City events, ranging from the tragedy of 9/11 to the electrical blackout of 2003. Though I lived in New York during a somewhat uneventful stretch, I did experience a transit strike and—even more personally impactful—a fire at my office building the week before an issue was due to the printer. Like the team at *New York* magazine, volunteers went in to salvage the computers and move them to a temporary office (graciously provided by our printer), where we all worked around a conference room table for the next week to get the issue out the door.

Like everyone around the world, I got another taste of working in crisis in March 2020 during the early days of the COVID-19 pandemic. As we all left the office for the last time on Thursday, March 12, VERANDA was scheduled to start shipping pages to the printer the following week. At that point, the common consensus across the U.S. was that it would be safe to return to the office in two weeks, so many took a bit of a pandemic vacation. I, on the other hand, was working 12 to 16 hours a day to get that issue out the door. Over the next two years, I would get COVID twice; both times the illness came during a week that we were shipping an issue to the printer. Though I would have liked to call in sick, I showed up (virtually) to get the job done, getting both issues to the printer on time without taking a single sick day.

EDITOR'S TIP

Treat every project like it is has your byline.

Though at times it's tempting to "phone it in," editors know that having passion for your craft *and* the work ethic to deliver your best every day is essential when your byline is attached to a story. This is a lesson that Heather Chadduck Hillegas brought with her when she left her role as style director at *Southern Living* to launch her own interior decorating and textile design firm. "I'm lucky to love what I do," she tells me, "but some days you work so hard, it's insane." On a recent installation, she and her team unloaded five moving trucks in a week, while averaging 18,000 steps a day. But when the client cried tears of joy upon seeing her newly designed home, the effort was worth it. "My mom and I are very similar, and something she always says is that we do everything wholeheartedly," Hillegas explains. "I'm not going to do a careless job because my name's attached to it, and you're only as good as your last project. You have to keep getting better and better."[61]

SHOW UP IN TIMES OF FAILURE

Before arriving for their first day at the United States Military Academy at West Point, cadets have already jumped through a number of hoops to be there, in a process that is arguably more difficult than getting into an Ivy League school. While having outstanding grades and test scores is a given for both sets of applicants, West Point hopefuls set their sights on admission as juniors in high school, a year before their peers. Not only must they have stellar references—from a member of Congress or other high-ranking official, no less—but they must also prove mental *and* physical fitness. Most West Point candidates are at the top of their class, as well as being varsity high school athletes (and often team captains).

Despite this rigorous application process, one in five cadets leaves West Point before graduating, with a sizable percentage dropping out their first summer, during an intensive seven-week training program known as Beast Barracks. When psychologist Angela Duckworth first heard this statistic, she was left with a nagging question: "Who spends two years trying to get into a place and then drops out in the first two months?"

To find the answer, Duckworth spoke to military psychologist Mike Matthews, who recalled frequent dropouts during his own days in Air Force boot camp. His similar experience provided a clue: The challenges presented to both groups of cadets were designed *to exceed* their current skills. For the first time in their lives, these West Point all-stars were being asked to do things they *couldn't* yet do—and many of these uncommonly bright and fit teens weren't used to failure.[62]

Figure skating champion Michelle Kwan, who started skating at the age of five, recalls that the first thing her coach taught her was how to fall. At first, Kwan was confused about why she was learning to fall *before* she learned how to skate, but looking back, she realized that her coach was very smart: "She knew that I was bound to fall many times throughout my career and that I'd need to learn how to handle it."[63]

Showing up in times of illness or crisis is important, but hopefully, these moments are few and far between. But showing up the day after you have failed at something may be the greatest act of perseverance—and the greatest indicator of further success. Founding IBM chairman Thomas J. Watson is often quoted as saying, "The fastest way to succeed is to double your failure rate."[64] Though it may be hard to hear that advice immediately after a failure, what makes great leaders great is their ability to brush themselves off after a fall and get back on the horse to try—and possibly fail—again.

"Show me a successful person, and I will show you someone who has failed more than most," author Donald Miller notes in his book *Business Made Simple.* "Show me an unsuccessful person, and I'll show you somebody who quit after failing a few times. It's counterintuitive, but successful people have failed more often than unsuccessful people. It's just that they had an optimistic attitude about life and got back up."[65]

LEARN TO FAIL BETTER

Prominent people who achieved their status more easily, perhaps because of advantages like generational wealth or family connections, may be reluctant to look back on their mistakes; their brand is built on having *always* been successful. On the other hand, those who came from more humble origins and fought adversity to reach the top spots in their given fields, often because of their own grit, take a different approach. They wear their missteps like badges of honor, knowing that without failure, there is no improvement.

Bucking the common wisdom of our perfection-oriented society, talk show host and author Tavis Smiley refuses to see *fail* as a four-letter word, believing that what we must learn to do is fail *better*. "Every day that you wake up, you get another chance to get it right. To fail better," he writes in the essay collection *The Best Advice I Ever Got: Lessons from Extraordinary Lives*. "We have to learn to think of failure in a different way. To think of failure as a friend, really. A friend who, if embraced, can usher us into new experiences, exposures, and excellencies."[66]

For most writers and editors, learning to handle failure and rejection is par for the course. Award-winning broadcast journalist Katie Couric often recounts the first time she was asked to report on air, when she was working in Washington, DC, as an assistant assignment editor at CNN. Nerves got the better of her, and after she reported about the U.S. President's daily schedule in a singsong voice, word came down from the head of CNN that he never wanted to see her on air again.[67] First-time novelist Kathryn Stockett also knows failure well; she received rejections from 60 agents before finding one who would accept her manuscript of *The Help*, which went on to become a bestselling novel and an Oscar-nominated movie.[68]

And just because we achieve some level of success doesn't mean that rejection is over. Years before founding The Huffington Post, Arianna Huffington gained acclaim for her first book, *The Female Woman*. Though she was offered book contracts to write on women again, she chose another path and decided to write about the role of leaders instead. To her surprise, 36 publishers turned down her second book. In her essay "A Lot of Greek Chutzpah," Huffington credits advice from her mother, who taught her to "accept failure as part and parcel of life. It's not the opposite of success; it's an integral part of success."[69]

According to Jason Feifer, editor in chief of *Entrepreneur*, the key is to stop thinking of setbacks as failures but rather as data. "If you 'fail,' it happens because you're further into the storm than other people are," he explains. "You're seeing change first—which means you have insights that others do not. That can be a powerful position if you're willing to recognize it."[70] This is easier said than done, but Feifer suggests stepping back and looking at the perceived failure from a bit of distance, then asking yourself: *What did I just learn that I didn't know before, and that other people may still not have learned?*[71]

Gaining insight from failures is something I learned about firsthand early in my career, as I attempted to transition from trade to consumer publishing. When I moved to New York City in early 2004, I dreamed about working at one of the top national consumer magazines, and there were two routes to climbing the ladder at one of these publications. Some people rose after getting a foot in the door as an assistant and working their way up, while others started at a smaller publication where they would be given more responsibility from the start, eventually transferring to a larger magazine, buoyed by their experience. I applied for both types of roles, and just a few weeks after moving, was offered a job at the small trade publication *Home Channel News,* setting me off on the latter path. It wasn't the big interior design magazine I had dreams of working for, but it was in an adjacent industry at least.

Throughout the next year and a half, I applied for all sorts of jobs at consumer magazines but was never able to get my foot in the door. I eventually moved on to another trade magazine, called *American Spa,* that was targeted to owners and managers of day spas, resort spas, and destination spas. The topic was much sexier than the building supply industry, and in some ways, the magazine was even more focused on interior design, as we covered the most gorgeous spas around the world. Each issue also included articles about travel and skincare, which were among my other interests. And most importantly for me as an art director, the subject matter allowed for more beautiful layouts than were possible at a magazine covering hardware and lumber.

American Spa was what Abe Peck, the chair of the grad school magazine program I attended at Northwestern, would have called a "sexy trade." Abe was and is still a big proponent of business-to-business (or B2B) magazines, urging students to consider starting or making a career at the less glitzy but equally important publications. The starting salary and amount of experience I would gain in the first few years would likely be better than those at a consumer magazine, he had told me, but there was one caveat: If your ultimate goal is to work for consumer magazines, only stay in a trade-press role for a few years, or else it will be harder to make the transition.

Though I enjoyed working at *American Spa,* I still had my eyes set on working at a big-name magazine, and over the next few years, I made finding that next position a top priority. At night, I pored over job listings, worked on résumés and cover letters, and applied to design jobs everywhere. Some of my grad school classmates and other friends had secured jobs at the larger publications, and I also used their contacts to try to get a foot in the door.

During my first four years in New York, I applied for jobs, met with hiring managers, or completed phone interviews at more than a dozen titles: *Martha Stewart Living, Women's Health, More, Fast Company, Departures, Domino, Men's Vogue, O, The Oprah Magazine, Every Day with Rachael Ray,* and the list goes on. Each of these experiences required a new cover letter and prep time, as well as sneaking out of my current job for an hour or two. I got my hopes up for all of them, and for the most part, I thought that I presented myself well. Though some interviews went better than others, I never bombed, and in the moments after the interviews, I often felt positive—only to receive a note of rejection via email a few days or weeks later. I usually heard some variation on the following: "We enjoyed meeting you, and your work is nice—but we went with someone else."

All of those interviews were failures—or were they? One of the last of these meetings was with Stella Bugbee, who was design director of *Domino* but went on to become editor in chief at The Cut, before landing in her current position as editor of *The New York Times* Styles section. When we met at the end of 2007, I was interviewing at *Domino* for an art director position, which is the same title I held at *American Spa*. We really hit it off during the interview, but she was frank: "I like your work and would love to see what you do with a design test, but I'll need to show your portfolio to our creative director first. I should let you know that we have dozens of résumés, including some from people with 10 or 20 years of experience at consumer magazines."

That night, I met a few friends for sushi, and though I tried to remain hopeful and upbeat, it wasn't easy. I was at the end of my fourth year in New York and still in trade publishing, with my professor's words ringing in my ears. When I heard nothing and followed up a few weeks later, Stella confirmed what I had feared: She had shown my portfolio and résumé to her boss, and they had decided to ask candidates with more experience to take the design test instead. To her credit, Stella reiterated how much she enjoyed meeting me and asked me to stay in touch.

I remember thinking: *This is impossible. Even when the interview goes well, and the hiring manager likes my personality and my work, it still is not enough.* I knew that I was talented yet still felt like a failure. But what if I had started to view all these setbacks as learning opportunities? Even though I wasn't consciously thinking of these rejections as rows of data, I did start thinking about the three things my job interviews all had in common:

- They were for designer or art director roles ...

- at major consumer magazine publishers ...

- located in New York City.

What if one of these variables in my job search changed? The first one was non-negotiable; though I enjoyed writing and editing, art direction was still my passion—and it's not like the competition for editor jobs was any less fierce! And the second variable was almost a moot point; I already had an art director job in New York City that *wasn't* at a major consumer magazine publisher.

But what if the third variable changed? After four years in New York, like many residents, I had a love/hate relationship with the city. It was the epicenter of magazine publishing, which meant there were lots of jobs—but also lots of competition. Some New Yorkers couldn't see themselves anywhere else, but that wasn't the case for me.

I was in my mid-20s and watched enviously as friends in other cities found partners, planned weddings, and bought homes. In New York, that all seemed so out of reach. Like the job market, the dating scene felt impossibly competitive, with people always waiting to see if there was someone better around the corner.

And buying a house? Forget it. I had spent my first two years living with roommates in Brooklyn, then my next two years in a 250-square-foot, fourth-floor walk-up apartment in Manhattan—and was now packing to move back in with a roommate in Brooklyn because they had raised my rent twice in two years, and I could no longer afford my Chelsea studio.

Maybe leaving the city wouldn't be so bad after all? I began considering jobs in other markets, and when I made it to the second round of interviews to lead the art department at *Spa* magazine—which was owned by a large consumer magazine publisher *but* based in San Francisco—I felt that my luck might finally be changing. In January 2008, I completed a design test and eventually traveled to San Francisco to meet the editor in chief and the rest of her team. By March, I had accepted a job offer, packed my tiny apartment into 10 boxes, and headed to California on an exciting new adventure.

Though I had no way of knowing it during all of my failures, my experience at *American Spa* made me the *perfect* candidate for this new role, ultimately setting me on a career path to lead art departments at several consumer magazines owned by the world's largest publishing companies— but all in satellite offices located in cities that weren't New York. It wasn't the path I had originally planned, but it ended up allowing me to live in many amazing cities (rather than just one), eventually meeting my husband and creating a life and career that I love.

THE TAKEAWAY

Practicing perseverance like an editor means **showing up when it's difficult:** during times of illness, crisis, and failure.

Whether you are leading a major company or going solo as a writer, artist, or entrepreneur, you must make the decision to **"go pro" with your pursuit,** treating it as any professional treats their craft and showing up every day.

Though having to show up during times of illness or crisis will hopefully be infrequent, showing up during times of failure may happen a lot more often. And that's actually a good thing, because **failing often also means that you are *trying often,*** even when the outcome is risky and not guaranteed.

Good leaders know that occasional failure is inevitable, but great ones **reframe each failure as another row of data,** asking themselves: "What did I just learn that I didn't know before, and that other people may still not have learned?" If you can look at your failures objectively and figure out what each taught you, these lessons can help improve future efforts, increasing the likelihood of eventual success.

CHAPTER 5

....

Lean into Change

n the last two chapters, I explained that passion and perseverance are the two traits that work together to give high achievers the grit necessary to make it to the top of their chosen fields. But there is one more skill that helps them reach—and stay at—the highest rung of the ladder: the ability to recognize change and quickly adapt to any situation life throws their way.

LEARN TO SLICE THE PIE:
How to adapt when facing immediate challenges

In her book *The Martha Rules,* Martha Stewart describes a lesson she learned early in her career. Before she ran a global media empire and became one of just a handful of people to have a national magazine named after her, Stewart was a small business owner. After spending her 20s first as a model and then as a stockbroker in New York City, she left the city for literal greener pastures, moving to a farmhouse in Westport, Connecticut, where she started a catering business out of her basement. Stewart was thrilled when two of the town's famous residents, actor Paul Newman and his wife Joanne Woodward, hired her to cater a Moroccan-style buffet for a party.[72]

The centerpiece of the menu would be eight *b'steeya,* or flaky Moroccan meat pies, that she planned to fill with chicken and squab. A few hours before the party, Stewart placed the pies in the oven but got distracted with other preparations while they were baking. When she returned to the kitchen to remove the pies, she was horrified to see that each pie had a badly burnt crust on the portion that was closest to the wall of the oven. Her mind filled with terrifying thoughts:

> My reputation as a caterer was at stake. The pies were time-consuming to prepare, and it would be impossible to recreate them. I took a deep breath and made an assessment. I saw that although the pies were no longer perfect, the vast majority of each was fine and undamaged. I picked up a serrated knife, cut each pie into wedges, discarded the damaged portions, gathered the perfect pieces, sprinkled them with crisscrosses of powdered sugar and cinnamon, arranged them on huge brass trays, took them to the party, and served them. I acted as though nothing were amiss, and the party was a huge success.[73]

By slicing the pie, Stewart was able to toss out the bad parts and salvage the good ones, creating a main course that looked a bit different from her initial expectation but that was just as tasty, ultimately saving the meal—and the reputation of her business.

I found my own opportunity to slice the pie about a year after I started working at *Coastal Living* (if you'll remember, this was my dream job after leaving *Parenting*). Our travel editor asked me if I would take a trip to the U.S. Virgin Islands to review a "new boutique waterfront hotel." When I landed in St. Croix, I asked for the hotel by name, but the cab driver had never heard of it. I told him the hotel was brand new and showed him the address. His face lit up—he recognized the address and said it belonged to another hotel, but that he could take me there.

When I arrived, the hotel didn't look very new. I was shown to my room, which I can only describe as fine. It had a view of the water—but the decor was more shabby than chic, and the tiled floor looked a little dated. The most disappointing thing was that the hotel was built around a pool that had an ocean view, but the pool was drained for maintenance and had a giant crack in the corner.

That night, the hotel's owner invited me to dinner, and I asked him to tell me his story. I was curious to know if he had recently moved to St. Croix and when he had bought the place. Again, they were billing themselves as a brand-new hotel, signaling to me that he may also be new to the island.

"No," he laughed. "I've been here for years, but we recently just changed our name and logo. Our PR guy said if we did that we could pitch it to the media as a new hotel." My jaw dropped as I realized why the taxi driver had been so confused. I muddled through dinner, and afterward, the owner took me on a tour of the more historic wing of the hotel, which oozed with real Caribbean charm. The guest rooms boasted beautiful red pine floors, historic plank-and-beam ceilings, and colonial-style four-poster beds. If these elegant accommodations were unoccupied and available, I couldn't fathom why they put a journalist in the outdated annex next to the drained, cracked pool.

After the tour, I went back to my room and tried to figure out what I could do to save the trip. I was in town for three days with nothing to do but report on this hotel, yet it was immediately obvious to me that while the historic rooms may warrant a mention, there was no way I could write a whole article on this place. I emailed my editor and told her that if we wanted to salvage the cost of the trip, and to make the most of my time out of the office, we should pivot from a hotel feature to a "Waterfront Weekend" article about Christiansted, the town I was visiting. She agreed and told me to get to work.

I immediately set about dining at restaurants, visiting a nearby brewery, booking a scuba lesson, and shopping in local boutiques to get a full sense of the town. I had secretly hoped for a bit of a working vacation, where I could sit poolside and soak up the sun with a paperback. Instead, I ended up running all over town trying to experience enough local culture for a completely different type of article. Travel writing is extremely rewarding, but also a lot more challenging than most people would expect.

Just like Martha Stewart, I "sliced the pie," salvaging my trip to write a better article with more information than a simple hotel review would have provided. In both scenarios, adapting to our circumstances helped us avoid failure, and no one was any the wiser. But is it possible to slice the pie even *after* others have seen us fail—and especially if we have done so publicly?

Stewart maintains that the answer is a resounding "YES." In fact, that is how she describes the actions she took when her perfectly manicured world was upended in the early 2000s by an exhausting legal battle. Accused of insider trading related to a personal stock market transaction, Stewart was the subject of an investigation that ultimately led to a trial. Throughout 2002 and 2003, her life was shaken to the core, and the stock price of her company plummeted. Stewart's board of directors and attorneys urged her to resign as CEO of the company she founded, which she did in 2003.

In March 2004, she was found guilty and shortly after was sentenced to a five-month term in prison and another five months of home incarceration. "Just as with my *b'steeya* mishap," Stewart notes, "it was time for me to fully evaluate the situation, cut the pie into wedges, gather the good parts, and move on."[74]

Stewart's lawyers were adamant that she appeal, and though she agreed with them, she also knew that an appeal could potentially drag on for years, and she may end up going to prison anyway. Though she had been the subject of much negative press during the investigation and trial, causing her company to be battered along the way, she had also received an outpouring of support from her most loyal fans. People were still buying her products and reading her magazines, and she felt that her company could weather the storm if she could somehow put this incident behind her.

"In order to save my company from irreparable harm, I knew it was time to slice my situation into wedges," Stewart writes. "I realized that it would be in everyone's best interests for me to complete my prison term and home confinement, even as my lawyers aggressively pursued my appeal."[75]

After taking actions to ensure that her company could run without her for a few months, Stewart reported to Alderson Federal Prison Camp in West Virginia on October 8, 2004. "Although my stay at Alderson had none of the fun and spice of a Moroccan buffet, it was a far better experience than I had anticipated," she recalls. Stewart found the inmates to be welcoming and was asked by them to lead an informal business seminar, teaching them how to become entrepreneurs themselves when they were released. The lessons she taught became the seeds of her book *The Martha Rules*.[76]

When she left Alderson in March 2005, famously wearing a crocheted poncho that one of her fellow inmates had gifted her, Stewart realized that although there were many things about her life that she had dearly missed, "there were just as many wonderful things that I had gathered during those five months: new friendships, so many ideas, and so much information and knowledge from fascinating books that I actually had the time to read. I also gained a new appreciation for the complexity of every single person's situation."[77]

In the almost two decades since, Stewart has unquestionably bounced back, launching multiple television shows, product lines, and other business ventures, including her first restaurant. A former model during the 1960s, Stewart reprised that role in 2023 at the age of 81, making history as the oldest person to appear on the cover of the *Sports Illustrated* Swimsuit Issue. "I hope this cover inspires you to challenge yourself to try new things, no matter what stage of life you are in," Stewart captioned the image on Instagram. "Changing, evolving, and being fearless—those are all very good things, indeed."[78]

FOLLOW THE CHEESE:
How to adapt when change is on the horizon

In 2006, when I was working at *American Spa* magazine, the vice president of our company created a contest. He had become enamored with the popular self-help book *Who Moved My Cheese?* by Spencer Johnson and wanted everyone in the company to read it. Although he couldn't require everyone to read the book on their own time, he said that if you did read it—and emailed him a short synopsis explaining what you had learned—you would be entered to win a free massage at a local day spa. He was even giving out free copies of the book! Well, I'm no dummy—a free book *and* a chance for a free massage caught my attention. (This particular executive may have been onto something; see Chapter 14 on offering perks when you can't afford raises.)

With the subtitle "An A-Mazing Way to Deal with Change in Your Work and in Your Life," *Who Moved My Cheese?* is a parable set in a maze that is inhabited by four characters. Sniff and Scurry are mice who are straightforward and action-oriented, driven purely by their desire for cheese. Hem and Haw, on the other hand, are mouse-sized humans known as "Littlepeople." For them, cheese symbolizes more than just food; it represents their self-worth. Their entire existence and belief systems are intertwined with the cheese they possess.

In the story, both the mice and Littlepeople find a large pile of cheese in the maze that sustains them for quite some time. But when their stash runs out, the mice adapt quickly and head off to find new cheese, while the Littlepeople struggle to accept the change. They wait for the cheese to return, expressing frustration and confusion when it doesn't. Eventually Haw, inspired by the mice, embarks on a journey to find new cheese, embracing the uncertainty despite potential dangers. But Hem digs in his heels, railing at the injustice of it all and refusing to accept this new change. It is only when he is nearly emaciated that he finally gives in and joins the others on the search for new cheese. At the end, Haw—who eventually finds his own new cheese—recounts the lessons he learned:

- **Change Happens:** They keep moving the cheese.

- **Anticipate Change:** Get ready for the cheese to move.

- **Monitor Change:** Smell the cheese often so you know when it is getting old.

- **Adapt to Change Quickly:** The sooner you let go of old cheese, the sooner you can enjoy new cheese.

- **Change:** Move with the cheese.

- **Enjoy Change!** Savor the adventure and enjoy the taste of new cheese.

- **Be Ready to Change Quickly and Enjoy it Again and Again:** They keep moving the cheese.[79]

Most readers can identify the cheese as something related to their career path or industry, but the author points out that it could also stand for more personal aspects of our livelihood, like health and relationships. Although our VP may not have been able to predict the financial crisis or the rise of social media and smartphones, he knew enough about consumers' evolving relationship with the internet to see that big changes were coming.

It's no secret: The rise of the internet in the first decade of this century, followed by the rise of social media in the second, drastically altered the way that people consume content. Newspapers were hit first and hardest, as people no longer wanted to wait a full day for a printed copy of the news when the internet would allow it to be delivered (and updated) in real time. Magazines held out a bit longer, largely, I think, because the early internet was not always a beautiful experience. People still wanted to see large photos and digest information that had been curated into a pretty package. Reading from a laptop at the beach or on the subway was not very convenient. Of course, with the advent of the smartphone and tablets, the delivery of digital information has come a long way—though I would argue that magazines still hold an important place in our culture and may experience a bit of a resurgence as people seek to limit their screen time in the future.

The media companies who recognized these changes first—seeing that the cheese was getting stale and less abundant—were the ones best positioned not only to find a new source of cheese but also to get there first, securing for themselves an earlier and larger share. We saw this as some companies created robust websites that became new sources of income, either from ad sales, e-commerce opportunities, or membership programs (i.e., putting most of their digital content behind a paywall for paying subscribers). Other brands explored completely different avenues, from launching in-person events to licensing their brand names to product manufacturers.

Similarly, some editors resisted the changes everyone in the industry was being asked to make, while others embraced the ever-expanding digital landscape, realizing that opportunities would open to them if they broadened their skill sets. Some of these editors became their own brands, starting blogs and podcasts focused on the topics they previously covered for national magazines, while also expanding their reach through social media. Others learned to apply their editorial skills to the business world, as they moved into marketing and communications roles in other industries, where they created content to help their new employers connect with audiences—a skill many of them knew quite well from their previous careers.

Those who did not think the cheese would *really* move, or who were too scared to think about what would happen if it did, fared the worst; many magazine brands that did not pivot—or did so too late—were forced to shutter in the face of declining subscriptions, newsstand sales, and ad revenue. Along the way, their editors often found themselves without jobs and competing with each other for even fewer editorial positions, unless they were willing to pivot to new roles that would utilize their skills to create digital-first content or branded content for companies in other industries.

At different points in my career, I have been similar to both the mice in the story who sniff out change and embrace it, and the Littlepeople who are slower to come around to the idea. The magazine business has long been known for having a revolving door when it comes to employment; often, the way an editor in the industry advanced their career was by moving to a new publication every few years, where they would usually receive a slightly higher title and salary. I definitely embraced this type of change, working for four different companies within my first decade in the business, which also meant learning to work with new bosses and colleagues every few years. Each of these moves helped contribute to my understanding of which leadership styles work best.

I've also tried to embrace changes in technology, designing the first few tablet issues of *Parenting* magazine just a few months after the iPad made its debut. And in 2015, when I left my job as design director at *Coastal Living* to start my own branding and graphic design company, that was me "looking for new cheese." After more than a decade of working almost exclusively on magazines, this new role allowed me to learn web design, as well as the intricacies of producing marketing and sales collateral.

Now, I am once again working for a magazine, owned by one of the world's largest media companies. But I have conquered the maze once and know that this is not the only corridor that has cheese waiting at the end. While I continue to refine my print design skills, I am also honing new ones, as we further expand the digital and social media presence of VERANDA, earning new revenue streams and learning new content creation and marketing skills along the way. Should the cheese one day disappear, I could lace up my sneakers and quickly head back into the maze to find new cheese that may be just as tasty—or even tastier.

EDITOR'S TIP

The only constant is change.

As the editor in chief of *Entrepreneur* magazine, Jason Feifer has found that the most successful entrepreneurs he meets all have one thing in common: They are good at change.[80] In his book *Build for Tomorrow,* Feifer reminds readers that many inventions—from the automobile to the elevator to streaming television—seemed bizarre at first but are now part of the way we live our lives. He advises people to ease their panic by considering what they could gain from a shift in direction; then, they can evaluate how a current skill set could be broadened to reflect the new normal.

Though these tactics make it easier to recognize and adapt to change more quickly, Feifer points out that there is an underlying belief that they are built upon: Nothing can—or should be—permanent. At times, change is scary, but that doesn't mean it's wrong. "Instead of defining ourselves firmly—I am *this*, I do *that*—we must recognize that everything we do, as well as everything we are, is simply the next thing in a long line of next things," he says.[81]

THE TAKEAWAY

When confronted with a problem, take a deep breath and evaluate the circumstances before making a rash decision. Then think about what actions you could take to **"slice the pie"** and salvage the situation, discarding the bad parts and making the most of the resources you have.

Just because things are going well doesn't mean they will never change. Learn to **anticipate any changes** on the horizon by constantly monitoring the condition of the "cheese" that nourishes you, which in business means your career, your company, and your industry.

If you notice the cheese seems less abundant or perhaps a bit stale, start to **adapt as soon as possible,** and be prepared to go off in search of "new cheese," whether that means finding new customers, new processes, a new job, or even a new career.

The most successful leaders realize that **change is inevitable.** Instead of being panicked by change, they seek out the positives and quickly learn how to use their skills and experience to bridge the gap between the old way and the new way.

PART TWO

Y is for

YOURSELF

"The pessimist complains about the wind. The optimist expects it to change. The leader adjusts the sails."

—John Maxwell, bestselling author, coach, and leadership expert

The day I was offered the role of design director at *Coastal Living* was one of the most exciting of my career. As I mentioned in Chapter 3, I had spent the past year and a half working at Bonnier's *Parenting* magazine, a publication that covered topics I really had no passion for. When I was finally offered my dream job, I was thrilled—but also a tad nervous to be leading a team that had already been working together for years. I was confident in my design abilities—but my leadership abilities? Not so much.

THE LEADERSHIP LEARNING GAP

Not many people start their careers wanting to be leaders. Sure, there are those brilliant few—the charismatic, visionary unicorns who have "The Next Great Big Idea" and know from a young age that they are destined to be innovators, industry leaders, and CEOs of their own companies. But for most of us, leadership positions appear mid-career and sometimes out of nowhere, when we have progressed far enough along in our work journey that the next logical step is a promotion into a management role.

The next thing we know, we are leading complex projects and even more complex teams of people, all of which may require an entirely different skill set than our core subject matter knowledge or competencies that got us to this point. By the time I was hired at *Coastal Living* at the age of 32, I had completed a bachelor's and a master's degree in journalism, and had also gained almost a decade of on-the-job experience, art directing and writing at several national publications. But the one thing I had never taken was a single course on leadership.

It remains baffling to me that this type of instruction, which is essential to almost any profession, is not taught more prominently in high school or college. (Along these same lines, I also don't understand why algebra, geometry, and trigonometry were drilled into my head in high school, but no one taught me about retirement accounts, credit card interest, or how to create a simple household budget.)

So in the three weeks between being hired and starting my first day at *Coastal Living*, my journalism training kicked in, and I did what I always do if I don't know how to do something: find the expert and learn from them. In this case, the expert was Kate White, the former editor in chief of five women's magazines, including *Cosmopolitan*, which she helmed for 14 years.

In her book *I Shouldn't Be Telling You This: Success Secrets Every Gutsy Girl Should Know*, White breaks down her advice into three sections, each targeting a different career stage: ambitious employees just starting out, mid-level managers who find themselves leading people for the first time, and executives who are at the top of their game and wondering what is next. Though I may not be the "gutsy girl" White had in mind, the book definitely resonated with me, and I had soon filled my copy with highlighter strokes, scribbled notes, and sticky tabs. The lessons contained in her book could bring value to any current or soon-to-be leader in corporate America, but they were especially helpful for me because White pulled most of the examples from her own career in the world of publishing.[82]

When it comes to being a good leader, she reminds us that there is one surefire technique that can turn every workday into an on-the-job leadership seminar: watching our own bosses and other bosses around us. It's a given that we've all had good and bad bosses over the years, but have you really taken a moment to think about what they did well and where they faltered? As you develop your own leadership style, consider how your current and past leaders have motivated—or failed to motivate—their teams. Did they seem approachable or aloof? Did they handle stress well or take it out on others? Which of their actions did you love and which ones made you feel unappreciated?

As I prepared for my first day at *Coastal Living*, I started thinking about the kind of boss I wanted to be. I had worked for a few great bosses along the way—and also a few lousy ones. But most of them, like all human beings, had areas where they excelled and areas where they fell short. I did my best to look back on past leaders and bring their positive traits into my own leadership style, while attempting to avoid any of their pitfalls that contributed to inefficient work processes and bad morale.

LEADING LIKE AN EDITOR

Though journalism has its share of good and bad bosses, there are three core leadership traits that all good editors must master to be effective leaders. The following chapters will explain why it is important that you:

- **Strive to have integrity of character,** which includes moral and ethical clarity as well as wholeness of self.

- **Embrace the truth** by vowing to know a little bit about everything, by asking clarifying questions when obstacles appear, and by getting expert help when you don't know the answer.

- Use this knowledge to **make informed decisions** about how to tackle problems, delegate responsibilities, and cut your losses if something just isn't working.

Despite taking such a considered approach to my first big management job, I still made plenty of leadership mistakes along the way and continue to do so in my current role. This is just a reality of managing others. But taking the time to work on yourself as a leader before focusing on your team, your customer, or your product is one of the greatest and longest-lasting gifts you can give to yourself—and to your business. So let's get started.

CHAPTER 6

....

Act with Integrity

To lead like an editor means, above all else, acting with integrity. Although having integrity is an admirable trait for anyone, it is essential in the field of journalism. In both my undergraduate and graduate journalism schools, ethics classes were required as part of the curriculum, and it was drilled into our heads that we must cover the news without fear or favor.

Journalism is not just about the business of selling newspapers or magazines, or in more recent times, digital versions of this information. In the way that I described the role of journalists as first responders in Chapter 4, reporters similarly have a duty to be the watchdogs of society, reporting the news without manipulating or sensationalizing the facts, and without allowing personal biases to cloud the truth.

Maintaining a lack of bias is taken very seriously by most good journalists and especially by those who report on hard news or politics. In extreme examples, some reporters register politically as independents, lest they be viewed as biased toward one party or another. Others, if attending a press conference, might refuse to accept a cup of coffee or doughnut offered in the back of the room, lest it be looked upon as accepting a gift from the organization or public figure holding the conference.

Journalists are storytellers, but our stories must always be based on a foundation of truth. Unlike novelists, whose only responsibility is to entertain the reader, journalists have a responsibility to deliver fair and accurate information to readers, while also holding their subjects accountable for their words and actions.

Before the internet, most of us got information from the same sources: "legacy" media outlets such as hometown newspapers, magazines, and TV stations; as well as national magazines and newspapers from larger cities, like *The New York Times* and *The Washington Post*. These outlets were usually run by editors with years of formal journalism training and on-the-job experience, who made it their mission to find and report the truth. In many cases, they also had fact checkers verify their words before they made it into the hands of the public.

Although the phrase, "Don't believe everything you read," is considered common wisdom, for many years, you really *could* believe most of what you read from these venerable sources. In the Internet Age, however, the speed with which news is reported can lead to more frequent errors; and even worse, because anyone can start a website without journalism or ethics training, "fake news" and "alternative facts" make it even more important for traditional journalists to maintain their integrity at all times.

WHY INTEGRITY MATTERS IN BUSINESS

Robert Chesnut has spent a lot of time thinking about the concept of integrity, especially as it relates to the world of business. As the chief ethics officer at Airbnb, he helped develop the company's code of ethics as well as an interactive employee program called Integrity Belongs Here, which helps drive company-wide compliance with that code.

For a business like Airbnb, having a sterling reputation when it comes to integrity is vital. The company's premise is based on the extremely personal act of hosting strangers in your home, and Airbnb also has access to a massive amount of data about where its customers live and travel. "Our business model relies on our customers' basic trust that this will be a safe, pleasant, as-advertised experience where both parties benefit," Chesnut explains. "The damage to our reputation can be swift and severe if any of us—the hosts, the guests, or Airbnb as the facilitator—do not act with integrity."[83]

While integrity has always been fundamental to building and maintaining trust, credibility, and a positive reputation, it is even more important in today's world where consumers and partners demand transparency from the companies they support, and a digital trail can expose indiscretions that may have previously been swept under the rug.

In a report called "The Bottom Line on Trust," the consulting firm Accenture notes that "in the not-too-distant past, trust was considered a 'soft' corporate issue" that companies focused on in theory but never made a top priority, at least in comparison to delivering profits. But today, the report continues, "companies need to execute a balanced strategy that prioritizes trust at the same level as growth and profitability. Those who do benefit from greater resiliency from trust incidents, making them more competitive. Those who don't are putting billions in future revenue at risk." The report finds that consumers may punish companies who publicly suffer trust-eroding incidents—from product recalls and SEC violations to major disasters, like an oil spill—by withholding their business temporarily or switching their allegiance to a more trustworthy competitor. Such incidents can also result in staffing issues, as both current workers and potential new hires may seek employment in other businesses that they view as having a stronger moral compass.[84]

INTENTIONAL INTEGRITY:
'IT ALL STARTS AT THE TOP.'

Though once defined as "telling the truth and keeping your word," integrity is more than that. It must be specific and purposeful. In his book *Intentional Integrity*, Chesnut explains that we must go beyond taking "a vow to be virtuous. It means making a serious and thorough effort to, first, identify an organization's purpose and the values it stands for; then develop specific rules that reflect those values; and finally, drive the importance of following the rules into every corner—and level—of the company."

Chesnut lays out a plan for creating, communicating, and enforcing a customized code of ethics for your organization. Most publicly held companies have these codes spelled out and available to the public on their websites, one of many stipulations of the Sarbanes-Oxley Act, which passed shortly after—and largely because of—the Enron insider trading scandal that came to light in 2001.

But before you can create a custom code of ethics, the most important part about perpetuating a workplace culture built on integrity is realizing that it starts with leadership. As leaders, we must make integrity a top priority not just for our companies but for ourselves, modeling the sterling reputation we would like our businesses to have. If we don't do that, how can we expect our employees to take integrity seriously?

Chesnut recalls meeting Jim Sinegal, the founder of Costco, in a hotel lounge and chatting with him about business for hours while winding down after a long day on the road. When Chesnut explained his concept of intentional integrity, Sinegal quietly said, "Only one thing matters. It all starts at the top." Chesnut suggests that having a leader who prioritizes integrity may be one of the reasons that Costco has never been involved in any scandals or accused of having questionable practices, but rather has one of the best reputations in retailing, with extremely low employee turnover.[85]

UNIMPAIRED AND COMPLETE:
THE OTHER DEFINITIONS OF INTEGRITY

As journalists, we define ourselves as "word people," and the origins of the word *integrity* are interesting to consider. Though the Merriam-Webster dictionary lists the first definition as a "firm adherence to a code of especially moral or artistic values; incorruptibility," it also lists two more definitions. Evolved from the Latin adjective *integer*, meaning *whole* or *complete*, the word *integrity* can also be defined as "an unimpaired condition; soundness" or "the quality or state of being complete or undivided."[86]

Most people use the first definition when describing a person who lives by a set of values and principles, while the second and third definitions are often used to describe objects or ideas, such as the "structural integrity" of a building or the "scientific integrity" of a study. But what if we used those definitions to describe people as well—and specifically, leaders?

Henry Cloud makes a case for doing just that in his book *Integrity: The Courage to Meet the Demands of Reality*. A person with integrity, he argues, has the ability to pull everything together, to make things happen no matter how challenging the circumstances. As a clinical psychologist and corporate consultant with a specialty in leadership coaching, Cloud worked for decades with CEOs and other high-level executives at companies large and small. Many of the people he encountered were honest, ethical people who were still struggling to achieve the next level of success.

"While we would say that they all were people of good 'character,' the reality is that their 'personhood' was still preventing their talents and brains from accomplishing all that was in their potential," Cloud writes. "Some aspects to who they were as people that they had never seen as important to develop were keeping them from reaching the heights that all of the other investments they had made should have afforded them."[87]

He notes that the high-level leaders who *were* successful and firing on all cylinders had six core abilities that either came naturally to them, or that they worked to develop. Successful leaders who seek to have the other

definition of integrity—unimpaired, wholeness of character—must be able
to do the following:

- **Gain the complete trust** of the people they are leading, capturing
  their full hearts.

- **Be oriented toward the truth,** operating within the realities of a given
  situation, even when it is not ideal.

- **Work in a way that gets results** and produces outcomes, by creating
  and then working to achieve goals.

- **Calmly deal** with problem people, negative situations, obstacles,
  failures, setbacks, and losses.

- **Create growth** in themselves, their organization, their people, their
  profits, and their industry.

- **Transcend their own interests** and themselves to larger purposes,
  thus becoming part of a larger mission.[88]

All of this sounds easy enough, but what does it look like in action?
Let's find out.

THE INTEGRITY LEADER IN ACTION: A CASE STUDY

From the time I got my first job in high school, I have had many leaders
over the course of my career. Looking at the six characteristics listed above,
I found that many of my bosses checked the mark for a few of the qualities,
maybe even four or five, but often they had at least one in which they were
deficient. It's to be expected; as humans, we aren't naturally wired to excel
at everything. But if a good leader recognizes a deficiency in any of the key
areas listed above, they should make an effort to grow in that aspect.

Of all the people I have worked for, the one that comes closest to meeting all of the qualities of a full-integrity leader is Steele Thomas Marcoux,
my current boss at VERANDA. Now I know what you are thinking: *How
convenient that he is full of praise for his current boss!* But look at it this way:
Over the last decade, I have had the pleasure of working with her on two
different publications (during my final year at *Coastal Living* and for more
than six years and counting at VERANDA). It is no coincidence that the
best boss I've had is also the one I've stuck with the longest.

But what makes Steele a good leader? Let's examine the way she checks
all of the boxes on Henry Cloud's list:

1. A high-integrity leader creates and maintains trust: Steele gains the complete trust of her teams by leading with empathy and also showing vulnerability. No one wants to work for a drill sergeant, or worse yet, a robot. When you have a problem—whether in your personal or work life—you can approach her with it, without fear of repercussion. Likewise, she is a transparent boss and is the first to admit when she doesn't have it all figured out. Rather than ruling from on high, she calls together small groups to talk through the implications of new initiatives or to brainstorm solutions when plans go awry. As Cloud points out, transparent leaders "let the reality of where they are and the situations be known. We can only ultimately trust people who are being real with us."[89]

2. A high-integrity leader is able to see and face reality: By being oriented toward the truth, Steele is always seeking out new information about how we can better serve our audience. Realizing that many of our readers are not only design enthusiasts but also professional interior designers, she recently started a newsletter called "Trade Secrets" that allows her to speak directly to this group, while also soliciting their feedback so we can serve them better. Like other leaders who exemplify this trait, Steele knows how to deliver difficult news as well, reframing less desirable developments as merely hiccups—or perhaps even opportunities—and not as catastrophes. When I asked for a promotion that was not financially possible at the time, Steele let me down easily while reiterating my value to the team and giving me hope that advancement may be possible the following year. (Thankfully, it was!) As Cloud explains, these types of leaders can take the "sting" out of the delivery when they are sharing bad news or negative feedback with a team member: "They neutralize negative truths with kindness. … Or, they just are not harsh in the delivery of it."[90]

3. A high-integrity leader works in a way that brings results: Good leaders take a "Ready. Aim. Fire." approach by taking stock of their resources and abilities and anticipating any obstacles that might come up along the way; then setting a specific goal toward which those resources will be focused or aimed; and only then, pulling the trigger to set the plan into motion. Steele is a planner who is more than willing to sit down and hash out every possible outcome before making a decision; but then, once she has all of the information, she trusts her instincts to take aim toward a goal. When obstacles pop up along the way, as they inevitably do, she finds a way to make things work. When tasked with essentially starting VERANDA's website from scratch, with a scant audience and a skeleton-crew team, she rolled up her own sleeves to help and spent much of her first year at VERANDA burning the midnight oil to crank out the type of SEO-focused stories that would eventually bring more traffic to our fledgling site.

4. A high-integrity leader embraces negative realities and solves them: In the Broadway musical *The Wiz*, the Wicked Witch of the West sings a song called "Don't Nobody Bring Me No Bad News," warning her minions that anyone bringing bad news will face her wrath. While it is played for humor in the musical, many of us have had bosses like this in real life, and the result is anything but funny. Steele is the opposite of this and actually excels at helping find solutions to her team's problems. (See her Editor's Tip at the end of this chapter.) When an article has the potential to be problematic because a lot of big personalities are involved, she offers to take the reins and write it. When a freelancer was unkind and harassing to a staff member, we stopped working with that person immediately. And back when she was the editor of *Coastal Living*, and Time Inc. was trying to sell the brand, Steele fought to get stay-on bonuses for key employees to ease their anxiety during an uncertain period of transition.

5. A high-integrity leader causes growth and increase: In 2018, Hearst made the decision to move VERANDA from its New York City headquarters to a satellite office in Birmingham, Alabama, where its sister title *Country Living* was already based. At that time, Steele was made editor in chief and given the budget to hire three full-time staffers (myself included), who would produce the magazine along with several additional employees who would be shared between *Country Living* and VERANDA. Although our print magazine seemed to be doing relatively well, we had a very limited digital and social media presence. While the past decade has seen the decline of many print-focused brands, under Steele's leadership, VERANDA continues to grow. Our full-time staff count has almost doubled since 2018, and our expansive redesign was a hit with readers *and* advertisers, resulting in the brand's largest print issue since 2008. Meanwhile, traffic to our website has increased significantly each year (unique page views were up 90 percent year-over-year 12 months after the brand refresh), and our Instagram presence has grown to well over a million engaged followers. New initiatives—from newsletters and video series to membership programs and editorial franchises (see a more thorough discussion of these in Chapter 10)—continue to launch every few months, furthering brand awareness and profitability.

6. A high-integrity leader achieves transcendence and meaning, serving a larger purpose: One of Steele's editorial goals for VERANDA was not only to showcase beautiful interior design but also to feature designers and architects who are committed to preserving historic buildings, shining light on their storied pasts through a modern lens. Under her direction, we have explored topics that go deeper than typical shelter-magazine fare; one essay, for instance, made the case for recasting Southern plantations as cultural sites that honor the stories of the enslaved people who lived there. VERANDA has also partnered with the National Trust for Historic Preservation to shine a light on significant buildings in Black history that have largely gone unrecognized for their importance in shaping our country.

EDITOR'S TIP

Honesty is the key to effective problem-solving.

Though no one *wants* to deal with drama, VERANDA editor in chief Steele Thomas Marcoux actually thrives when helping her team find solutions to problems—and she prefers to know about them as soon as possible. "I feel like I'm at my best if someone is coming to me with a problem, but what I don't like is when I *perceive* that there's a problem but nobody is actually talking to me about it," she explains.

Steele says that her ability to help her team solve problems effectively depends on three basic human principles: respect, transparency, and—perhaps most important—honesty. "If we're being honest, we can remove personality, ego, and emotion because we are just dealing with some facts," she says. "There's always a solution that can work, even when things get sticky, even if we have to make hard choices, even if we have to give people bad news that they don't want to hear. As long as we lay all the cards on the table, then we can work through it."[91]

THE TAKEAWAY

To lead like an editor means, above all else, **leading with integrity.**

Integrity has always been important in journalism, as newspapers and magazines have historically served as "watchdogs" for the interests of their readers. It is even more important today, in the era of "fake news."

Integrity is also more important than ever in business, as modern consumers and potential partners demand transparency from the companies they do business with.

Rather than just having a vague sense of "doing the right thing," companies today should practice **intentional integrity** by mapping out a code of conduct for themselves and their employees. Everyone in the company should embrace and be held to these standards—including the CEO.

The most effective leaders also display the other definition of integrity: **completeness of character.** They maintain the trust of their teams through kindness and empathy, while staying focused on the truth and demonstrating the courage to meet the demands of reality, even when it isn't pretty. These leaders are growth- and results-oriented, but can also see beyond the numbers, serving a larger purpose or mission outside of themselves.

Visit **LeadLikeAnEditor.com** to download a free workbook that includes **The Integrity Leader Self-Evaluation** as well as other templates and resources.

CHAPTER 7

Embrace the Truth

Walking into a grocery store in 1950 was a much different experience than it is today. Most Americans shopped at neighborhood grocers, where the footprint was significantly smaller than today's mega supermarkets. The layout was usually simple with fewer aisles, offering a more limited selection of brands and products compared to today's stores. Fresh produce sections were also smaller in both size and variety, and many products were sold loose or in bulk, bearing little resemblance to the colorful packaged goods we see today.

At that time, the Great Atlantic and Pacific Tea Company, also known as A&P, was the largest retail organization in the world, while another grocery retailer called The Kroger Company was merely half its size, barely keeping pace with the general market performance. Now flash forward to today: Kroger is the country's largest supermarket operator by revenue[92] and fourth-largest retailer.[93] Meanwhile, A&P is now a distant memory. After decades of decline, the company filed for bankruptcy in 2015, eventually selling off its remaining stores to other chains the following year.

That a struggling retailer can rise to such amazing heights while a stronger and more established competitor eventually falls from grace begs the question: How did such a dramatic reversal of fortunes happen? In the end, it all came down to a simple trait that Kroger's leaders had and A&P's leaders did not: a willingness to embrace the truth.

In his book *Good to Great: Why Some Companies Make the Leap ... and Others Don't,* Jim Collins does a deep dive into this case study and comes to an interesting conclusion.[94] In the first half of the 20th century, which included the Great Depression and two World Wars, a small, utilitarian store with limited-but-inexpensive offerings served the American consumer just fine, and companies based their retail models on this fact. However, by the second half of the century, Americans had grown more affluent, and many had also moved to the suburbs. They wanted nicer, larger stores with lots of parking and a wide range of offerings, including specialty foods, all types of fresh produce, and even things they may have traditionally gone to other retailers for: fresh-baked bread, flowers, cold medicine, and more.

The problem wasn't that Kroger knew this and A&P didn't. Both companies conducted their own research and found that consumers preferred this new type of supermarket. But instead of using the information to their advantage and adapting their locations, A&P's leadership fought this trend and tried to win business by lowering costs. During an economic boom, this proved less important for customers than having nice stores. Collins describes the vicious downward spiral that A&P entered: "The price cutting led to cost cutting, which led to even drabber stores and poorer service, which in turn drove customers away, further driving down margins, resulting in even dirtier stores and worse service."[95]

Kroger's leaders, on the other hand, realized that "supercombination" stores were the way of the future—and also that if they couldn't be number one or two in any given market, it made more sense to exit the area and focus their efforts elsewhere. And then they took action, changing, replacing, or closing every store that did not fit the new realities. It wasn't a fast process, but it was an effective one. Flash forward a few decades, and by the end of the 1990s, Kroger had rebuilt its system, becoming the country's top grocery chain.[96]

According to Collins, it is this ability to embrace the truth—even when it isn't what you want to hear—that separates the most innovative leaders from the status quo. "When, as in the Kroger case, you start with an honest and diligent effort to determine the truth of the situation, the right decisions often become self-evident," he writes. "And even if all decisions do not become self-evident, one thing is certain: You absolutely cannot make a series of good decisions without first confronting the brutal facts. The good-to-great companies operated in accordance with this principle, and the comparison companies generally did not."[97]

KNOW A LITTLE BIT ABOUT EVERYTHING IN YOUR BUSINESS

When I applied to enter the master's degree program in magazine publishing at Northwestern University's Medill School of Journalism, one of the things that appealed to me most was that we would learn not just about writing and editing, as was the case at many journalism schools, but also about art direction, advertising sales, and the business side of running a magazine. Lessons in these areas would be taught—and put into practice—during a group project in the final quarter.

For the capstone project, our 16-person class was split into four teams and given a few weeks to research and present an idea for a new magazine. The concepts were approached from all aspects, as we studied our target market, potential competitors, and even the distribution model that made the most sense for each new title. Sample articles were written, covers were mocked up, and editorial calendars were plotted out. (I'll talk more about the importance of calendars in Chapter 10.)

We then pitched the ideas to our peers, along with a team of advisors and professors with specialties ranging from new media (the internet!) to business to design to circulation; then, each faculty member asked questions and weighed in on our concepts. After the feasibility of each idea was debated and holes poked in its merits, the class was left to vote among ourselves on which project we would choose to focus on exclusively for the next three months. In the end, we chose a concept called *Fuel*, which was essentially a smart magazine about youth culture—a teen *Vanity Fair*, if you will.

Once our topic was chosen, we dove into creating a prototype issue and business plan from scratch. From September to December of that year, we lived and breathed the magazine business for 10 to 12 hours a day, five to six days a week. Each of the 16 students was assigned a role, ranging from editor in chief to advertising director to business manager to design director, and we all wrote stories for the prototype as well.

I had always loved reading magazines, but throughout the next 12 weeks, I learned more than I ever thought I could about the business itself. We had lectures on market research, distribution models, and writing cover lines that sell; we went on sales calls to top media buyers and hit the phones, calling potential readers in our target demographic to ask what they wanted from a magazine. We even created a five-year business plan and website for *Fuel*, before reconvening at the end of the quarter to present the fruits of our labors to a mix of faculty, friends, and family, as well as media bigwigs who flew in from New York for the occasion.

I learned a lot from this program (including that a career in telephone market research was not for me). But more importantly, I realized that in business, it is vital to know a little bit about all aspects of your company. When the publisher and business director attended a photoshoot, they saw the sweat and heavy lifting that went into producing a fashion feature. (Forget any notions you may have of how glamorous a magazine photoshoot is; I always say they are one part creativity, nine parts manual labor.) As the design director, I went on sales calls where I learned that no matter how beautiful my layouts were, they wouldn't make it very far if we weren't working as a team to create a product that the advertising department could sell.

This information served me well throughout my career, including when I left the world of magazines to start my own branding business. As a solopreneur, I knew better than to concentrate exclusively on the creative aspects of my job, even if they were what I loved most. I also had to focus on winning new clients, retaining the ones I already had, and following up to make sure all of them paid their invoices on time—or else I wouldn't have money to buy food and pay my bills.

When you're running a business, be it a one-person operation or a major corporation, it's vital that you get your hands dirty learning a little bit about all aspects of the operation. Even a small business is like a machine—when one part stops working effectively, the whole enterprise suffers.

The popular TV show *Undercover Boss* was great at showing the importance of this. By putting CEOs into disguises and embedding them in different locations of their businesses, the show helped executives discover what—and who—was and wasn't working in their companies. This willingness to seek out and embrace the truth about all aspects of your business can be vital in making decisions about what problems to fix and how to fix them, and can help squelch potential disasters early on, before they grow out of proportion or before it is too late.

WHEN YOU'RE STUCK, GET EXPERT HELP

Shortly after starting my own business, I took on a few freelance writing assignments for a new Florida-based lifestyle magazine called *Flamingo*. For my first story, the editor asked me to cover freediving, an extreme sport that involves diving without an air supply. Because the sport is not particularly well known, the article would need to explain what it was, how people trained for it, and how our readers could try it locally.

Over the years, I had written about a lot of travel-related topics, reporting on everything from weekend getaways to the latest luxury spa treatments. I had also written stories on the arts, covering theater, music, and even interior design. Extreme sports, however, was a new genre for me. Still, I was excited to write about something different—and also genuinely curious about why people would participate in what I thought must be a terrifying and dangerous sport. So I did what any journalist would do; I said yes to the assignment, and then started calling the experts.

Throughout the next few weeks, I read two books on freediving, making notes about the names and concepts that appeared in them. I called Performance Freediving International, one of the leading training agencies, and spoke to the founder, who was also a champion diver herself. Next, I found local divers and instructors, and had several phone calls lasting an hour or more, where they meticulously explained the sport to me. Finally, I found a Freediving 101 class that was being held in a city that was 45 minutes away and went to observe several sessions, including classroom training, pool training, and a final session taught in the open water a few miles off the coast.

Journalists and editors who read this chapter are probably thinking, *Well, duh! Of course he called the experts.* But in business, and especially in start-ups led by first-time entrepreneurs, it is shocking how often we think we must go it alone when that simply is not the case. There are lots of ways you can seek expert help:

- Searching for articles in print or online, which often quote or are written by experts.

- Reading books by prominent leaders in your industry.

- Contacting a trade organization in your industry.

- Emailing or calling an actual person who is an expert on the topic.

Googling a problem and going down a rabbit hole of information can solve some questions, but for others, there is no substitute for picking up the phone or sending an email. The CEO of SelfPublishing.com Chandler Bolt knows this better than anyone. As a 20-year-old college dropout, he had no idea how to create a thriving business from scratch—but he did have a dream of helping people all over the world learn how to publish their own books, delivering their messages to audiences that needed to hear them. When he started his business in 2014, Chandler relied on what he calls a "Triple F" round of financing: money borrowed from "friends, family, and fools." As he launched and grew his business, Chandler made it a point to reach out to experts and other entrepreneurs for advice, while also investing in a library of business books, which he calls "$15 mentors."

"I'm a big fan of asking *Who?* not *How?*," he says, referring to a concept popularized by author and leadership coach Dan Sullivan. In other words, when facing a challenge he has not previously encountered, Chandler asks, "Who has done this before that I can learn from?" and not simply, "How do I do it?"

For almost any problem, chances are high that someone else has dealt with the same issue before, so why not learn from their mistakes? Many professionals—from lawyers and accountants to graphic designers and marketing experts—offer a complimentary initial consultation, but even those who don't will often be glad to answer a simple question free of charge. People love talking about two things: their own experiences and subjects they are passionate about, which is often their chosen business.

When all else fails, don't be afraid to hire someone. When I started my own business, I did a good deal of the daily bookkeeping myself, but I quickly learned that having an accountant I could turn to with my tax questions would save me hours of time Googling to find answers that may not fully address my specific situation.

REPLACING 'NO' WITH 'KNOW'

Editors love words in their many forms, but one that we simply cannot tolerate is *No*. Unfortunately, it happens to be a word we hear a lot. When planning a magazine issue, it is conceivable to hear the word hundreds of times:

- **From PR agents:** No, you cannot feature our product in your magazine.

- **From celebrity handlers:** No, you cannot interview my celebrity client in person for your profile.

- **From town councils:** No, you cannot shoot on the beach next week without a permit—and no, we will not grant you one.

- **From a source, for any type of story ever written:** No, I will not answer that question.

When most people hear "No," especially from someone in a position of authority, they automatically assume that it's the final word. But journalists and editors aren't like most people; we are more like precocious children who hear our least favorite word and immediately respond with our favorite question: "Why?"

"No" is an easy word to say, but rarely is it the whole story—and journalists always want to get the whole story. You see, the thing about "No" is that it almost always implies a "because." And once you know the "because"—or the reason for resistance—you are armed with the information necessary to change someone's "No" to a "Yes." Whenever you hear the word *No,* you must always find out the *Why* behind it. Then when you come back with a response, attempt to validate the person's concerns and place yourself on their side. Make them a friend who will conspire to help you get what you want.

Let's take the above examples and play out how the rest of the conversation might go if you didn't take "No" for any answer but rather teased out the "because," or the reason behind the "No":

- **From PR agents:** No, you cannot feature our product in your magazine … because we have given another magazine an exclusive for next month. **Response:** That's okay! I completely understand that you have a prior commitment and would love to honor it. We can feature your product at the end of the year in our Holiday Gift Guide, so that it is top of mind during the busiest shopping season.

- **From celebrity handlers:** No, you cannot interview my celebrity client in person for your profile … because she is only in town for a few days and has a very busy schedule. **Response:** I can't imagine how hard it must be negotiating her schedule! What if I hopped in her car on the way to the airport for a 30-minute chat—or I could meet you both at the next stop on her tour? If all else fails, we could try for a Zoom meeting instead.

- **From town councils:** No, you cannot shoot on the beach next week without a permit—and no, we will not grant you a permit … because we require three weeks' advance notice. **Response:** Oh, we definitely want to make sure we have all the legal requirements in place! How about we move this story from our June issue to our July issue, and shoot next month instead of next week? That should work with your time frame.

- **From a source, for any type of story ever written:** No, I will not answer that question … because I could get fired if my boss knew I was talking to you. **Response:** I completely understand and would never want to jeopardize your job. Why don't you give me that piece of information off the record, and I will find another source to corroborate it?

Objections and resistance are a part of doing business; they will inevitably come up despite your best attempts to avoid them. The same holds true whether you are trying to broker a deal with a prospective partner or sell your product to a potential customer. Just remember: Behind every

"No," there is a reason. Identifying and then addressing the reason behind an objection can drastically change the final outcome.

EDITOR'S TIP

Get ahead of objections and have a backup request in mind.

Former editor in chief Kate White points out that an even better strategy than fielding objections is trying to anticipate them, so that you can deal with them ahead of time, without sounding defensive. She learned this when trying to get Adele on the cover of the December 2011 issue of *Cosmopolitan*, which would have been the singer's first U.S. magazine cover.

Adele's team was enthusiastic, but there was just one issue: They had already promised that she would appear on the March 2012 cover of *Vogue* and said they would have to ask that magazine if it was okay for Adele to run on *Cosmo*'s cover four months earlier. White decided to get ahead of the problem as best she could, as she recalls in her book *I Shouldn't Be Telling You This*:

> I knew in my bones that the other magazine would demand to go first. ... So I had my entertainment editor make a list of all the times this competitor had followed us with cover subjects and send it to Adele's reps before they went back to our competitor. The entertainment editor told the rep, "As you can see, they often follow us, so it shouldn't be a problem." That way if the competitor said they didn't want to let Adele pose for us, her management would have viewed *them* as being difficult. I don't know what happened in the conversation; all I know is that Adele posed for the December cover.[98]

White also advises that even if you do get a "No," there may be a way to salvage something from the ask. "Never scurry away with your tail between your legs," she says. "You want to walk away with something. ... The trick is to have your backups clearly in mind so you can bring them up at the right moment." She gives the example of comic Amy Schumer, who, as a somewhat unknown comedian, was on the short list to write the Charlie Sheen roast for Comedy Central. When she was not chosen, Schumer asked: "Well, can I be *on* the show, then?"[99] The station agreed, and her jokes that night were hilarious. Just 18 months later, Schumer had her own TV series on Comedy Central.

THE TAKEAWAY

The best managers don't hide their heads in the sand. Instead, they **embrace the truth** about themselves, their business, their team, and their industry.

Make it a point to understand a little bit about all aspects of your business. If you are a numbers person, spend some time with the creative team; if you are a sales wiz, learn about how your products are manufactured. Ask your team questions about their processes, their most difficult challenges, and their biggest successes.

This advice applies to even the smallest of businesses. If you are a solopreneur, schedule dedicated time to focus on the aspects of your business that you find least interesting. For creative types, perhaps you sit down quarterly to dig into the financials of the past three months, evaluating what product or project brought in the majority of your income—*and* what you could do to create more opportunities like that.

When people tell you "No," it's rarely the whole story. There is almost always a reason behind this resistance. Respond to the dreaded "No" with the journalist's favorite question: "Why?" Information is knowledge, and knowledge is power; **learning the reason behind the "No" empowers you.**

Use the information you receive to **counter the reason for the objection.** Be sure to placate the person you need a "Yes" from and assuage their fears. **Conveying empathy** for their situation and positioning yourself as a friend who is on the same side will often give you the best results.

CHAPTER 8

Make Informed Decisions

n the last chapter, we learned how embracing the facts of any situation—even if they aren't what you want to hear—is essential to making sound decisions. If, as in the case of Kroger, this means that you have access to data that lights a new way forward, you should use that insight to drive your decisions. But according to top leaders like Disney CEO Bob Iger, that isn't always enough. "No matter how much data you've been given, it's still, ultimately, a risk," he writes in his memoir *The Ride of a Lifetime*. "And the decision to take that risk or not comes down to one person's instinct."[100] In this chapter, we will look at three editor-approved frameworks for how to make tough decisions, as well as three common decisions you may encounter as you lead your business.

THREE FRAMEWORKS FOR MAKING TOUGH DECISIONS

Leaders must make difficult decisions constantly, which can be exhausting. But using these frameworks can help make the process less agonizing—and the best choice clearer.

Framework 1: Listen to your gut.

In August 2010, I was living in San Francisco and working as the art director at *Spa* magazine, which was owned by the niche publisher Bonnier. Though the editorial team had always been based in California, our parent company's U.S. headquarters was in Orlando. Other folks from the company rarely visited our office, so when our publisher flew in for a few days, we put together a small happy hour so she could meet the team. The evening was nice but uneventful—until we were leaving for the night, and she asked my editor in chief Julie Sinclair and me if we would come in for a meeting with her at 8 a.m. the next morning.

I tossed and turned all night, wondering just what news she would share. It couldn't be good if we had to discuss it before the rest of the staff arrived. The next morning, we sat before our publisher, who wasted no time beating around the bush. "The company wants to move your magazine to Florida," she said. "Anyone on the team who would like to stay with the brand is welcome to relocate as well."

It wasn't the first time I had been given the opportunity to make a move for work nor would it be the last. However, I can say this: In my entire life, I don't think I've ever had as strong a gut reaction so quickly to a decision—and surprisingly, what I thought in my head was *YES.*

Of course, some may say that keeping a job versus becoming unemployed is an easy decision to make, but out of our team of seven, I was the only person who took Bonnier up on the offer. To this day, the strength of my gut reaction shocks me. I wouldn't characterize my response as, *Oh this sucks—but I'll do it.* Rather my exact thinking was, *I have no idea why this is supposed to happen, but I know with certainty that it is the right thing for me right now.*

Although a gut reaction like this is impossible to ignore, there is a caveat. Even if your immediate inclination about a decision feels primal, that doesn't necessarily mean your gut is always leading you toward the right choice. According to Laura Day, author of *Practical Intuition: How to Harness the Power of Your Instinct and Make It Work for You,* gut reactions can be used to point us in a direction, but we should still utilize all other available information to make the final decision. "When you have an instinct, it doesn't mean you should blindly follow it," she advises in an article for *Cosmopolitan.* "It's a message that you should examine the situation a little bit more."[101]

In the case of my job being relocated from California to Florida, I had a strong gut reaction but still made use of all available resources to make my decision. First, I did cost-of-living calculations and discovered that my salary, which wouldn't be changing, would go a lot further in Orlando. Then I planned a visit, spending a few days in the office and meeting with other art directors and editors. They all seemed super friendly, and one even invited me to her birthday dinner, followed by drinks later that evening. Finally, I went and looked at a few nearby neighborhoods, so that I could see what my housing options might be like. Although no decisions are guaranteed, after this trip, I could soundly say that my initial gut reaction lined up nicely with the data I had collected. The offices, staff, and neighborhoods I had seen were all lovely, so moving now seemed like the best decision for me.

And it was. We received the news in August, and by Thanksgiving, I had traded my bare-bones studio apartment in San Francisco (which I could barely afford) for a spacious one-bedroom loft, complete with a washer and dryer, dishwasher, patio, and even a parking spot for my new car—all for hundreds less each month. Aside from improved housing, I discovered what my gut may have known all along: that there was a life-altering encounter waiting for me in Orlando. After years of hapless dating in Chicago, New York, and San Francisco, I met my future husband Craig just six weeks post-move, and we have been together ever since.

Framework 2: Get outside yourself.

In his book *Build for Tomorrow,* Jason Feifer references a conversation he had with Katy Milkman, who he calls a "walking, talking library of every smart study ever done about behavioral change." A professor at the Wharton School of the University of Pennsylvania, Milkman told him that the best way to see a choice more clearly is to take an outside perspective, which "can make you more dispassionate, a clearer thinker, a better observer."[102]

"When we're thinking about someone else's problems, they don't feel so personal," she explained to Feifer. "We can see the pros and cons more clearly." This can be easier said than done, so Milkman offers a few tips for doing so—and both involve looking outside of yourself.

First, you can borrow someone's decision. If you are facing a tough choice between two things, chances are someone else has been faced with the same decision before. Depending on the specifics, this could mean looking at a decision made by someone at your company, someone in your industry or another industry, or even a friend or family member. If you can, talk to that person to ask if he or she was happy with the final choice. But even if you can't, see if you can dissect their decision from an outsider's perspective. Did what they chose seem to work out for them? If not, are there variables in your situation that might result in a more positive outcome? If it looks like a positive decision could have similar results, try "copying and pasting" that choice into your own situation.

Another option is to pretend you are trying to solve someone else's problem—and then offer advice. Milkman points to the work of psychologist

Lauren Eskreis-Winkler, who found that when people give advice to others about a particular decision, it makes it easier to take that same advice about a similar decision in their own lives. This happens in three steps: First, giving advice puts us in a position of authority, which builds confidence. Then, as you figure out what you would say to the other person, you are forced to introspect more deeply about what you truly want and need to happen. Finally, this leads to a "saying is believing" effect, where you can now suggest actions to a hypothetical friend that you might not initially have recommended to yourself.

For instance, if you are considering whether or not to apply for a job that might be slightly outside of your current skill set, it can be easy to talk yourself out of it, essentially losing the position before you've even applied for it. "Should I really take the time and effort to apply?" you might ask yourself. "There are probably hundreds of applicants who are more qualified than I am."

But we are often harder on ourselves than we are on others. If a friend asked you if *they* should apply for a role that was a bit out of reach, you might take a different approach, offering a pep talk and reminding them that there is no harm in throwing their name in the ring. Once you realize the actions you would suggest to your friend—apply for the job while also reaching out to the hiring manager with a thoughtful cover letter—it becomes clear that those same actions are likely the ones you should take as well.

"Once we suggest them, we start to believe them," Milkman explains. "We start to feel hypocritical if we don't do them. So it's this magic sauce where you get yourself to get behind a risk that you wouldn't necessarily be comfortable telling yourself to take. And in the end, you convince yourself to take it."[103]

Framework 3: Look into the future.

In her book *How to Decide: Simple Tools for Making Better Choices,* author and former professional poker player Annie Duke lays out a framework for better decision-making that involves creating a decision tree, where each branch is a possible outcome. She recommends weighing each potential outcome in terms of the three P's:

- **Preference:** What is your personal goal in the situation?

- **Payoff:** How would each outcome affect your progress toward or away from that goal?

- **Probability:** How likely is each outcome?

By using these three barometers—and honing our precision over time by noting how past choices turned out—Duke believes that we can make an educated guess about almost any decision that comes our way.[104] This is a great way to carefully and systematically weigh decisions by truly analyzing future outcomes, and I recommend reading her book for a more in-depth discussion of the process.

That said, there is another way of looking into the future that relies not just on potential outcomes but also on how much of an impact those outcomes may or may not have on our lives in the immediate and distant future. Author and former *Harvard Business Review* editor in chief Suzy Welch recommends a method that has helped her make a lot of tough decisions in both her career and her personal life. The idea is simple—and may be my favorite framework. Every time you find yourself in a situation where there appears to be no solution that will make everyone happy, ask yourself three questions:

- What are the consequences of my decision in **10 minutes?**

- In **10 months?**

- And in **10 years?**[105]

The beauty of this framework is that if you make the decision based on just one of these time frames, you might choose a different outcome. But by looking at all three of them together, you can weigh how dramatically a choice might alter your day or even year—which could be significant—but then also place that choice in the context of the next decade of your life.

By looking into the future—both immediate and distant—the right answer may become more clear; and not only that, it can also help suggest a line of reasoning that you can use to explain your choice to other people who are affected by your decision (and may not love what it means for them). In an article she wrote for *O, The Oprah Magazine*, Welch explains this concept by giving three examples from her own life:[106]

Situation 1: After promising her kids she would be home for dinner and promising the babysitter the night off, Welch encountered a 5 p.m. crisis at the office. Her boss needed her there, but when she called home to test the waters, the babysitter nearly burst into tears, as two kids were fighting and another was sulking. Her daughter even grabbed the phone to shout: "You love work more than us!" As she weighed the pros and cons, the 10-10-10 method was officially born:

I slowed my thought process down and systematically began to pick it apart. "What exactly," I asked myself, "were the immediate repercussions of staying at work versus rushing home?"

If I stayed, my boss would jot it down in her little book of good deeds, and my children and babysitter would turn purple. If I rushed home, my boss would get someone else to help her, and my triumphant arrival at the front door would be greeted with the usual grunts and sighs. ...

In 10 months? Assuming I didn't make staying late a daily feature of our lives (which I knew I wouldn't), the kids would be fine. As for the babysitter, she would be back at school, and I would be but a distant memory. At work, though, if I left, my boss might start to question my commitment and my availability, not the impression I was eager to encourage.

In 10 years, the fact that I worked late (or not) would be irrelevant. My career would be someplace I couldn't foresee. The babysitter would be working on Wall Street. And my kids would love or hate me for reasons much bigger than one late night at the office.

And so I stayed without flinching. I got my gold star at work, and the home-front grumbles faded as anticipated.[107]

Situation 2: At times, the scales of Welch's work/life balance swung the other direction, also because of the 10-10-10 method. Once, she was asked to lead a Saturday meeting for the company's top executives—but the meeting was scheduled on the same day that her son would be going for his junior black belt in karate, for which he had been training for four long years.

Again, she ran through the time frames. In 10 minutes, her sensitive son would be devastated and teary; her boss, she reasoned, wouldn't cry but would definitely be disappointed. In 10 months, she figured the pain would be buried by extra efforts with the losing party. If she attended the off-site, she would love her son extravagantly for months, apologizing profusely and spoiling him with gifts; if she didn't go, she would put the same kind of effort into her work performance, pleasing her boss. But when she thought about 10 years, the choice became more clear:

My kids would be gone and my career at full-throttle, whether I had gotten one promotion or not. But on some visceral level, my son would still know that I had chosen to miss one of the seminal events of his life for my own advancement. That was damage I could never undo. So I skipped the off-site. And late that Saturday afternoon, I cheered as my son received his black belt, his face pink as he tried to hold back tears.[108]

Situation 3: Though the 10-10-10 method helped Welch make both of these important but somewhat minor decisions, she finds that it is even more invaluable when making truly big life choices. "Like many marriages, mine took a long time to come apart," she says. "The stakes of doing something—that is, ending it for real—seemed unbearably high: the children, the friends, the house, the backyard barbecues. And so we waited, and waited, for something to unfreeze us—a decision, one way or another."

When the problem wouldn't go away, Welch took a quiet morning alone to go on a hike for some self-reflection. As she thought about her marriage using the 10-10-10 framework, she realized that the 10-minute question would be easy to answer: Telling her husband and then kids that she wanted a divorce would be extremely painful. Once lawyers, upheaval, and moving came into the picture, the next 10 months looked even worse. "All I could think was, 'Awful, awful, awfulness—not just in 10 months, in 20, and maybe more,'" Welch explains. "In 10 years, though—in 10 wonderful years—we would have our lives back. … That night, after a long talk about how things would unfold over the coming days, months, and years, my husband and I agreed we'd found a shared reason—and a road map—to say goodbye."[109]

THREE TOUGH DECISIONS YOU WILL HAVE TO MAKE IN BUSINESS

No matter which framework speaks most to you, there are common decisions that all leaders must make at one time or another. Here are three of the most universal, progressing from the least to the most serious:

Tough Decision 1: What to delegate

I've never known how to answer the ubiquitous job interview question, "What is your biggest weakness?" For years, I would say that I am a perfectionist, which I always thought was great because it sounds like it *could* be a weakness, but in the detail-oriented world of publishing, where every photo is meticulously color-corrected and every statement is verified by fact checkers, it is actually a strength. After years of using this in job interviews, I eventually found a new weakness I could discuss: At times, it is hard for me to delegate.

I started my career in trade or B2B publishing, which is known for having smaller staffs where everyone pitches in to do everything; often, there is no one to whom tasks *can* be delegated. Sometimes we had interns, but their skill level was inconsistent; some were super-talented "eager beavers," who could complete any job you handed over. But many were so green that more complex assignments required a lot of hand-holding and sometimes redoing the work yourself. For this reason, I was often reluctant to delegate anything other than the most menial tasks.

But at *Coastal Living*, I led a staff of two that would soon grow to a staff of four, plus several freelancers; I also spearheaded a redesign of the magazine while still putting out the monthly issue. After weeks of staying at work until long after the sun had set, and then taking more work home with me, it quickly became clear that I didn't have a choice—I *had* to delegate.

Hank Gilman, the editorial manager at Yahoo Finance and former deputy editor of *Fortune*, advises managers to keep the tasks that they do well and delegate what they don't do well.[110] I think that is a great start, but what if you do a lot of things relatively well? Or what if you do something well but still don't have time to do it? There are three questions you must ask yourself when deciding whether or not to delegate a task:

- Do I *like* doing this?

- Am I *good* at doing this?

- Do I *need* to do this—or could someone else do it just as well?

When I first started my career, one of the parts I had liked about my job was attending photoshoots. It provided a chance to get away from my desk while also exercising a different creative muscle; art directing a photoshoot while working with a photographer and stylist is a collaborative process, and much different than sitting alone at a computer, designing a page. Plus, when art directors are on set, we can make sure we are truly getting what we want and need for the story to be successful. We have a vision for how the final page will look and have also been in meetings with our editors, so we know what our boss is expecting from the shoot. Some of this can be conveyed by sending the photographer a brief that includes a sketch of the final page, but oftentimes, the details are best worked out on set. That said, the downside of shoots is that they can be time intensive, taking you out of the office and into a studio for days on end.

After a few harried weeks at *Coastal Living*, I ran through my three criteria and realized that although I liked going on studio shoots, I didn't *love* it and didn't necessarily *need* to do it every month. Yes, I was good at art directing on set, but so was the art director who worked for me—and she truly loved it, especially when we shot recipes. (For more on leveraging your team's strengths, see Chapter 13.) Ultimately, I concluded that to achieve the best results, we needed *someone* on set—but it didn't have to be me. By not going on every shoot for the magazine, I was free to spend more time working on tasks that did require my presence: mocking up pages for the redesign, honing our new cover strategy, and being available for impromptu meetings with our editor in chief.

That's not to say I never went on another shoot. Some of our most important shoots were not in the studio but rather on location in coastal towns around the country. The same art director who loved studio shoots was less enthused about their on-location counterparts, because she had to board her dog and spend a day in transit on each end of the trip. These shoots were also less predictable due to the variables of weather, travel, and personality that came into play, especially if a celebrity was involved. That said, on-location shoots were still very important in that we usually had lined up cover tries (photo setups planned specifically with the cover in mind). I often *did* go on these shoots because, when potential covers were being shot, it upped the ante on whether my presence was necessary.

As you can see, delegating doesn't have to be an all-or-nothing approach. While I delegated most of the photoshoots, I went on many of the most important ones. Similarly, when I started my own business, I knew I wanted to delegate some—but not all—of my financial recordkeeping. Because I owned a small, one-person business, I felt like I could adequately do my own bookkeeping; reconciling my income and expenses only took a few minutes a week, and I actually enjoyed the process of reminding myself just how I had made and spent my money each month. However, since I now owned a corporation, that meant that I needed to prepare a corporate tax return in addition to my personal tax return, which didn't sound like much fun. I delegated these tasks to my accountant, who did a better job than I could have, saving me hours of frustration in the process.

Tough Decision 2: When to kill a project

When I worked at *Coastal Living*, we had a big feature planned that involved sending a writer and photographer to a picturesque seaside retreat in Canada to learn how to build stone walls. Reporting this story wasn't for everyone—to me, it sounded like signing up for a week of hard labor. But we found an eager writer and photographer, both of whom had worked for the magazine before, and sent them off to document the experience.

When the text and photos came in, the results were less than stellar. The writer spent more time focusing on the logistics of getting to the remote camp than on the actual experience. The images were equally uninspiring, as it seemed the instructor had tasked this particular class with working on a different type of creation, one that ended up looking less like a wall and more like a scary, abstract dragon sculpture. The story was sent back for rewrites and our executive editor refined the copy as much as she could; on my end, the art and photo team culled the ho-hum images, trying different crops and preliminary color corrections.

But alas, the piece just didn't hold together. Our team—and in the end, our editor in chief Antonia van der Meer—was left with a tough conundrum: Should we be "in for a penny, in for a pound," and take whatever steps necessary to make the story work? Or was that line of thinking an example of "sunk cost fallacy," a cognitive bias that pushes us to keep trying something because we have already put so much time, hard work, or money into it—even if the end result may not be worth the effort?

As with the delegation decision, I have also found that there is a simple three-question framework that can help determine whether or not we should, in editor-speak, "kill the story":

- **Have we truly tried our best to make this work?** In the case of the stone wall debacle, we had spent time researching the workshop, eventually choosing an eager writer and photographer, both of whom we had worked with before. Once the text and images came in, the executive editor and I met to review them and spent time editing them to make the best possible version of the story and layout, which still wasn't terribly compelling.

- **What would it take to make this work?** If we *really* wanted to make this work, we would probably need to send the photographer and writer—or a different photographer and writer—back to the retreat. This would require a second round of plane tickets and accommodations, plus waiting until the retreat was offered again, and this time insisting to the retreat leaders that they would need to build an actual stone wall—not an abstract creature that looked more like a haphazard pile of rocks.

- **How badly do we need this to work?** In the case of the stone wall story, not terribly badly. Though we had it slated for a future issue, it wasn't planned for a cover, so we could replace it with something else.

When you have invested a lot of time and money into a project, as we had with the story, you desperately want to see it succeed, and it can be hard to be objective and know when to cut your losses. But in this case, the story's editor and I both felt like we were beating a dead horse that just wasn't worth bringing back to life. In the end, our editor in chief recognized that the story just didn't warrant the time, energy, and money that would be needed to redo it. Although we were disappointed that it hadn't worked out, I think everyone on staff was relieved that a subpar piece wouldn't be going into the magazine and that we could just let this one die.

EDITOR'S TIP

Utilize your team when making tough decisions.

As a leader, there will be many times when you have to make a tough call. But even if the buck ultimately stops with you, that doesn't mean you have to reach your final decision in a vacuum. Use *all* of the information and resources available to you, including one of your biggest resources: your team. Every decision doesn't need to be crowdsourced, but when the stakes are high and you find yourself needing a bit more input to make an informed decision, gather thoughts from trusted people on your team. Sometimes a fresh set of eyes can offer a new solution, or at the very least, a different perspective that you may not have considered.

Tough Decision 3: What to do when the shit hits the fan

Though deciding what to delegate and knowing when to kill a project are big decisions, they aren't necessarily life-altering ones. Delegation can always be course corrected along the way, and although a failed project can be annoying, it will rarely derail a whole career. However, there are a few decisions, especially ones made in times of crisis, that can alter the course of your company, your career, and even your legacy.

Although Airbnb now prides itself on its "intentional integrity," at one point in its first few years of operation, the company was placed in a situation that would test its values. In June 2011, a host named EJ published a lengthy blog post about returning from a business trip to find that the person she had rented to had trashed her San Francisco apartment. The damage was obviously intentional and went beyond a reasonable mess from having a few houseguests or even a full-blown party. They had removed her clothes from the hangers and left them in a wet pile in the bathroom; had sprinkled powder and a mysterious crud all over her kitchen and bathroom; had burned wood and a set of sheets in her fireplace with the flue closed (despite the fact that it was summer); and had punched a hole through the wall of a locked owner's closet in order to steal her jewelry, laptop, camera, and credit cards, the last of which were then used for online shopping.[111]

At that time, it was Airbnb's policy that it was not liable for any damage inflicted by a guest; the company would aid hosts in contacting the guests, but it was the hosts' responsibility to reach out and seek restitution. When EJ's post went viral, prompting other hosts to talk about their destructive guests, Airbnb began to experience a PR nightmare that went on for weeks. At one point, someone from the company reached out to ask EJ to remove the blog post, which offended her, prompting her to write a second post.

As reporters continued to cover this unfortunate incident and Airbnb's less-than-ideal response, Airbnb founder Brian Chesky had an epiphany. "At one point, and out of desperation, frankly, I thought, screw the outcome," he recalls in the book *Intentional Integrity*. "I am going to think about how I want to be remembered. I decided to make a business decision to do the right thing. The principled decision."[112]

Airbnb issued a public apology to EJ and its other hosts, provided restitution to her, and worked with law enforcement to identify and track down the suspect, who was arrested and charged with possession of stolen items. Most importantly, it made the decision that, going forward, hosts would be insured for $50,000 to make things right in the event of damage. In the process, Chesky learned an important lesson: "If you don't know how a situation that's complicated is going to play out, figure out how you want to be remembered," he says. "That is different from making a decision because you believe it's going to play out a certain way."[113]

Chesky's decision helped restore guests' and hosts' confidence in Airbnb; it also set a precedent for executives doing the right thing in times of conflict, years before the company had its formal integrity code. Employees noticed that their boss took the high road, and the story is still talked about today.

As a leader, you will be faced with countless decisions each year. When a choice is complicated, figuring out how you would want to be remembered can be the best way to reach the right decision—making you a model for your direct reports and others in the company to follow.

EDITOR'S TIP

———

Accept that your decisions may not please everyone.

While using these recommended frameworks will help make decisions easier, that doesn't mean that your choices will be popular with everyone. As a former VP at Netflix and former editor in chief of *Allure* and *Nylon*, Michelle Lee knows this all too well. Her top advice for new leaders? When it comes to making tough decisions, "it's better to be respected than liked," she told me.

"That's not to say, *Don't be liked*," she is quick to clarify. "I'm definitely not saying that. It's just that when we feel like we need to please everybody, we end up not pleasing anyone. You have to have strong convictions and believe in your decisions. Sometimes, that means you're going to make choices that make someone unhappy—and that's okay."[114]

THE TAKEAWAY

As leaders, we must **use the information we have available** to us to make the best possible decisions for ourselves, our businesses, and our teams. Start by listening to your gut—but don't follow it blindly. **Use your gut instinct** to point you in the right direction, while also considering any other data you might have.

If you don't have a strong gut instinct, **try stepping outside of yourself,** either by seeing if someone you know has faced a similar decision and "copying and pasting" their choice; or by pretending that someone you know is currently facing the same decision and offering advice to them.

If all else fails when making a tough decision, **look into the future** by making a list of outcomes and ranking them based on the three P's: Preference, Payoff, and Probability. You can also ask yourself: "Based on the likely outcomes, how will I feel about this decision in 10 minutes, in 10 months, and in 10 years?"

When deciding what to delegate, ask yourself if you *like* the task, if you are *good* at the task, and if you *need* to do the task—or if someone else could do it just as well.

When deciding whether to kill a project, ask yourself if you have truly tried your best to achieve success, what it would take to achieve success, and how badly you *need* the project to be successful.

When the shit hits the fan and you aren't sure what the outcome will be, **think about how you want to be remembered** and make the decision that best aligns with your principles.

PART THREE

S is for

STRUCTURE

**"To achieve great things, two things are needed:
a plan and not quite enough time."**

—*Leonard Bernstein, award-winning composer and conductor*

In many ways, making a magazine is like a group art project that's been cranked up to hyperspeed. Each month there are new stories to be told, new photoshoots to be styled, and new layouts to be designed. Think about the creativity that goes into publishing a high-end coffee-table book or a beautifully photographed travel guide—and then imagine trying to find a fresh way to do it all over again the next month, while producing daily digital content as well.

It's easy to forget that artistic expression—at a breakneck pace—requires a lot of hard work and careful planning. At their best, great photography and sharp prose make the process look easy, masking the oodles of outtakes or umpteen rewrites that brought them, kicking and screaming, to fruition.

As you might imagine, all of this right-brain creativity needs a healthy dose of left-brain structure to make sure that deadlines and budgets are met. But before any creative work—or even planning for the work—begins, the editor in chief must first lay out a vision for the publication that gets everyone on board and working toward the same goal.

PLAN LIKE AN EDITOR BY CREATING THE RIGHT STRUCTURE

To truly succeed as a leader, you must start with a framework that can support your business pursuits. In the following chapters, you will learn how to:

- Create a **vision, mission, and pillars** that will reinforce your brand and help you gain buy-in from both your team and other stakeholders.

- Zoom out and **plan your year** in a way that meets the needs of your business and your target customer.

- Zoom in and **plan your day** for optimal efficiency and enjoyment.

Achieving award-winning results consistently is as much science as art, and behind every truly great publication—or business—there is a well-organized infrastructure. Build the right structure first, and the rest will fall into place a lot more easily. Now, let's start planning.

CHAPTER 9

....

Establish Your Vision, Mission, and Pillars

When Lindsay Bierman was named Chancellor of the University of North Carolina School of the Arts in 2014, both the media and academic worlds were abuzz. Throughout the previous two decades, Bierman had ascended the ranks of Time Inc., serving as editor in chief of *Cottage Living, Coastal Living,* and eventually *Southern Living.* A talented leader, he had thoughtfully shaped and improved each brand he helmed, while racking up a shelf of awards along the way.

Bierman's latest wins as editor of *Southern Living* included helping transition the title from a stalwart magazine favored by Southern grandmothers to a modern print *and* digital powerhouse, with a number of successful brand extensions and a growing audience of 18- to 34-year-olds. In fact, the year before Bierman moved into academia, the thriving publication had been named the country's "Hottest Home Magazine" by *Adweek.*[115]

Bierman was at the top of his game, helming one of the largest titles at Time Inc., so many wondered: What made him want to leave the glamorous world of media for the decidedly less glitzy realm of nonprofit education?

Bierman wondered that himself. In his installation address at the school, he recalled psyching himself up in his office at *Southern Living,* just before his first interview for the new job:

> I sat in silence with the door closed and locked for 15 minutes, trying
> to listen to what my inner voice was telling me. I enjoyed my role as
> the face, champion, and steward of such a beloved, iconic, and highly
> profitable cultural brand. … But I knew that it was time to move on,

time to serve a higher creative purpose, time to find greater fulfillment in a community that brought me closer to my roots as an artist. ... Time to give back. Time to leave the comfort zone of my longtime employer, Time Inc. I answered the call from the recruiter that morning, and in doing so I answered a calling to serve.[116]

Though this calling to serve propelled him forward through the interview process, once he started the position, Bierman was met with a daunting hill to climb. He had to get everyone on board quickly, while also articulating a path forward for the school, which had faced budget cuts and a bit of an identity crisis after a name change. "The faculty was so skeptical of me," Bierman told me. "They thought, *What the hell does a magazine editor know about running a school?* Many saw *Southern Living* as just fluff: cake recipes and houses and gardens. They didn't think of it as a $100 million business that I had been running."[117]

Sometimes a fresh perspective can be crucial. Bierman had a vision for how the institution could be improved, which he outlined in a five-year strategic action plan that—like all of the magazines he had run before—was ambitious in both its content and design. But before the real work began, Bierman knew he needed to get everyone on board by laying out a vision.

"You have to get the whole institution—with all of the different perspectives and backgrounds and agendas and ideas—aligned around a shared vision," he says. "There's only so much time and money, and they're always in short supply, particularly in the nonprofit sector. ... You need to have strong alignment around the institution's purpose to help you focus your work, understand what you should keep doing, what you should stop doing, and what maybe you should be doing instead."[118]

Having a clearly outlined vision is crucial in organizations large and small, as a way to make sure everyone is on the same page. It also helps when it comes time to deciding whether or not to allocate financial or human resources to a potential new initiative, by asking if the new opportunity aligns with your stated mission and whether it moves you toward your clearly spelled out vision.

Now the executive director and CEO of San Francisco's popular Exploratorium museum, Bierman still follows his own advice. "We can't do everything, so we want to be amazing at a few things," he explains. "I look for a way to be really clear about what *our* work is, as opposed to what is the work for other organizations to do. Does a new idea move us toward our long-term vision?"[119]

START WITH A VISION THAT INSPIRES YOU

Most people wouldn't consider a road trip without a destination in mind. In the same way, if you are launching a business—or rethinking an existing one—you must start at the end by knowing exactly where you want to go.

Founded in 1850, *Harper's Magazine* has the distinction of being the oldest continuously published general interest magazine in the U.S.[120] From the beginning, the founders of *Harper's* had a big vision for their publication. In the inaugural June 1850 issue, managing editor Henry Jarvis Raymond wrote an article entitled "A Word at the Start" in which he laid out a lofty goal for the new publication: To "reach the great mass of the American people" and to "make its way into the family circle of every intelligent citizen of the United States."[121]

It would have been easier for the founder of this magazine to launch out of the gate with a smaller vision, but he knew that to succeed, he needed to aim high. As *The New York Times* bestselling author Grant Cardone says in his book *The 10X Rule*, to be successful, "You must set targets that are 10 times what you think you want, and then do 10 times what you think it will take to accomplish those targets."[122]

WHAT MAKES A GOOD VISION?

People often confuse a *vision* statement with a *mission* statement, which I will discuss shortly. Simply put, a vision statement should express your ultimate end goal for the company. If there is a core value or pie-in-the-sky dream that you hope to achieve, put it in the vision statement. A vision statement must be positive, decisive, and clear. And like its name suggests, it should be something tangible and specific, something that people can easily *envision* in their mind's eye.

To return to the road trip analogy, saying that you are driving from the East Coast all the way "out West" is a lot different than saying you are driving from Manhattan to the Las Vegas Strip. The first trip is amorphous and vague. How will you know when you have reached "out West"? When you see the Rocky Mountains? Or perhaps a desert landscape? The second trip gives not only a clear direction for where you are headed but also a highly specific vision. While "out West" can mean different things to different people, we can all picture the flashing neon lights of the Las Vegas Strip.

A vision statement is aspirational, providing a literal vision for what tomorrow will look like for your company. It may answer one or more of the following questions:

- What are our hopes and dreams?

- What problem are we solving for the greater good?

- Who and what are we inspiring to change?[123]

Author and leadership expert Simon Sinek often refers to Martin Luther King Jr.'s "I Have a Dream" speech when explaining how a clear vision—delivered by a charismatic leader—can inspire people to take action. In that speech, King did not present a comprehensive 12-point plan for how to achieve civil rights in America; instead, he told us that he had a dream that one day "little Black boys and Black girls will be able to join hands with little white boys and white girls as sisters and brothers." The specificity of that image, which we can easily picture, makes for a clear and inspiring vision.[124]

Like editors who must have a strong vision to know where their publications stand in a competitive marketplace, businesses in all sectors can benefit from creating these statements early on. Many companies that are now household names have been guided by vision statements that reference how they will make a difference to humanity:

- **Tesla:** To create the most compelling car company of the 21st century by driving the world's transition to electric vehicles.

- **Google:** To provide access to the world's information in one click.

- **Uber:** Smarter transportation with fewer cars and greater access. Transportation that's safer, cheaper, and more reliable; transportation that creates more job opportunities and higher incomes for drivers.[125]

- **Amazon:** To be Earth's most customer-centric company; to build a place where people can find and discover anything they might want to buy online.[126]

As you can see, fortune favors the bold. If any of these companies had written about serving a small audience, it is doubtful that they would have grown to be the empires that they are today. Ask yourself what the reason behind your business is and what you ultimately hope to accomplish from all the hard work that will be required to reach your end goal. Though specificity is good, Medill dean Charles Whitaker cautions against making your vision too narrow; it should still allow room for your team to bring *their* ideas and creativity to its interpretation. And if you are articulating a new vision for an existing organization, he suggests that you pay some homage to what came before. "While it is important to have a North Star," he told me, "the vision can't be so narrow and so prescriptive that it's a straitjacket for everyone."[127]

Once you have a draft written, think about it for a few days to make sure it feels right in your gut. But remember: An inspiring statement locked away in a drawer does no one any good. After you have a clear vision, share it with your team and consider posting it somewhere visible, so that everyone understands the common goal they are working toward.

DEVELOP A MISSION STATEMENT THAT GUIDES YOU

Revisiting the road trip analogy, if the vision statement presents a dream destination for where your company will be *tomorrow*, then the mission statement describes the route (or process) you will take *today* to get there.

Many times, companies set about their business with a vague idea of who they are as an organization and an even vaguer idea about who they are going to serve and how they are going to do it. It's no wonder that they find themselves getting lost along the way. For large corporations, this can include developing offshoots to chase trends that ultimately do not serve the core vision of the company—like Frito-Lay's unfortunate Cheetos-flavored lip balm or Harley-Davidson's poorly received line of perfume, cologne, and aftershave. For smaller businesses, this can mean saying yes to every project or idea, diluting their message and spinning wheels on actions that don't move the needle or add to the bottom line.

At magazines, editors are pitched stories every day by PR agencies and publicists, who are trying to get coverage for their clients. These people can make a convincing case for each idea, but magazines have limited space for content, and their readers depend on them to curate only the best and most relevant information. For these reasons, having a strong mission is absolutely essential. Magazine editors refer to it constantly until they have read it so many times that it becomes ingrained in their way of thinking, allowing them to evaluate a new story idea in a split second, before determining if it is right for their readers.

CRAFTING THE MISSION

In journalism school, fledgling reporters learn that a good story must always convey "the Five W's and the H." That is:

Who   What   When   Where   Why   How

The best news stories answer these questions quickly and thoroughly, to present all the most important information to the reader. Mission statements can take on many forms, but they generally follow a similar, although more concise, format. According to *Forbes*, a good mission statement should answer these four questions:

- What do we do?

- How do we do it?

- Whom do we do it for?

- What value are we bringing?[128]

Ideally, all of these questions can be answered succinctly in one or two sentences. When writing your mission statement, it is important to keep it focused and specific, but at the same time, make sure all essential elements of your business are covered. Start by brainstorming answers to each of the four questions above, and then begin crafting them into a statement that follows the four C's:

- **Concise:** Usually one or two sentences is plenty.

- **Clear:** When possible, use specific language, especially if you serve a niche demographic.

- **Comprehensive:** The mission should be broad enough to cover the full suite of products or services you offer.

- **Current:** As companies evolve over time, it is sometimes necessary to review and revise the mission statement to include a change in either direction or focus.

Here are two examples from prominent publications that cover very different subject areas:

Men's Health

As the world's largest men's magazine, *Men's Health* considers itself a bible that the modern man can use to navigate all aspects of his busy life. Although the print magazine is the flagship product, the brand's portfolio also includes a website, books, apparel, and exercise gear. While much of the mission refers to editorial content, it also is careful to call itself "a source of information" and "the brand for," making the mission inclusive of its non-magazine ventures:

Men's Health is the #1 source of information for and about men. It's the brand for active, successful, professional men who want greater control over their physical, mental and emotional lives. We give men the tools they need to make their lives better through in-depth reporting, covering everything from fashion and grooming to health and nutrition as well as cutting-edge gear, the latest entertainment, timely features and more.[129]

Although editors have come and gone, and the magazine even changed ownership when Hearst acquired it from Rodale in 2018, the mission has remained essentially the same for many years. That said, missions can—and sometimes must—evolve, as you can see in the next example.

The Atlantic

Founded in 1857 as a literary and cultural commentary magazine called *The Atlantic Monthly*, this well-regarded publication has continued to grow and change throughout the past two centuries, officially dropping "Monthly" from its title in 2007. Its original mission statement, still referenced on its website, highlights the magazine's position as a neutral commentator:

The Atlantic will be the organ of no party or clique, but will honestly endeavor to be the exponent of ... the American idea.

Although this is still an important part of the magazine's DNA (it has only endorsed four presidential candidates since 1857), a new mission statement was needed to keep the focus current. This revised statement from 2014 expands upon the brand's increased offerings, both in terms of the types of media, breadth of its content, and diversity of audiences served:

The Atlantic is America's leading destination for brave thinking and bold ideas that matter. *The Atlantic* engages its print, online, and live audiences with breakthrough insights into the worlds of politics, business, the arts, and culture. With exceptional talent deployed against the world's most important and intriguing topics, *The Atlantic* is the source of opinion, commentary, and analysis for America's most influential individuals who wish to be challenged, informed, and entertained.[130]

Ever-evolving, the publication's mission has since reverted to a more succinct version, as espoused by editor in chief Jeffrey Goldberg in recent media kits:

Our mission is to be big, not small; independent, not partisan; and above all, rigorous.[131] *The Atlantic* leads the way. We illuminate the most complicated issues; we ask the hardest questions; and we host the best writers and the most urgent conversations, here and around the world.[132]

CONSTRUCT PILLARS TO SUPPORT YOUR BRAND

As a creative director, I am naturally a visual person; as such, I always love talking about pillars, because when it comes to describing the structure of your organization, they are one of the easiest aspects to visualize. Just picture many of the great monuments of the world: the Parthenon in Athens, the Pantheon in Rome, the Lincoln Memorial in Washington, DC. Without strong pillars, each of these monuments would easily crumble.

When it comes to magazines, pillars represent the subject areas that make up the brand's DNA, giving each title its signature mix of topics and unique editorial focus. As issue size and advertising pages fluctuate, publications often expand and contract, adding or removing pages depending on the month; as a result, for the lean issues, it can be hard to know which stories to run and which ones to cut or hold. Having a clearly designed set of pillars helps hone the focus by setting a list of topics that are essential to make the magazine's concept work. Sometimes these topics are listed in the table of contents or hinted at in the section names, but often they are not spelled out quite so directly.

For a general interest magazine like *Reader's Digest*, having a clearly defined set of pillars is very important to its positioning. With an audience of more than 14 million readers, it must be broad enough to appeal to a wide variety of people but specific enough to distinguish itself from other mass-market publications. On the first page of its media kit, *Reader's Digest* lists its six pillars so that potential advertisers know just what they are buying into:[133]

Health Family Heroes Humor Home Food

By determining this clear list of pillars, *Reader's Digest* pledges to have elements of these six topics in every issue. In some issues, there may be multiple health stories, while in other issues there may be multiple stories about heroes or about issues affecting families. But we know—and the magazine's editors know—that every issue will have at least one story that speaks to each of these subjects in order to stay on-brand.

PILLARS AS COMPANY VALUES OR BRAND VALUES

For media brands, it is helpful to have a specific list of content pillars that you know you will cover each month; this unique mix of topics will deliver on your vision and mission statements, while also engaging your readers and helping define your brand in a crowded marketplace. For other businesses, it may be more helpful to determine key values your company or brand will need to embody to deliver on your mission and vision.

Company Values

As the world's largest hotel chain, Marriott International is a leader in the hospitality industry. The company lists its five core values as declarative statements on its website:

- We Put People First.

- We Pursue Excellence.

- We Embrace Change.

- We Act with Integrity.

- We Serve Our World.[134]

Beneath these values are examples of programs and initiatives that show how each is put into practice. At Marriott, it is expected that everyone—from the C-suite at corporate headquarters to the housekeeping team at the company's smallest hotel—models these values in their work and interactions with customers.

Brand Values

While the overarching values above extend to all areas of the company, each of Marriott's 30-plus brands has its own list of characteristics and values that set it apart from its sister brands. Take the St. Regis, "where exquisite immersive experiences, impeccable service, modern indulgence and refined taste define every stay."[135] In practice, this translates to elegant hotels that offer luxurious selling points, like 24-hour butler service, exquisitely designed suites, and a daily champagne sabering ceremony, where guests are invited to enjoy a glass of bubbly together.

On the other end of the scale is Marriott's description of Moxy Hotels: "With cozy rooms and social spaces, Moxy offers a fun experience at the right price."[136] Geared toward 20-somethings who appreciate cool design but may not have large budgets, these properties offer small and minimalist rooms, focusing instead on the bars, lobbies, and other spaces where young travelers will enjoy hanging out. (In fact, the bar even serves double duty as the front desk—meaning it is always open.) Mirroring the language on the corporate site, the brand's own homepage says it best: "At Moxy Hotels, we don't take ourselves too seriously."[137]

EDITOR'S TIP

Maintain focus with a strategic plan and check-ins.

When Lindsay Bierman started his new role as Chancellor of the University of North Carolina School of the Arts in 2014, he began work on a five-year strategic plan, just as many of his predecessors had before. "These previous plans had been announced with some amount of fanfare and then went into a drawer and were never looked at again," he told me. "This is not unusual." What was unusual, at least for this school, is that Bierman brought in consultants who worked with his team over the next five years to make sure the plan stayed on track.

"We had continuous check-ins where we looked at what we said we were going to do and asked: What *did* we do? Let's celebrate the wins and accomplishments, but then also look at what we didn't do and *why* we didn't do it. What was getting in our way: Time? Money? Staffing? Or something else? And were there any emerging or conflicting priorities that we needed to address?" Bierman says that this adaptive and responsive approach to work—with the aid of an outside facilitator—helped hold the school accountable and focused on what was truly important over the long haul.

"There are ten thousand things we *wanted* to do," he says. "But when deciding what to focus on, it came back to the question: What are we uniquely positioned to do? What is on-mission, what is *our* work to do, and what is within our power to change? My mantra has always been relentless incrementalism; we can have a big, grand vision that may seem overwhelming and impossible to achieve. But you must ask: What are we doing *today* to move the institution forward? What part can *I* play in advancing us toward this long-term goal? Change is made through small things, every day, every week. And then over time, you will look back and say, 'Wow, I cannot believe how much we accomplished.'"[138]

THE TAKEAWAY

Create a **vision statement** that represents that largest possible goal you have for your company, either in terms of size, reach, or the way it will better the lives of your customers—and even change the world. Think of it as the destination you want to reach, and write something that is grand enough to last for years to come, as your business grows and changes. Make the language visual, so that anyone who hears the vision can picture it in their mind.

Create a **mission statement** that tells *how* you will reach the destination set out in your vision. It should answer what you do and how you do it, as well as who your customers are and what value you bring to them. Make it as specific as possible, while also leaving it broad enough to cover the most important aspects of your business as it stands today. Be sure the statement is concise, clear, comprehensive, and current; it can always be updated later. This statement will create an effective compass to keep you laser-focused when evaluating new ventures or making difficult decisions.

Finally, create a set of **pillars** that further define what your business stands for. For a publication, these are topics it covers that uniquely position the brand and are central to the mission. For other types of companies, it may be more useful to create a list of **core values** that dictate the spirit with which you conduct your business. For a larger corporation, it may be helpful to articulate one set of overarching values for the entire company and different characteristics or **values specific to each brand.**

Visit **LeadLikeAnEditor.com** to download a free workbook that includes templates for crafting your **Vision, Mission, and Pillars,** as well as other resources.

CHAPTER 10

Zoom Out: Planning Your Year

ave you ever tried shopping for pumpkins in July? If not, then let me assure you: They are nearly impossible to find. Though timing can vary by region, most farmers with the goal of a fall harvest plant pumpkin seeds in late spring or early summer, which means that during July, the nearest pumpkin patch is likely filled with nothing more than seedlings. The only thing harder to find than pumpkins in the middle of summer is crunchy red, yellow, and orange fall leaves—unless you are shipping them in from South America or somewhere else in the Southern Hemisphere. During the North American summer, they just don't exist.

But you know what *does* happen in July? Magazines all around the country begin working on their October issues. Let's back up a second and see how this works. Generally, each issue of a monthly magazine hits newsstands and is mailed out to subscribers midway through the prior month.

This means an October issue would be available starting around September 15. But all of those copies need to be printed and shipped ahead of time, which means the editorial team probably sent the issue to the printer around August 15. But before printing can happen, each story had to be photographed and written; then both the images and words had to be designed into carefully edited magazine pages. This means the team probably began working on the stories in July (if not earlier!).

Producing spring and summer stories out of season is definitely possible; I've shot outdoor entertaining stories in the middle of winter by traveling to either Florida or California. But for lifestyle magazines that want to show Halloween parties complete with crunchy leaves and expertly carved pumpkins—or charming farmhouses decorated for Christmas, complete with a picture-perfect dusting of snow—the better option is to shoot these stories a year in advance. For this reason, magazines excel at planning at least a year at a time to make the most of each season when it actually happens. To optimize your business, I recommend that you do the same, plotting out what you plan to accomplish for the next 12 months with key moments as well as mini-goals—and corresponding deadlines—added in throughout the year.

FIND A CYCLE THAT WORKS

Try planning a vacation with someone who works at a magazine. If you pick the wrong week, you'll hear the dreaded words: "Oh, I can't go then; that's when we ship." Pick the same week in the next month, and you'll likely get the same response. Sometimes it is called shipping week, sometimes it is called blockout week, and during my last year at *Coastal Living*, we even gussied up the name with the nautically inspired moniker "Ship-Shape Week." But no matter what you call it, the fact remains: During one week a month, magazine pages ship to the printer, and late nights, lots of nail-biting, and copious amounts of coffee are usually involved.

Love it or hate it, there is something comforting about ship week coming back every few weeks, just like clockwork. Paradoxically, human beings are creatures of habit, but we also need constantly changing stimuli to keep us from getting bored or complacent. The magazine cycle is perfect for this.

For editors, story lineups have to be decided each month, then assigned to writers, then written, edited, put into a layout, and edited some more. For designers, story concepts are nailed down, then photoshoots are scheduled and layouts designed, as pages are tinkered with and images are retouched until everything looks perfect. Finally, the whole issue is uploaded to the printer as high-resolution PDFs. Digital proofs are reviewed to make sure that no typos snuck in, and then everyone takes a deep breath for about 15 seconds, before starting it all again.

When working at a magazine, each month is a new project, a clean slate, a chance to make the best thing you possibly can. And if you aren't 100 percent happy with the results, that's okay—you'll have the chance to do it all over again next month. That's the beauty of having a consistent cycle.

Depending on your business, there may be different cycles that you could employ. For me, the monthly cycle has always worked well, within the larger yearly cycle of an editorial calendar (see the next section, below). Thirty days allows a project to have a proper beginning, middle, and end with different aspects to focus on each week. At VERANDA, we publish issues bimonthly, so our cycle is approximately 60 days, allowing for a less frantic pace.

For some companies, a three-month cycle is ideal, allowing more time to see trends or changes in your business. For publicly held companies, this is a popular cycle because it corresponds well with releasing quarterly data to investors. For a new business, it may take time to figure out the cycle, or you may have multiple cycles with quarterly goals, monthly mini-goals, and weekly status checks. But either way, adopting a cycle creates a sense of order and makes it easier to implement deadlines.

PLAN YOUR YEAR WITH A CALENDAR

"It doesn't really fit anywhere in our editorial calendar."

These dreaded words are the fear of every magazine freelance writer who has ever pitched a story to an editor. (The only response that is worse: "That's a great idea; in fact, it's so great that we ran a story just like that in our last issue. Don't you *read* our magazine?")

Most people who have never worked in publishing are surprised to learn just how planned out every issue is, and often, like I mentioned above, a full year in advance. Like teachers who decide each summer what lessons they will cover in both the fall and spring semesters, or meeting planners who secure the venue and date for next year's conference before this year's has even begun, magazines must be forward-thinking and highly organized to manage the sheer volume of content that they produce each month.

This is where the editorial calendar comes into play. Each magazine usually has a bare-bones version with overarching themes and a few marquee stories for each month, as well as a more detailed version that, in some cases, has every single story planned, issue by issue, for the entire year. It is easy to get lost in the day-to-day chaos of any business, but creating a detailed calendar allows you to keep the big-picture goals in mind, while predetermining what you will focus on each month.

For years, I've helped create these calendars for every magazine I've worked at, and although each was different, they all covered many of the same bases:

- **January:** Starting the year strong with self-improvement and goal setting.

- **February:** Stories about love and relationships (and often chocolate), timed with Valentine's Day, along with cozy stories or travel stories to escape the cold.

- **March/April:** A focus on spring, new beginnings, and cleaning or decluttering. Often these issues include stories about flowers as well as spring fashion, inspiring the line that Meryl Streep as Miranda Priestly sarcastically delivers at a pitch meeting in *The Devil Wears Prada*: "Flowers for spring? Groundbreaking."[139]

- **May/June/July/August:** Not surprisingly, these issues include everything related to summer, from vacations, to a skincare story on sunscreen, to a roundup of beach reads.

- **September:** The home of early autumn, fall fashion, and back to school.

- **October:** Fall proper, and of course, Halloween. (Just go to the newsstand and count how many magazine covers show a pumpkin or the color orange in October!)

- **November:** Thanksgiving, including stories about feeling grateful and recipes for the holidays.

- **December:** Christmas and the holiday season, including decor, gift guides, recipes, and heartwarming stories; end-of-year recaps and "best of" lists are popular as well.

Every business has its own unique cycle, including different peaks and valleys in terms of workflow and busyness. Creating a similar calendar reminds us what to focus on each month. Things always change, and there will definitely be surprises, which a nimble editor (or businessperson) must face when they arrive. However, having this basic framework allows us to shuffle ideas and content, and know how a new piece of information will affect us not only immediately but also in the months that follow.

Although I had worked off of an editorial calendar for years, I failed to make one for myself the first year that I left my full-time job to start my own branding business. Rookie mistake! As a result, I found myself being reactive rather than proactive. I accepted every project that came my way, without actually spending any time planning for future projects. It's no wonder my first year as an entrepreneur found me setting the alarm at 4 a.m. each morning to tackle my heavy workload, and often working late into the night. This continued from January through the end of June—and then suddenly, it stopped.

I had heard other freelancers talk about the "summer slump" but had not prepared for it by securing projects for these slower months. As a result, I nearly killed myself for the first half of the year, and then suddenly found I had nothing to do. In the end, I used this time to reach out to potential new clients, polish my portfolio, and teach myself web design. (Learning new skills is a great use of downtime in any profession.) I also created a detailed calendar, so I would have a framework for the peaks and valleys of my business going forward.

A calendar with clearly marked tentpoles is essential for magazines, but it can be invaluable for other businesses as well. Since 2011, Apple has released a new version of its iPhone every September. The company is able to plan the release of other products around this launch, and consumers are also able to decide whether to buy a phone midyear or wait for the next version in the fall. The release is very well timed: The latest iPhone premieres in September but often is not available until a few weeks later, meaning that it is still "new" when holiday shoppers begin hunting for gifts. But by debuting in September rather than November, it avoids being lost in the fray of all the other holiday releases. People have time to see it online or try it in an Apple store, and add it to their wish lists *before* the big holiday shopping craze officially begins on Black Friday.

By plotting your company's year on a calendar, you're able to prepare for one-off events, and in some cases, schedule them at specific times. Perhaps, like Apple, you plan a big product launch in the fall, so that it is available for the holiday season. In this case, you know that you need to plot out deadlines for prototyping, testing, producing, photographing, and writing a press release for the product, plus getting it out to potential reviewers—all well before the actual release date.

On the other hand, perhaps your company is in the health and fitness niche. If you own a gym or personal training company, the holiday season will likely be slower, as clients focus more on celebrations with friends and family than on fitness. December may be a prime time to run promotions to get people in the door; or perhaps it is a good month to plan an off-site company retreat or allow employees to burn through any unused vacation time because your business will be slower anyway. Just make sure that everyone is back and ready to hit the ground running by January 1 for the New Year's Resolution crowd.

The timing of slow and busy cycles will vary in each industry, but if you anticipate and prepare for these shifts ahead of time, you can avoid knee-jerk reactions that may fail to capitalize on the opportunities these fluctuations can provide.

CREATE FRANCHISES TO BUILD EXCITEMENT AND BOOST SALES

When you hear the word franchise, you may think of a large chain like McDonald's that licenses its branding and product to franchisees. Or, if you are a movie buff, perhaps your mind goes to entertainment franchises, like the Marvel Cinematic Universe, Star Wars, or Harry Potter.

But when magazine editors talk about a franchise, what we mean is a recurring and highly branded editorial package, often built around a yearly event or list. When done well, these content engines bring increased advertising, newsstand sales, and PR buzz. When I worked at Time Inc., discovering the next game-changing franchise was always top of mind for its editors—and with good reason. After *Time* magazine put Charles Lindbergh on the cover in early 1928 with the words "Man of the Year," the company became known for launching some of the most successful franchises in the history of publishing:

- *Time*'s Man of the Year (later renamed Person of the Year)
- The *Fortune* 500
- The *Sports Illustrated* Swimsuit Issue
- *People*'s Sexiest Man Alive

Finding a franchise that consumers respond to is like searching for the Holy Grail: It can be a difficult and grueling pursuit, filled with trial and error, but when you find it, all the effort is undoubtedly worth it.

These ownable tentpole moments can be applied to other businesses as well. The seasonal flavors offered by Starbucks are a delicious example. Dressed in festive red cups, piping hot peppermint mochas and eggnog lattes are practically mandatory accessories during the holiday shopping rush. And for many coffee lovers, fall does not begin in late September with the autumnal equinox, but rather in late August, the first day that pumpkin spice drinks appear on the menu at their local Starbucks.

While seasonal cues can inform a great franchise, some of the best ones go the other direction, creating buzz during slower "off-season" periods. Many stores operate in the red throughout much of the year, finally turning a profit during the holiday shopping season that begins the day after Thanksgiving—hence the name "Black Friday." But smart retailers create their own exclusive Black Fridays at slower times throughout the year.

Fans of the department store Nordstrom, for instance, eagerly await the Anniversary Sale each July, which gives loyal customers first access to deep discounts on new fall styles from top designers; the unique event often results in more revenue for the company than its holiday sale.[140] Similarly, Amazon shoppers log on in droves that same month to catch Prime Day deals; the past few years, results were so strong that the company repeated this sale a second time, in October.[141]

FIVE KEYS TO A SUCCESSFUL FRANCHISE

Creating a franchise that attracts and excites customers involves a bit of trial and error, but as you begin to brainstorm, keep in mind these five characteristics that almost every successful franchises embodies:

1. It builds expectations. By occurring at the same time every year, the franchise becomes something customers expect and eagerly await. In the case of annual lists, like the *Travel + Leisure* World's Best Awards or the *Condé Nast Traveler* Top 500 Hotels, it also builds excitement within the industry to see who will be named each year.

2. It boosts slow sales. The *Time* magazine Man of the Year cover was first rolled out during a slow time for news just after the holidays, and the *Sports Illustrated* Swimsuit Issue was brought in to boost sales during the period between college bowl games and baseball's opening day.[142] Similarly, Amazon Prime Day and the Nordstrom Anniversary Sale occur not during the holidays but during the summer months, when people are spending their money on travel and experiences, and may be less likely to turn their discretionary income to retail.

3. It's easily repeatable. Franchises based around seasons are great, because people know exactly when to expect them each year. They can even work more than once a year, like the Nordstrom Half-Yearly Sales (another franchise the retailer has successfully rolled out). That said, franchises that happen too frequently aren't ideal (see the next point), and those that aren't frequent enough, such as ones based around the Olympics or elections, risk being forgotten during the two- or four-year gaps between those events.

4. It creates scarcity. Although it may be tempting to turn a good franchise into a common event, I believe that making these events once or twice a year is the best practice. If the pumpkin spice latte was served all year long, would people turn out en masse to buy it each fall? Nordstrom's president of stores Jamie Nordstrom puts the topic front and center when speaking about his company's famed Anniversary Sale, which is offered for just a few weeks each year and with limited inventory. "Anniversary is an event of scarcity. That creates excitement," he says. "You've got to get there first to get the best selection. It's like concert tickets—you've got to get them before they're sold out."[143]

5. It builds media buzz. Even if you didn't read the *Time* magazine article proclaiming Taylor Swift its "Person of the Year" in 2023, you likely read another article or headline that referenced it. Similarly, even if you don't shop regularly on Amazon, you are likely to hear about Amazon Prime Day in the weeks leading up to it, as media outlets around the country cover what has become a major shopping day for many consumers. When you have a unique franchise, it is easier to get people buzzing about it.

HOW TO BRAINSTORM NEW FRANCHISES

When I worked at Time Inc., each brand set aside special "Editorial Development" days to brainstorm new franchise ideas throughout the year. Several members of the editorial staff would participate, but we would also invite employees from other magazines for a fresh perspective, as well as staffers from other departments—sales, marketing, circulation, etc. Once we had a good mix of 10 to 20 people, the group would be divided into two teams in different rooms and given a prompt, such as: *Come up with a new franchise that could be rolled out during a summer issue.*

The two teams separately brainstormed ideas for the first hour or two, then spent the next day and a half determining what their chosen idea would look like. Some team members worked on producing quick mock-ups of a cover and feature layout, which we called "rapid prototyping," while others drafted a business plan that showed how the idea would bring new readers, new press coverage, new revenue, or—in a perfect world—all three. Each team then presented their idea to the editor in chief, publisher, and other top brass at the end of the second day.

One or both of the new ideas were often adopted, tweaked slightly, and rolled out the following year as a test. Sometimes they were a hit and repeated for years to come, as was the case with *Coastal Living's* Happiest Seaside Towns franchise. Other times, they turned into a one-off experiment, as was the case with the *Coastal Living* Design Awards. But either way, there was excitement in the air; as the two teams worked on their pitches, you never knew if you were actually creating the next game-changing franchise for Time Inc.

Although this particular process was very magazine-specific, it can be applied to any industry. Gather a group of your smartest and most creative employees from across various disciplines and departments and divide them into two teams with a task: Come up with a new franchise that fills a particular need at a particular time of year, and that embodies most or ideally all of the "Five Keys to a Successful Franchise."

Give them the rest of the day and the following morning to work on a presentation that shows how such an idea could impact the company's bottom line. The teams could mock up examples of new product packaging or promo ads, along with a rough business and marketing plan that shows how the venture could garner new customers, larger orders, and media buzz. If you are a clothing retailer, is it a new sales event that brings people in during a slower season? If you are a company that sells hot tea blends, do you create a new limited edition line of iced tea formulations for summer?

When you gather a group of your best and brightest and encourage them to let their imaginations run wild, you may be surprised by the brilliance of the ideas that are generated. As a bonus, empowering your team to lead the charge for a potential new venture will give them ownership over the results, making them more invested in the business as a whole.

EDITOR'S TIP

—

Make the most of franchise brainstorming sessions.

If you take the time to schedule one of these brainstorming sessions, follow these five suggestions to maximize productivity:

- Plan ahead to make it a fun event, almost like a retreat. Order breakfast and lunch, have drinks and snacks available, and ask participants to block their calendars so they can be fully focused on the task at hand.

- Include staff members with a variety of skill sets and specialties on each team, and consider grouping people who don't often work together.

- Make the brief you give each team as specific as possible to ensure the objective of the exercise is clear and focused.

- Appoint yourself or someone else as an independent moderator who checks in on the teams throughout the two days, and especially during the first few hours. If the two teams are leaning toward similar ideas, it may behoove you to steer one of them toward a backup idea so that you don't end up with two presentations and concepts that feel the same.

- Invite key stakeholders to the final presentation so that they can hear the ideas, ask clarifying questions, and offer feedback on how an idea could be optimized with a slight tweak.

THE IMPORTANCE OF DEADLINES

You've found a monthly or quarterly cycle that works for your business, planned out a yearly calendar, and incorporated a few franchises through-out the year. But the day-to-day operations haven't stopped, and each day feels busier than the last. How do you ensure that all of your big plans and exciting new ideas come to fruition? The answer, as every editor knows, is that you must set—and stick to—a series of deadlines.

Have you ever noticed that if you have a week to do something, it takes a week to finish? But magically, if you have just a day—or even an afternoon—somehow the same task can be completed in a fraction of the time? This is called Parkinson's Law, a term coined by 20th-century naval historian and author C. Northcote Parkinson, who stated that "work expands so as to fill the time available for its completion."[144] As someone who has been a lifelong procrastinator, I can tell you from experience: Parkinson's Law is a very real thing. Sure, there are Type-A superachievers who make a to-do list every day, and joyfully check off each task as quickly as possible. But for the rest of us, there is no reason to do today what can be put off until tomorrow. The problem is, without a strict deadline, tomorrow literally never comes.

As any writer can tell you, in the days before your story is due to the editor, there are a million things that seem more pressing. Emails to be answered, phone calls to be returned, files to be organized, and of course, social media accounts to be checked. For freelance writers working from home, the distractions are even greater. As you stare at a blank screen, your mind can take you for a wild, unproductive ride that looks something like this: *Hmm, it's hard to finish writing this article— maybe it's because I have a slight headache. Have I drank enough water today? I think I'm thirsty … While I am getting water, maybe I will have a small snack … Oh, this refrigerator is such a mess! I really should take ten minutes to reorganize it … Now that the fridge is in order, the kitchen would look much better if I mopped the floor as well …*

Fortunately, everything in the world of publishing has a due date, and the stories must eventually be written, edited, designed, and printed—even if it takes a bit of desk-cleaning, internet-surfing, or—God forbid—floor-mopping to actually get to that point.

The problem in business (and life) is that sometimes deadlines are less pressing. When I started my own company, I knew that I needed a killer website to bring in new clients. But because building it wasn't a paid project with an actual launch date, my site languished for almost a year while I attended to more pressing matters.

It's the same with personal projects. While I rarely turn in work assignments late, life goals that truly felt important to me—like writing this book—often seemed to get pushed to the side, sometimes for years. In business and in life, deadlines need to be self-imposed. Just as the squeaky wheel gets oiled, the project with a due date gets completed. Perhaps the biggest lesson about success that I have learned from the magazine world is that deadlines are essential to get anything done—and done is better than perfect.

EDITOR'S TIP
—
Make your procrastination productive.

If you are going to procrastinate—and at times, we all do—consider engaging in what I call "productive procrastination." If you need to work on a project but the inspiration just isn't coming, for goodness sakes, *don't* retire to the sofa and turn on the TV. Instead, tick off another task on your to-do list that will make you feel equally accomplished at the end of the day, even if you didn't tackle the project you intended. If you are feeling uninspired to finish working on a sales presentation, for instance, perhaps you gather your receipts and finally submit that expense report that has been lingering for weeks. And yes, sometimes even organizing your desk counts!

HOW TO SET DEADLINES—AND STICK TO THEM

Taking on a big project can be daunting; I certainly felt intimidated when I started writing this book. But you must remember that in order to run a marathon, you don't go from running zero to 26.2 miles in one day. To do so would be setting yourself up for disappointment, failure, and injury. The only way to ensure you achieve a gigantic goal is to break it down into smaller tasks along the way.

Often, leaders set ambitious goals that we hope to accomplish in one year. This is a natural time frame, as it corresponds to the fiscal year that businesses of all sizes use for accounting. Also, within corporate America, we are often either given direct financial goals or asked to create our own personal performance goals that we work on over the course of a year. At Hearst Magazines, each employee writes a list of three or four personal and business goals during Q1, with a deadline of achieving them by end of year.

The best way to make sure you can achieve a big goal is to break it down into smaller actions. For this reason, I like to divide a big yearly initiative into smaller 90-day goals, 30-day mini-goals, and daily and weekly tasks that will help me reach these deadlines. I have found that when I do this exercise at the beginning, I set myself up for measurable success. And when I don't?

Well, let's take this book for example; I started writing it in late 2016 and set a goal of having the first draft finished in four months. At the time, it seemed reasonable; I had completed my college thesis in a similar amount of time. (Notably, my thesis had a hard-and-fast deadline—if I wanted to graduate!) What I didn't account for was that I started writing this book during the first 12 months of running my own business full-time, and specifically during a once-in-a-lifetime period that saw my husband traveling around the world for his job, while I accompanied him.

In the first month I started working on the book, we visited Greece, Hong Kong, Singapore, Thailand, China, Australia, and New Zealand. Though I thought that I would have lots of time to write on planes, I didn't take into account jet lag, time spent sightseeing, and a particularly gruesome bout of food poisoning that lasted a week—not to mention the difficulty of scheduling interviews from a time zone that was six to 15 hours ahead.

I missed my deadline, which was a bit too ambitious, but then never set a new one. This resulted in my puttering around with the book throughout 2017 and 2018, writing a page here and a page there, but not really making any concrete progress. Despite my own knowledge about the goal-setting process, I never set a deadline for its completion. And surprise, surprise— five years later, I still hadn't finished it.

EDITOR'S TIP
—
Make your goals SMART.

Many companies, including my employer Hearst, encourage team members to use the SMART framework when setting yearly objectives for themselves. SMART goals should be:

- **Specific:** Clearly define what you want to accomplish.

- **Measurable:** Establish criteria to track progress and measure the outcome.

- **Achievable:** Develop aspirational yet attainable goals.

- **Relevant:** Ensure the goals matter to you and align with business needs.

- **Time-bound:** Set a deadline to achieve them.

Using this framework helps you create a clear, structured, and attainable list of objectives, increasing the likelihood of success.

Then, in June 2023, I attended a virtual conference for first-time authors. Afterward, I was reinvigorated and decided to dust off my half-finished manuscript, which I had not touched in more than five years. I set an ambitious—but attainable—goal of publishing the book just over a year later, by late summer or early fall 2024. And instead of crossing my fingers and hoping that happened, I broke down all of the steps that would need to occur in order to meet my deadline.

This time, I gave myself quarterly and monthly goals, all of which used the SMART framework (see sidebar):

- **Summer 2023 (June–August): Outlining and Starting the First Draft**
  Create an outline, start research, and salvage the rough draft that I had started in 2016.

- **Fall 2023 (September–December): Finishing the First Draft**
  Complete interviews with editors and other experts, adding their insights to my research as I finish the first draft.

- **Winter 2024 (January–February): Self-Editing**
  Begin self-editing in January; move on to developmental editing by the end of February.

- **Spring 2024 (March–May): Editing**
  Continue developmental editing in March and progress to copy editing by May.

- **Summer 2024 (June–August): Production**
  Begin proofreading in June, production in July, and initial promotion in August.

- **Fall 2024 (September–December): Publication and Promotion**
  Officially launch the book and continue promotion throughout the fall.

Based on this, I was able to create a list of weekly tasks to ensure I hit my monthly and quarterly goals. I also set myself up for success by organizing the project in several spreadsheets and text documents, as well as a detailed calendar. This time I didn't just wish for success but rather planned for it—and if you are reading this book, the plan worked.

EDITOR'S TIP

Adjust your sails when you veer off course.

A carefully planned calendar is a framework that helps you organize your year. That said, surprises can and will pop up, so you'll need to remain nimble, adapting to unexpected speed bumps. In the case of this book, writing my manuscript actually took a bit longer than intended, requiring me to push everything back by a month or two. This was followed by a few delays in the editing process as well. Fortunately, I had anticipated these hiccups, which is why I optimistically hoped to have the book published by the end of summer (mid-September) but set an *actual* launch goal of fall 2024—meaning that I had until mid-December if need be. Because I had built a bit of wiggle room into my schedule, I was able to adjust the editing and production dates slightly and still hit my fall launch goal.

THE TAKEAWAY

Determine what **cycle** best fits the needs of your business and team; often, this is a monthly cycle within larger quarterly and yearly cycles. Creating a detailed **calendar** for the year allows you to know what your business will be focusing on each month, both in terms of product and content.

List some **franchises** that you love, and ask family, friends, or coworkers to do the same. Using these successful examples as a guide, brainstorm potential franchises that could heighten sales during slower times. For each idea, ask yourself if the franchise could build expectations, boost sales, be easily repeatable, create scarcity, and garner media attention.

The amount of work we have will always expand to fill the time allotted. To accomplish tasks efficiently, **deadlines are essential.** For projects that could languish on forever, set firm deadlines and share them with others on your team, so that everyone knows the date and can hold each other accountable.

If you have an ambitious dream for the year, **start by breaking your big goal down into smaller goals** for each quarter. Then break those down further into monthly mini-goals or deadlines. Use these to determine which tasks you need to complete each week—and even each day—to meet the big goal's deadline for completion.

When creating goals both large and small, use the **SMART framework:** Each goal should be Specific, Measurable, Achievable, Relevant, and Time-bound.

Whenever possible, build in some wiggle room so that you can **remain nimble,** adjusting your mini-goals slightly when setbacks arise, while still hitting your final deadline.

CHAPTER 11

....

Zoom In:
Planning Your Day

F or most of my life, I was a night person. As a kid, I loved to stay up late and hated waking up early for school. This continued into college, where I rarely scheduled classes before noon, if I could help it. In my freshman year, I discovered that several of my required classes had an option with an evening time slot after 5 p.m., geared toward students who had full-time day jobs. I would schedule myself into these classes whenever I could because I felt more alert at night. My night owl tendencies remained throughout my 20s—the majority of my thesis was written in the middle of the night—and even in my first few magazine jobs, I found that I would much rather roll into work at 10 a.m. and stay until 7 p.m. or later than show up at the crack of dawn.

Then in my mid-30s, something flipped. I had resigned from *Coastal Living*, but because I was leaving to start my own business and not another job, I gave my boss a 10-week notice. During that time, I continued working on the magazine but also started ramping up my own business on the side. In order to work both jobs successfully, I began setting my alarm for 4 a.m. each morning. This way, I could get in a few hours of freelance work before showering and heading to the office.

To my surprise, I found that I loved my new schedule. There was something about being awake before everyone else that made me feel like I had gotten a head start on the day. Much of my job at *Coastal Living* involved planning sessions for magazine layouts, whereas my new freelance clients were paying me for creative designs in the realms of marketing and advertising, spaces I was less experienced with. These projects required slightly different thinking, and I found that I was most alert and able to do my best work in the early morning hours, before the distractions of the day had begun. At that moment, a morning person was born.

ADAPT YOUR WORKDAY TO YOUR BUSINESS NEEDS

As part of my grad school magazine project at Northwestern, we had to call media buyers for some of the largest brands in the country and attempt to secure ad placements in our prototype. Because the school is based just outside of Chicago in the Central Time Zone, we reasoned that if we got to school at 8 a.m., it would be 9 a.m. in New York City—the perfect time to reach busy advertising executives and catch them fresh, before their meeting-filled days began.

There was just one problem: Almost everyone we called, in industries ranging from fashion to entertainment to beauty, was never in the office. Morning after morning, breathless assistants, who had probably just walked in the door, grabbed the phones at 9:01 a.m. Eastern Time, only to inform us that their bosses weren't in yet, and probably wouldn't be for a while.

When I moved to New York, I soon realized that the 9-to-5 schedule rarely applied to the world of magazines. Yes, Wall Street was buzzing early, and some professionals, including doctor's offices, also got an early start, squeezing in morning appointments with patients who were eager to be seen before their own workdays began. Even newspaper reporters may be at their desks early, ready to get the scoop first and have their stories in to their editors and copy chiefs by early afternoon.

But magazines were a different animal, following what I call "The Creatives' Schedule." At my first job, the hours were 10 a.m. to 6 p.m., allowing everyone to avoid the rush hour commute. I even knew people at other magazines who adopted a 10:30-to-6:30 or even an 11-to-7 schedule.

And why not? The magazine industry at that time was less digitally focused and was based on monthly or weekly—not daily—news cycles. The beauty of this schedule is that it allowed employees to finish their morning tasks—dropping off the kids, exercising, or running errands—before 10 a.m., so that they arrived at the office rested, alert, and ready to work.

Magazine editors, especially in New York, often find it necessary to attend evening events as well, ranging from product launches to dinners and cocktail parties. Depending on the mix of people, these events can either be terrible or a lot of fun, but nonetheless, they are work—and they frequently occur at night. "The Creatives' Schedule" allows editors to attend these events, schmooze as late as necessary, and still get enough sleep to arrive bright-eyed and bushy-tailed the next day.

Adapting your workday to your business needs is a small concept to borrow from magazines, but it can have a big impact on the experience of both your employees and your customers. So many businesses automatically adopt a 9-to-5 schedule by default, but if you run a business that caters to busy professionals, perhaps you open a bit earlier and stay open a bit later, or offer weekend hours. For years, Fifth Third Bank ran advertisements about staying open late and on the weekends, catering to people who may not be able to visit during regular banking hours. If you have the type of business with extreme peaks and valleys, you could even follow the "fitness class" model by offering early morning, lunchtime, and evening availability. If mornings and evenings are quiet but midday is slammed, you could hire some employees on a 7-to-3 schedule and others on an 11-to-7 schedule, to allow for optimum double coverage during the busiest time.

CONSIDER HOW YOU WORK BEST
AND PLAN ACCORDINGLY

Regardless of what hours best fit the needs of your business, as a leader, you also need to figure out what time slot is best for you to complete your deep work, whatever it may be. For many of us, morning is when we are at our freshest and most alert. That time should be used for completing our crucial tasks, or the tasks that require the most creativity or concentration.

As a leader, this often means blocking your calendar to maximize your productive hours. Jason Feifer, the editor in chief of *Entrepreneur*, calls this "knowing yourself as a resource," and it makes sense.[145] Our brain power and ability to come up with good ideas is a finite resource each given day—although, thankfully, it is also a renewable resource that replenishes itself again after a good night's sleep.

Recognizing the importance of sleep and how alert we feel after it, some high-achievers double their "power hours" by taking midday naps. Chandler Bolt, the founder of SelfPublishing.com (who was also named to the *Forbes* 30 Under 30 List—another great franchise!), has taken a 20-minute after-lunch nap for years, finding that it gives him two "fresh and alert" windows each day, making him twice as productive.

Whether I am focused on design or writing, my deep work requires intense concentration and freedom from distraction. For this reason, I start my day by getting out of bed by 6:30 a.m. most days (and often earlier), before diving into my deep work as soon as possible. I try to plow through as much as I can before others are online, finding I can often continue working free of distractions for the first hour of the workday, as my colleagues spend the morning getting coffee and checking email.

Though important, meetings are usually less dependent on my being at my freshest. (Brainstorming or "big idea" meetings are the exception.) For this reason, if I am the one scheduling the meeting, it will almost always be as late in the day as possible, when I no longer feel creatively sharp enough to produce new work but *do* feel alert enough to review work or plan future work with others. Such a schedule is not uncommon for editors and for writers of all types. An array of novelists from Stephen King to Barbara Kingsolver have reported that their best writing is usually done first thing in the morning, while they reserve afternoons for less creative tasks.

USE TIME-BLOCKING TO CONQUER YOUR TO-DO LIST

I am a longtime proponent of to-do lists and have varied the ways I've used them over the years. On legal pads, I've written long rambling lists of things I want to accomplish or places I want to visit in the next five years; I've also jotted short daily checklists on Post-it notes and stuck them to my computer monitor as a reminder. For the past five years or so, I've used a weekly list that is the size of a half sheet of paper with a column for each day of the week, plus an extra spot to write monthly or long-term goals, which I cross off when completed or carry over to the next week's list when they aren't.

Some productivity articles suggest that you focus on three priorities each day, which I believe is a great strategy—if you can make it work. But for most of us, there are way more things we need to accomplish on any given day. For this reason, high-achieving editors take the to-do list to the next level by figuring out which tasks they need to accomplish and then blocking out exact times to work on each, while grouping together tasks that are of a similar nature.

Think of these as mini-work sessions with mini-deadlines. It goes back to Parkinson's Law: Our "work expands so as to fill the time available for its completion." So if you have all day to complete three priority tasks, it may take you all day to do it, as you fit them haphazardly between emails, phone calls, and meetings. But with time-blocking, you will find that each hour has a set goal, making haphazard days a thing of the past.

Seven Steps to Effective Time-Blocking

Time-blocking can be a game-changer when you have a long to-do list to accomplish each week, but the results are only as good as the process. Here are my top tips to make the most of your new time-blocking habit:

1. Set clear goals and priorities. Before you start time-blocking, identify your key goals and priorities for the day, week, or month. This will help you allocate your time more effectively.

2. Define time blocks and assign tasks accordingly. Using a physical or digital weekly calendar, break each day into blocks (typically in 15- to 90-minute increments), and assign specific tasks or activities to each time block. (If you use Microsoft Outlook or Google Calendar to schedule meetings, that is probably a good place to start.) Be specific about exactly what you will work on during each block, while also being realistic about how much time each task will take.

3. Prioritize tasks. Schedule important and high-priority tasks during your most productive time of the day, which for many people is in the morning when they are most alert. As you map out your day, think about energy level, attention span, and other factors: For example, does your whole team need to be involved in a task? If so, what works best for their schedules?

4. Batch similar tasks and avoid multitasking. Group similar tasks together in the same time block to avoid "switch cost," which is the lost time that occurs when we mentally shift our focus from one task to another. For example, schedule all of your meetings back-to-back with short breaks between them. Avoid multitasking, especially during blocks of deep work. The best way to do this is to silence notifications, close unnecessary tabs or apps, and schedule a 15-minute breather to get water, use the restroom, and check email immediately after the block ends.

5. Be realistic. Avoid overloading your schedule, and don't forget to plan short breaks in your day to rest and recharge. Also, be honest about the requirements of your specific job and what you can accomplish in a day. Some experts advocate just checking email twice a day, but if that doesn't work for your role, maybe you schedule four shorter email blocks. If a particular task requires three hours to complete but your schedule is already jam-packed, it may be best to work on it in 60-minute blocks over three days.

6. Keep some flexibility. Few of us have complete control over our days—things come up or our boss schedules a meeting during our deep work time. If possible, try to keep one "flex" time block later in the day, in case something comes up and you need to shift a morning task to that slot.

7. Adapt and review. Regularly review your time-blocking schedule at the end of the day or week to see how well it's working for you. Make adjustments and improvements as needed.

EDITOR'S TIP

—

Time-block your calendar *and* remain available.

You may be thinking, *This sounds great in theory, but I can't block my whole calendar.* If you can, it's best to communicate your new time-blocking schedule to colleagues and family, so they understand that you may have limited flexibility during the workday. But if you are hesitant to do so, and are also hesitant to have your entire day show as blocked on your digital calendar, consider this work-around: For a chunk scheduled for my most important and time-sensitive tasks, I will often have Outlook show that time as *Busy* for other users who are trying to find time on my calendar to book a meeting. Then, for my more flexible time blocks (assigned to checking email or working on a less pressing project), I block the time on my calendar in the same way but have the time block appear as *Free* to others. In that way, I am carefully scheduling every minute of my time in my own calendar view, while still allowing my boss or direct reports to book time with me if needed. If someone books a meeting during one of these less crucial slots, I can redirect the work I had planned to do during that time to another "flexible" slot later that afternoon or the following day.

HOW TO OPTIMIZE MEETINGS

Meetings: a subject that has launched a thousand memes, *Saturday Night Live* skits, and episodes of *The Office*. Love 'em or hate 'em, meetings are a fact of life when you have a group of people who are working collaboratively to produce or sell a product. Though I had attended meetings throughout my career, I entered a new level of meeting fatigue when I started as design director at

Coastal Living. In most of my past roles, I had worked on very small teams of six or seven people, which meant that most meetings could happen quickly in hallways or standing in someone's office. Although my job as art director at *Parenting* brought me to a much larger staff, I was still spared from the lion's share of meetings because I was not yet in the top spot on the art team.

At *Coastal Living,* that all changed. As the person overseeing the look of the entire brand, I was invited to almost every story and photoshoot meeting. In addition to the day-to-day work of the magazine itself, there were also meetings about our other ventures (coffee-table books, as well as furniture, accessory, and stationery lines), plus management meetings, planning meetings, budget meetings, and so on.

After my first two weeks on the job, I realized that most of my deep work—designing pages of the magazine—would need to be done early in the morning before everyone had arrived, or in the evening after everyone had left for the night. In fact, there were so many meetings requiring my presence that I bought a box of meal-replacement protein bars to keep at my desk, since I sometimes had to eat lunch while walking from one meeting to the next.

Throughout my career, each of my managers has had a different relationship with meetings and has run them differently. Some bosses loved meetings and thought the more the merrier; others saw them as a necessary evil that should be kept to a minimum. Over time, I have compiled five tips to make unavoidable meetings less painful—and, in some cases, even enjoyable:

1. Choose the right day and time.

Weekly staff meetings have been a reality at almost every job I've had, and they have almost always been scheduled for the first thing Monday morning. It seems like a good idea on paper: Kick off the week with a bang and ensure everyone has their marching orders! But in reality, I have found that Monday morning staff meetings are often problematic. First of all, Mondays suck. People are tired and grumpy, so why make it worse? Because staff meetings are often used for status updates on projects, they can also be fear-inducing and lead to the Sunday Scaries, especially if your projects aren't as far along as you had promised the previous week.

Ana Connery, my editor in chief at *Parenting,* scheduled our staff meetings for Tuesday morning, and I thought it was brilliant. You could show up on Monday, keep your head down and work hard, and usually be ready for a positive update on your assignments the following day. Another advantage to Tuesday meetings is that everyone is usually there. Six U.S. holidays occur on Mondays, meaning that more than a tenth of all staff meetings scheduled for Monday will need to be moved before the year even starts. Many employees will also take Monday off if they are planning a weekend trip, while it's less common to take Tuesday as a vacation day.

2. Choose the right people—and the right number.

While it might be tempting to have a "big ideas" meeting with your whole staff, keep in mind that the larger the group, the more likely it is that some people will become wallflowers and not share their ideas. For this reason, it is sometimes better to invite a smaller group of five or six people for the best brainstorming results.

Now, that doesn't mean that the five most senior employees should always be the go-to's for these meeting. A former editor at *Good Housekeeping* and *Money*, Margaret Magnarelli transitioned to the corporate world in 2014 and since then has held executive director and vice president roles at Monster, Morgan Stanley, and Baldor Specialty Foods. Although she has attended countless meetings throughout her career, there is one recurring meeting from an early job that she still remembers. "When I was at *Seventeen*, the editor in chief would have monthly meetings to determine cover lines for the magazine," Magnarelli told me. "She brought together a group of people from all different levels, people who she identified as talented at cover line writing. I was invited even though I was an assistant editor."[146] Decades later, Magnarelli still remembers how it felt to have been given a seat at the table based on her talents, despite being lower on the masthead.

When deciding who needs to attend a meeting, remember that often the person who doesn't need to be there is *you*. In some cases, your presence may not be necessary, and in others, it could even hinder the flow of conversation, since people may wait to see what your reaction is before expressing their own thoughts about new ideas. In his book *Clone Yourself: Build a Team that Understands Your Vision, Shares Your Passion, and Runs Your Business for You*, bestselling author and leadership coach Jeff Hilderman recommends pulling yourself out of unnecessary meetings by explaining that there is something else you need to be working on during that time and offering to contribute in another way, such as by providing talking points in advance or by reviewing the minutes later and giving feedback. "The last thing you want to do is give others the impression that you're too important to be in the meeting, you're not a team player, or that your time is more valuable than everybody else's," Hilderman writes. "Sell them on why it's just as important that you're not in attendance."[147]

3. Keep them short.

There are certain types of jobs where meetings are the main priority—think project managers, who are tasked with getting updates and making sure everyone is on the same page. But for most of us, our priority is the deep work we were hired to do, so to allow the most time for this, we should keep meetings as short and to the point as possible. Consider holding stand-up status check meetings, which encourage people to speak briefly and to the point, rather than settling in for long monologues. When I first started my own business, I worked on branding initiatives for several hotels and found that a daily, 15-minute "stand-up," led by the hotel general manager and attended by directors and managers from every department, was customary—and quite effective for relaying key information quickly.

For first-time managers, it's important to remember that meetings may be dragging on because *you* let them. Kristin van Ogtrop learned this lesson during one of her first layout review meetings after she took over as editor in chief of *Real Simple*. "The meeting was just going on forever, and we were running out of things to talk about," she told me. "It was getting really boring. Later, I asked someone who had been there why the meeting dragged on so long, and she said, 'Well, we were waiting for you to stand up and end it.' Then I realized: *Oh … I'm the person who ends the meeting now*."[148]

4. Distribute a prioritized agenda.

In Chapter 9, I compared launching a brand without a vision to starting a road trip without a final destination in mind. Similarly, scheduling a meeting without an agenda is like starting out on a road trip without a map. You may know the point of the meeting/trip—the destination you have in mind—but if you don't have a detailed map for how to get there, will you actually arrive? Even if you do, there will likely be wrong turns, wasted time, and confusion along the way.

Part of your job as a leader is managing your time and helping your staff manage theirs, which means communicating clearly and letting them know your expectations. If you are hosting a brainstorming meeting, make that clear in advance. Some people think well on their feet, but others do much better work with a bit of preparation, research, and time to ruminate. If the meeting is to review upcoming projects or initiatives, let the attendees know which topics you are going to cover ahead of time, so people can plan brief statements about their progress, rather than being caught off guard and rambling a lengthy update out of nervousness. Using an agenda to prioritize topics ensures that the most pressing subjects will be covered first, even if you run out of time to discuss everything on the list.

5. Whenever possible, make meetings fun.

Aside from the invite list, the other thing Margaret Magnarelli remembers about those cover line meetings at *Seventeen* is that people actually enjoyed them. "The meetings were really fun," she recalls. "People laughed a lot, and I felt like that was something I always wanted to have in a workplace. It was the collaborative nature of people being creative together." Today, she puts that lesson into practice at her own meetings. "If you can instill a positive feeling about creativity, where you say 'Yes, and …' rather than 'No' to people's ideas, then it becomes fun. Those are the moments that make people want to keep going back to work. A meeting doesn't have to be miserable."[149]

We have all been in plenty of meetings over the years where we wanted to poke our eyes out or crawl under the table and hide. And while certain meetings must be more serious, often the tone is simply set by whoever is leading the meeting. So if that person is you, why not make it fun and encourage people to laugh a little? As the saying goes, we are not curing cancer here—unless you run a hospital or medical research company, in which case humor may be even more necessary!

EDITOR'S TIP
—
Listen to what is said after the meeting.

In his book *You Can't Fire Everyone: And Other Lessons from an Accidental Manager*, Hank Gilman spends several pages ranting about how much he hates meetings. And as the editorial manager of Yahoo Finance and former deputy editor of *Fortune* magazine, he's certainly sat through his fair share. Although Gilman advocates keeping meetings minimal, brief, and with as few people as possible, it's the "after-meeting meetings" that he finds the most useful. "That's when things break up and you just talk about anything that comes to mind. Then you stumble, invariably, into an important topic and you get work done. Always happens. So if you want to have a good meeting, end the old one quickly and just hang out."[150]

THE TAKEAWAY

When creating a **daily schedule,** consider the basic duties of your employees, and ask yourself: Do these need to be completed at a certain time of day or is there flexibility? Next, think about the needs of the people you serve. Would potential customers benefit from having hours that do not fit the typical 9-to-5 model?

Know yourself as a resource and plan your most important, high-priority work during the time of day when you feel most fresh and alert. (For many people, this is early or mid-morning.)

Use **time-blocking** to take your to-do list to the next level. Prioritize your tasks, group similar activities together, and then assign a block of time for each item. Protect your time by sticking to this schedule as much as possible, but allow some wiggle room for breaks and flexibility if an unforeseen meeting or other issue that needs your attention comes up.

Make the most of any meeting by choosing the best day and time; inviting the right people (fewer is usually better); and using a prioritized agenda that will allow you to keep it brief yet productive. And whenever possible, make it fun as well.

Visit **LeadLikeAnEditor.com** to download a free workbook that includes a guide to **Time-Blocking Your Calendar,** as well as other templates and resources.

PART FOUR

T is for

TEAM

"Business is a team sport."

—*Robert T. Kiyosaki, entrepreneur and author of* Rich Dad Poor Dad

A common platitude heard in business is that "people are your greatest asset." Many would argue that this maxim is so ubiquitous as to have become a cliché. But search the internet for the phrase and you will find a multitude of contrarian arguments seeking to debunk this statement.

Harvard Business Review makes the distinction that it is how we empower people that is our greatest asset.[151] *Inc.* magazine takes it a step further, saying that a company's greatest asset is its business beliefs as a whole, which in turn, empowers its employees.[152] And when the top brass are asked to weigh in, their staffs are often left out of the equation altogether. A *Wall Street Journal* article, for instance, points to a survey of 800 CEOs who, when questioned about their companies' most valuable asset, prioritized technology above all else. Their employees didn't even make the top five.[153]

But here's the thing: I have seen businesses run without a great mission, without empowering leaders, and even without up-to-date technology. But I have yet to see one run without people. For years, Southwest Airlines did not have the largest jets, the most dazzling website, or the best in-flight amenities—but it did have employees who were passionate about their work. And the company took care of them, making them feel protected, which led to more enthusiasm on the job. Although Southwest is known for its friendly customer service, it does *not* believe the customer is always right, and will not tolerate travelers who are rude or combative to its staff.[154]

It may be obvious that a large company, especially one based on customer service, would be crippled without its deep roster of employees. But in many ways, small companies are even more dependent on their teams. If your business has fewer than five employees, there really is no room for dead weight. And even if you are a solopreneur, you will likely need to hire contractors to help in certain areas, like bookkeeping or accounting. It's rare that we can do everything by ourselves.

CREATING YOUR TEAM LIKE AN EDITOR

In the following chapters, we will cover the three most important aspects of leading other people:

- Hire intelligently to **build a dream team** that has the skills—and personality traits—needed to take your business to the next level.

- **Lead that team** by motivating them through a five-step process that includes assessing people's strengths, teaching them what success looks like, empowering them to make choices, and offering frequent constructive feedback, as well as rewards for good work.

- **Keep your team happy** by creating a company culture that makes a job feel like more than just work. To do this, provide perks, purpose, fun, and opportunities for growth.

People are at the heart of every successful business, and taking time to focus on hiring and developing your team is one of the best investments you can make. So let's start building your dream team.

....

CHAPTER 12

Build Your Dream Team

Most people learn about the concept of teamwork early in life when they sign up to play their first sport. Take football, for example: Although quarterbacks may get all the glory, and running backs score a lot of touchdowns, these players know that without the offensive linemen blocking for them, they would be toast.

It's the same in most businesses—and especially in journalism. Creating a publication from scratch every month simply cannot happen without having the right team in place. I got my first taste of this as the co-editor of my high school newspaper, *Xavier News*.

When the year started, I hoped for a staff of students who were just like me: hardworking, strong writers who were obsessed with grammar. I quickly learned that in order to get the newspaper out on time, we needed people who were interested in an array of topics and who possessed a variety of skills that I had not considered. First, we needed a good photographer; I tried my hand at photographing a varsity soccer match once, and all of the images—on film back then—turned out blurry. But we also needed an illustrator, designers, and people who were interested in writing about all sorts of topics, including sports, which (despite the football analogy above) was definitely not my forte.

Although I had a defined talent pool—the students who had signed up for journalism classes—I was also able to recruit a few more student "stringers" to fill in some holes in our coverage. For you, team building could mean hiring someone to fill a current role or a newly created one; or if you are starting a new business, it could mean creating an entire team from scratch. Regardless, you will quickly find that the hiring process can be confusing and time-consuming, with lots of room for error along the way. But resist the urge to rush through it. Building your dream team can take time and effort, but ultimately, may be the most important thing you do as a manager.

HOW TO WRITE A KILLER JOB DESCRIPTION

Good job descriptions can take on many different forms. I've seen—and posted—ones that are just a few sentences long and ones that have multiple sections with bullet points in each. To some extent, it can depend on the role you are seeking to fill. If you are hiring for a part-time cashier or receptionist, keeping the description short may be fine. But for most professional roles, I like using a longer four-part structure:

- **About the Job:** This is a great spot to tell the candidate a bit about the role, the team, and the impact they will have. If there are important selling points—like a pet-friendly office—you may want to include them here. When hiring for roles at Hearst's office in Birmingham, I hoped to attract local as well as national talent, who may not be aware of just how cool Alabama could be. To woo big-city candidates who might be on the fence about moving to the South, I mentioned that the "loft-style office" was located in a "vibrant urban marketplace surrounded by local shops, restaurants, bars, and even a weekly farmer's market—all just minutes from several charming residential neighborhoods." Remember, this is the time to sell them not only on the job and brand but also on what their new home will be like, if relocation is required.

- **What You'll Do:** Here, list job responsibilities, objectives, and other key performance indicators (KPIs). This is also a good spot to list other departments that the role interacts with and who the position will report to. (Fair warning: This could potentially set you up for a few new requests on LinkedIn if your title matches the one listed as the hiring manager.) Of course, you want to strike a balance between being concise and including enough info. Aim to have five to 10 bullets, and if you find yourself with more, consider combining a few, if possible.

- **Who You Are:** In this section, list any relevant degrees or certifications the ideal candidate would have, as well as any software or systems they need to know. You can also list key attributes of an ideal candidate, whether that be attention to detail or being a collaborative team player, as well as any interests you are looking for; an interest in interior design, for instance, is a big plus for someone hoping to work at VERANDA. In past positions, I have listed the number of years of experience I am looking for, as it can sometimes be difficult for an applicant to tell whether a position is entry level, senior, or somewhere in between—though obviously if you list "at least five years of experience," a superstar candidate with three or four years could also be a great contender. For creative roles, I also point out that to be considered, any candidate must link to a portfolio of past work or attach a PDF of examples.

- **About the Company:** Finally, end with some details about the company. Consider including your mission, values, and market position—but keep this part somewhat brief. If a candidate is truly interested in the role, they can (and probably will) do their own research. In this section, sell them on the culture, as well as any perks or benefits the company may offer. Do you have happy and engaged employees with very low turnover? Say it (but only if that is true, of course!). Has your business been recognized as one of the best places to work by a publication or organization? Say it. Be sure to list if the workplace is diverse and if there are any uncommonly great benefits, such as fully covered medical insurance, unlimited vacation days, or a high 401(k) match. Even smaller companies can offer low-cost perks, like flexible hours or remote work. I once saw a role that included a monthly housekeeping service; although that benefit may have only cost a few hundred dollars per employee each month, it definitely caught my attention.

FOUR RULES FOR RECRUITING AND HIRING

Recruiting and hiring, especially for multiple roles, can sometimes feel like a second full-time job when you are already knee-deep in the day-to-day responsibilities of your work. Now that you have the job description written, follow these four steps to make the hiring process as smooth and effective as possible.

1. Figure out what you actually need.

This is obviously an important step for hiring in any role, but it is especially true when hiring for smaller teams where people may need to wear many hats on any given day. It can be tempting to hire people who are a lot like us. We can often relate to these candidates' skills and work history, making for easy conversation in interviews—but sometimes that's not what the role requires.

In their book *The ONE Thing: The Surprisingly Simple Truth About Extraordinary Results,* authors Gary Keller and Jay Papasan—who also work day jobs as executives at the national real estate firm Keller Williams— encourage figuring out your "one thing" at work: the thing that, if you do it, makes everything else easier or unnecessary.[155] While this can be an important question for you to ask yourself, it is also a great way to really clarify the top skills or traits of the position you are hiring for. If you need someone who can sell, place your focus on experience, personality, and results rather than expensive educations or flashy degrees. If you need someone to complete a series of highly technical tasks, hiring a candidate who possesses laser-like focus and an obsession with accuracy is more important than finding a "big ideas" person.

When I was searching for a new art director at VERANDA, I knew that I needed someone who could do three things well: collaborate with our style department to conceive ideas for studio photoshoots, lead the team on set at the shoots, and design short but creatively challenging stories using the photos that were produced. This requires a slightly different skill set than designing longer features of eight to 10 pages about an individual house or travel destination, using photography that was commissioned months before. I enjoy and excel at the latter type of stories, so although my new art director may occasionally design something in this realm, it was the highly collaborative stories shot in-studio that I really needed someone to own.

2. Use HR or a recruiter to help, but remember that hiring the best candidate is ultimately your responsibility.

If you work at a large or mid-size company, you will likely be working with human resources throughout the hiring process, or you could also be using an outside recruiter to help you find and vet candidates. It's easy to look to these people as hiring magicians, who can demystify the process and find you perfect candidates. But like the rest of us, they are imperfect people too, with varying levels of experience and talent. Furthermore, they are likely juggling multiple job postings, often in multiple departments for candidates requiring different skill sets.

Just remember that no one is as invested in hiring for this role as you are, and you are the one who is going to have to work with and manage the new hire, possibly for years to come. So by all means, take advantage of these resources if they are available to you, but proceed with a bit of optimistic caution. If HR combs through résumé submissions and sends you their top five—but you don't love the options—ask to see their top 10 or 20, or in some cases, all of them. After all, it could be that you and your HR partner prioritize slightly different things when looking at a résumé. If this is the case, be sure to share *why* you liked any résumés they had left out of the first batch.

If your human resources team is still not finding the right potential candidates, take an hour or two to poke around on LinkedIn yourself, researching people in your network or at a competitor who might be a good fit. Just because you are working with a recruiter doesn't mean you shouldn't be recruiting as well. The best leaders always have an eye on top talent in their field; by constantly monitoring the talent pool, both on LinkedIn and at industry events, they can be prepared with a list of potential candidates when new jobs become available.

3. Take your time with the interview process.

There is an old adage that says to hire slowly and fire quickly. Although I agree with the second part to some extent, I wholeheartedly agree with hiring slowly—even when I am the one being hired. I fought hard for the *Coastal Living* gig, completing three phone interviews; an in-depth design test that took a week to finish; and a three-day trip to Birmingham to meet with the editor in chief, the editorial director, and other key members of the team. In addition to several in-office meetings, I also met different staff members for breakfast, lunch, and dinner at three different restaurants, so that everyone could get an idea of how I interacted in social settings. Then, after all of that, for my final follow-up, I was asked to create a plan for how I would improve the design of the magazine, using "tear sheets" (pages ripped from other publications) as examples, all of which needed to be annotated and assembled in a giant binder.

The whole experience lasted three months from application to job offer. At the time, the process felt never-ending, but in hindsight, it actually progressed at the perfect pace. Along the way, I met or spoke with almost a dozen different people, ranging from the recruiter to potential colleagues to my boss, and even her boss.

A single interview provides a helpful snapshot of a person, but it doesn't give a full picture. John W. Mitchell, author of *Fire Your Hiring Habits: Building an Environment that Attracts Top Talent in Today's Workforce*, recommends employing the Rule of Three: narrowing the final pool to three different candidates, who should each be interviewed three different times, by three different people, at three different locations.[156] Though Mitchell specifically recommends this process for hiring managers and executives, I think it is advisable for roles at all levels, if time and resources permit.

At these interviews, you will of course want to ask candidates about their qualifications and work history, but also try to gauge as much as you can about their attitude, interests, and principles. Do their personal values align with company values? Are their hobbies related to the brand? Legendary *Vogue* editor Anna Wintour is a big fan of culture, so she will often ask what books, movies, or plays candidates have enjoyed recently; although they may not be directly covering such topics for the magazine, it is important to her to find editors who are abreast of what is going on in the cultural zeitgeist.[157] Even if a candidate's interests are not an exact match with your industry, hobbies like playing in a softball league, running marathons, or even building houses with Habitat for Humanity can help tell you about their teamwork capabilities and grit.

Watch for clues about how well candidates may fit in on your team. Do they make disparaging comments about their current employer? While we hope for honesty from all candidates, these types of honest statements can also be red flags. Immediately after the interview, jot down any highlights but also any comments, actions, or body language that rubbed you the wrong way. These aren't necessarily deal breakers but are definitely worth noting.

4. See how they work by giving them a test.

Before she was a bestselling author and *Project Runway* judge, Elaine Welteroth recalls interviewing with founding *Teen Vogue* editor Amy Astley for the role of beauty director back in 2012. (Astley went on to become editor in chief of *Architectural Digest*.) They first connected during an easy yet in-depth 45-minute conversation that ended with Astley asking her to complete a follow-up assignment: At some point in the next two weeks, did she mind jotting down a couple of ideas she might like to write about for the magazine?

"Did I mind? Hah! Two weeks!?" Welteroth writes in her memoir, *More Than Enough: Claiming Space for Who You Are (No Matter What They Say)*. "I had gotten so used to hiring managers handing me these lengthy multi-part edit tests—assignments that assess your qualifications for an editorial job—that I never had more than a few days to complete. … I saw [this] edit test as an opportunity to feel out whether it was a role I could truly fall in love with."[158]

Anyone in the final stages of consideration for an editorial role at a national magazine is familiar with the edit test. I have given and taken several over the years—and for good reason. It is the only way you can *really* see if candidates in creative fields have the skills to succeed in a given role. Yes, you can review their portfolio or read about successful projects they worked on. But often these projects were team efforts, so it's impossible to know how much they really contributed. In the case of people applying for writing roles, seeing their past clips can be helpful, but there's no way to know how much editing those articles required before they were fit to publish.

After an HR prescreen and an initial phone interview, I usually ask the top three candidates to take a multi-part design test. For art director and designer roles, this may include designing a mood board that encapsulates the brand, as well as a longer feature story and a shorter "front of book" article. In addition, something that requires a bit of research—such as listing three photographers or illustrators we should consider commissioning—is a great way to see how resourceful and organized each candidate is. Ideally, the candidates will be given at least a week to complete it, as they will need to fit it in between their current job and any personal or family commitments.

This may sound like a lot, but it's nothing I haven't been asked to do myself. For more advanced roles, I've done all of this and more, also designing several covers, mocking up new logo treatments, and writing a comprehensive "design philosophy" for the brand. It isn't easy, but for a high level creative job, it is extremely helpful in weeding out those who can talk a good game from those who are truly talented. It also helps narrow down those who "get" the publication from those who may be great for this job title—but at another brand.

If assigning several job-related tasks sounds like too much to ask, consider a simpler test that can help assess the "one thing" that you really need your new hire to rock. For a salesperson, is it writing out a detailed pipeline plan for how they will qualify a certain number of new customers each month? Or perhaps a persuasive email that shows how they would seal the deal with a lukewarm client? For someone in marketing or corporate communications, giving the candidate a topic and asking them to prepare an executive summary of five to 10 PowerPoint slides could be extremely telling, if such presentations constitute a large part of the job. And if all else fails, asking for a list of several new ideas (as Astley did) helps you determine if you have an "ideas person"—an asset in many roles.

If your line of work is more hands-on, see if it is possible to have a candidate come and work with your team for a single day. Mark Adams, the managing director at the furniture maker Vitsoe, does this to see who truly has the skills and how they fit in with the rest of the team. Sometimes it can reveal an attention to detail—or the opposite, in the case of a prospective employee who knew how to install a shelf correctly but then threw his tools haphazardly into the box at the end of the day rather than carefully putting them away. Whether this action should provide a teaching point once the candidate is hired *or* serve as a reason not to hire him is debatable, but either way, it is good information to have before the decision is made. (In this case, Vitsoe decided not to hire the candidate.)[159]

EDITOR'S TIP

Make the most of the candidate test.

If you are still on the fence after multiple interviews and giving a test, ask your top three candidates to walk you through their tests and explain their choices. This extra step can serve two functions: It gives you a further peek into the candidates' thought processes, and it can also be a great way for you to provide feedback on their work while evaluating how graciously they accept critiques.

MAKING THE FINAL DECISION

Sometimes, after multiple rounds of interviews and tests, it starts to become very clear who to hire. Other times, there still may be two candidates who have risen to the top. Here are a few more things to keep in mind throughout the interview process, but especially as you home in on your final choice:

- **Remain open-minded.** Sometimes the candidate who rises to the top is not who you expected. Hopefully you have been considering a diverse group of candidates throughout the process, but at this stage, keep in mind that assembling a team with a mix of different genders, sexes, ages, races, sexual orientations, religious affiliations, and even education levels can bring perspectives that you may not have previously considered. Such diversity of thought can be invaluable when marketing a product to a wide range of customers, and it may even improve the bottom line. Using the percentage of revenues coming from products introduced in the last three years as a proxy for innovation impact, a study of more than 1,700 companies across eight countries found that companies with above-average total diversity had 19 percent higher innovation revenues; overall, those companies led by diverse staffs had fresher product portfolios, and unsurprisingly, they turned out to be more profitable too.[160]

- **Carefully consider any internal candidates.** I strongly believe in promoting from within when you can to encourage loyalty and reduce turnover, but just because someone has been working at the company for a few years does not necessarily mean they deserve a promotion.

That said, if someone from your department or another department *would* make for a natural fit (and has been willing to undergo the same test and interview process as external candidates), please resist the "shiny new object" syndrome that some companies have, ignoring talent from within and assuming fresh blood will always result in the next big idea. Sometimes the candidate right in front of you is perfect for the role.

- **Ask how promotable each candidate is.** This is especially true when hiring someone who will be or could be a manager eventually. Does the person have executive presence and communication skills? Could you see delegating some of your responsibilities to this person? Do they have a special skill or proficiency that, even if you don't need it now, could come in handy down the road? For instance, as technology continues to evolve, an early adopter with a penchant for all things tech-related could be a great asset in ways you can't foresee.

- **Do your due diligence.** When two candidates are neck and neck, every piece of information is another row of data to help make your decision easier. At this point, if you haven't already, please do your due diligence in researching everything you can about your top choices. If they listed references, make sure that you or HR has contacted them. Do you have mutual friends or connections on LinkedIn? If it looks like a person you know has worked with the candidate before, get their off-the-record opinion as a former manager or colleague. And last but definitely not least, be sure to Google the candidate and see what their online presence can tell you about them.

- **Ask other people's opinions but go with your gut.** Eventually, you will need to make a decision, and you should carefully consider the opinions of everyone who has interacted with the candidate thus far. I've seen candidates who were bubbly and energetic with me, the hiring manager, but yawned their way through interviews with other colleagues. Take all of these points of view into consideration, then make a choice that you feel comfortable with. At the end of the day, you will be the one leading this person for the foreseeable future. If you go against your gut and follow someone else's advice, you will kick yourself if the person ends up not being the right fit, as you suspected.

EDITOR'S TIP

—

Be as honest as you can about compensation.

Compensation is the elephant in the room throughout almost every interview process. Some companies forbid managers from even mentioning it, while others require all candidates to name a desired salary to be considered. If you work for a corporation, this is one area where you will want to work closely with an HR partner who will often have a very specific number in mind that depends on the salary range allowed for the role and, in the case of internal hires, on the candidate's current salary.

But if you are running your own business or do not need weigh-in from HR, my advice is to be as candid about salary as you can be, and to do so as quickly as possible. In my first magazine role out of grad school, the editor in chief told me exactly how much the position paid at our first meeting, and it immediately instilled a sense of trust in him. Online applications, interviews, tests, follow-ups—it's a lot to go through if you aren't even sure how much you will be making. For years, corporate America has thrived on a culture of secrecy and vagueness about compensation, but in the past few years, several states and metropolitan areas (including New York City) have begun requiring that salary information be listed in any job posting—and more states are considering it. Though some national companies only list salaries for roles based in those states and cities, as required by law, others have changed their policy and now list salary ranges for every role, regardless of location.

THE TAKEAWAY

Building your dream team can take time and effort, but ultimately, it may be the most important task you do as a manager. **When recruiting and hiring for a role, start by figuring out what you *actually* need.** Determine the one skill or ability that the ideal candidate must possess to be successful, which may be very different from your own skills and abilities.

Next, **write a killer job description** that outlines key job requirements and responsibilities, while also selling prospective candidates on the position and the company. Work with HR or a recruiter to help with the recruiting process, but remember that hiring the best candidate is ultimately your responsibility.

Don't rush the interview process. For your top three candidates, have them interview with three different members of your team, in three different locations (if time and resources permit).

To see how they work, **give the top three candidates a test** composed of a few tasks that they might be asked to complete in the role. This could also be achieved by inviting the candidates to come work with the team for a day.

When making your final choice, consider diversity and growth potential, along with any benefits of choosing an internal candidate, if one exists. Do your due diligence by checking references, Googling the candidate, and asking the other interviewers (or any mutual connections) their thoughts on the person. Use all of these data points to make your decision, but in the end, **go with your own gut.**

Visit **LeadLikeAnEditor.com** to download a free workbook that includes a guide to **Writing the Perfect Job Description,** as well as other resources.

CHAPTER 13

....

Lead Your Dream Team

Now that you've assembled the perfect team, what does it mean to actually lead them? While many of us may dream of one day holding a high-level position at a major company, or even breaking out on our own to start a new business venture, few actually consider what it will be like to lead other people. We usually choose our paths because we have a strong passion for the subject matter or a devotion to the purpose of our work. We do our work well, advance up the ladder, and then one day it happens: In order to take the next step in our careers, we must move into roles that require us to manage other people. As Hank Gilman points out in his book *You Can't Fire Everyone*: In journalism, "we find bosses by taking talented writers, waving a wand, and saying, 'Hey, congratulations, you're now supervising a dozen people. And by the way, good luck.'"[161]

But good writers don't always make good bosses right off the bat, and it's the same in other fields as well. The best nurse does not necessarily make the best hospital administrator; the best salesperson does not necessarily make the best director of sales and marketing. With a lack of management training in many professions, it is up to these new managers to figure out how to do their jobs well. Some are naturally suited to the task, while others—like myself—take it upon themselves to learn more, either through books, outside training, or mentorship. Others never take these steps and plod along blindly, often at the expense of the teams they manage.

"At this point in your career, your only possible promotion is to management, where you will stop doing the work you love and use a skill set you don't have and we don't teach."
Illustration by Kendra Allenby / The New Yorker Collection / The Cartoon Bank

HOW TO MANAGE PEOPLE LIKE AN EDITOR

After decades in the workforce as both an employee and manager, I've spent a lot of time watching and learning from those around me, while also immersing myself in books and articles about how to lead others. Based on all of this data, I have created a five-step process that explains how to STEER your team in the right direction, setting them up for success:

- S - **STRENGTHS** should be leveraged.

- T - **TEACH** them what success looks like.

- E - **EMPOWER** them to make choices.

- E - **EXPLAIN** the results through constructive feedback.

- R - **REWARD** good work.

1. STRENGTHS should be leveraged.

Veteran editor Hank Gilman says that playing to people's strengths is his top piece of advice for managing others, and I have to agree—even if I didn't always want it to apply to me.[162] You see, in my early days at *Parenting* magazine, the team had two art directors (myself and a super-talented woman named Amanda Bardwell) reporting to a creative director, Jerry Pomales. Jerry had been working on sample pages for an upcoming redesign, and now it was time for Amanda and me to put them into practice, using his mock-ups to create the first issue.

As we met to go over the story lineup, Jerry said that for the next few issues, he wanted Amanda to focus on designing all of the features, plus one small "back of book" section that came just after the features, while I would design all of the "front of book" departments that came before the features, while also reworking each issue into an enhanced digital format with extra bells and whistles for the iPad.

In most magazines, features are the longest and most high-profile stories, usually grouped toward the back of the magazine and shown as full spreads without ads, allowing for more complex designs. Departments are the shorter stories that appear earlier in the magazine. They are generally shown as single pages adjacent to ads, giving designers less leeway visually. Because they are more templated, departments are (in theory) easier to design; they are often assigned to junior staffers, while features are reserved for the senior designers.

Understandably, I was disappointed. I had previously worked as the sole art director on two smaller brands—*Spa* magazine and *Caribbean Travel + Life*—and designing lush features with gorgeous travel photography was one of my favorite parts of those jobs. Now I had progressed to working on a much bigger brand but was relegated to the type of pages usually given to those with a lot less experience.

Although I felt slighted at the time, looking back years later, I understand that our creative director was making the best decision for the brand. Jerry had recently taken over and redesigned a magazine with a very small art team, especially given the amount of content we were producing. *Parenting* published 22 issues a year, which meant that we had printer deadlines almost every other week. He had worked with each of us for a few months before we started on the redesign issue and had learned our strengths and weaknesses—even if we didn't fully realize them ourselves.

Amanda and I were both good designers but brought very different skills to the same role. I was an art director with a journalism and copy editing background, which contributed to my love of consistency, templates, and order. When it came to photoshoots, I excelled at still-life and food photography, where you create a setup, photograph it with the camera resting securely on a tripod, scrutinize the photo on a computer screen, and then make a hundred micro-adjustments until it is perfect. I also enjoyed the challenge of making beautiful layouts using existing photography, such as stock photos or press images, which are often used for departments when time and budget do not allow for a new photoshoot.

Amanda, on the other hand, had an art school background. She excelled at photo illustration, which involves combining several images in Photoshop, and adding filters and textures to create a new image. She also loved working with illustrators and had a long list of artists she had successfully collaborated with in the past. And last but definitely not least, she was great with children. Directing little kids on set—including toddlers and infants—came naturally to her. For these shoots, there was no time to take a photo and scrutinize every detail; the photographer often roamed with a handheld camera getting as many shots as possible to ensure we had ones with the models smiling, laughing, and making eye contact with the camera. Amanda was able to roll with the punches and get great results from our mini-models, which—you guessed it—were largely utilized in the longer feature stories.

Although I didn't see it until years later, Jerry was triaging in the best way he could—by making the most of the two designers available to him. Eventually, I did work on some of the features, but I never excelled at creating complex photo illustrations or art directing toddler photoshoots. Instead, I excelled at—and also enjoyed—working on the redesigned departments and figuring out how to be creative within their defined templates, even if the subject matter did not match my passions in the long run.

A Gallup study found that people who get to use their strengths every day are three times more likely to report having an excellent quality of life and six times more likely to be engaged at work, making them more productive and less likely to quit their jobs.[163] Certainly there are times when we want our team members to learn new skills and grow, but if there are certain tasks that they are best suited for—and others that could be removed from their plates or delegated to someone else—why not make the most of everyone's natural abilities?

2. TEACH them what success looks like.

People are not mind readers. You have to tell them how you like to work and your expectations for their role before they can excel. In one of my first Monday staff meetings at *Coastal Living*, I informed my editor in chief Antonia van der Meer that while she had been out the previous Friday, I had met with the style director and photo editor to choose the photographer for an upcoming story. We had picked a great one, so we could check that off the list! "Not yet," she told me. "If you have a photographer you would like to use, let's discuss before you hire them."

At another point in my first few weeks, I tried to pop into her office and show her a layout during the five minutes she had between meetings. She stopped me at the door, saying that it would be better to *schedule* a one-on-one layout review once I had a handful ready. In the moment, each instance felt like I had made a mistake, but later I realized that I was just learning how my boss preferred to work—a natural part of starting a new job. I was also learning the nuances of being on the leadership team at a larger brand, where processes and procedures were essential for optimal efficiency.

Though obvious now, these lessons were new to me. At *Parenting*, I'd had minimal interaction with our editor in chief, as my creative director reviewed layouts and photographers with her. Prior to that, I had led art direction on tiny staffs, where my editors usually did not weigh in as much on photographers, and it was common to drop into people's offices through-out the day.

When you start a new role, it's a bit like jumping into a river: The current of the business is strong, and there is little time to figure out how to swim. You spend the first few weeks trying to keep your head above water before eventually learning to go with the current. Still, it may take months or even years before you're swimming in the most efficient way.

This is true both for us and for other people who join our team. But what if, instead of throwing people into the deep end, we pulled them to the side of the river and into a quiet inlet for some swimming lessons? Sure, they may have swum up a river before, but every river is a bit different; as leaders, we know the specifics of this one and can help them navigate the waters much more easily by providing a few key tips.

By communicating clearly from the beginning, you can help new employees excel quickly. As soon as they start, have a meeting to discuss expectations, what success looks like for them, and how you like things to run. It is easy to assume that if someone has come from a similar company, they may already know these things, but often the nuances of processes and procedures are vastly different. Obviously, there may be things you forget to mention in this meeting, and if this is the case, be sure to explain these preferences as soon as possible, as Antonia did at *Coastal Living*.

Clarify expectations to improve performance.

As a professor of game design and VP of engineering for a major game studio, Curtiss Murphy has managed people for three decades and finds clarity to be at the heart of employee success. In his book *What Makes Great Managers Great,* he offers a four-step process for setting expectations with your team members, giving them ownership over their roles. He suggests that you help them brainstorm what their responsibilities are, organize those into groups, shrink them down to the essential, and then place them in order of importance. By doing this, you can work together to create a list of expectations that you both agree on, making goal setting—and ultimately reviews—clearer as well.[164]

At this initial meeting, you should also go over any KPIs, goals, and priorities. Taking an hour for this type of conversation can provide invaluable clarity going forward, as there may be things they thought were priorities that are actually outside the scope of their role or just not that important to you.

3. EMPOWER them to make choices.

Once you are on the same page, you have to empower people to make their own decisions. This can be tough, especially for first-time managers. If you have a Type A personality, you may be inclined to micromanage your team members, asking to be copied on every email and for all decisions to be run by you. But as tempting as it can be to keep a tight hold on the reins, you must learn to let go for two reasons: First, being involved in every tiny decision is not the best use of your time and will ultimately lead to your own burnout. And second, making decisions for themselves and trying new ideas is the only way employees can learn to trust their own instincts.

"The first time I was a boss, I was really hard on myself, thinking that I needed to know all the answers—but that's not what you're expected to do as a leader," former *Fitness* and *Runner's World* editor in chief Betty Wong Ortiz told me. "Your success as a leader is in the enablement of your team to do their best work."[165]

In publishing, writers and designers have thousands of choices to make each day as they craft stories and design pages. Wong Ortiz found that trusting her team and giving them ownership to make decisions using their own sense of judgment—rather than just choosing what would make her happy—usually led to the best results.

"Your job is to help your team problem-solve, experiment, and execute with a sense of ownership and responsibility," she explains. "You can be there to facilitate it, but you're not there to do it for them. Do whatever you can to clear roadblocks, get answers for them, steer them, and point them in the right direction—but then really empower them to do the work."

At the beginning, you may want to be more involved in the decision-making process, but as you learn how your individual team members work and where they excel, there will be decisions or steps that you can let go of completely. For instance, when I hired a new art director at VERANDA who would be leading in-studio photoshoots and designing stories using those images afterward, I asked to see the briefs she wrote up for on-set stylists and photographers as well as the templates she created for how the story would be laid out. I may have made a tweak or two along the way, but after several issues of seeing that we were generally on the same page, I eventually allowed her to send these on to the photographers without running them past me first.

4. EXPLAIN the results through constructive feedback.

One of the most important things a manager can do is provide timely and constructive feedback to his or her team members. It can be easy to do this when things are going well, but that won't always be the case. Remember that as a manager, you are a coach—not just a cheerleader. Though both want their teams to win, the coach is the one that shows them *how* to do so.

When providing feedback, the coach's job is not to pass judgment or make players feel small but rather to develop their skills and teach them how to win. If you feel that your manager doesn't care about you, or worse, is trying to belittle you, their feedback will feel like scolding, and it is natural to shut down and become unreceptive. However, when you feel that your manager genuinely wants what is best for you, both in your career and in life, you become hungry not just for their praise but also for the wisdom of their critiques.

My close friend (and former roommate) Alice Oglethorpe worked for years as an editor at magazines like *Shape* and *Fitness,* before becoming a prolific freelance writer. Two decades later, she still remembers a critique she received early in her career, as an editorial assistant at *Good Housekeeping.* "The managing editor took me aside and told me that I rolled my eyes in meetings—and that I needed to stop," she recalls. "I was mortified! I didn't even realize I was doing it." After tossing and turning that night as she thought about the critique, Alice went into the editor's office the next morning and thanked her for the feedback. "She told me that I had a long career ahead of me, and she would hate for something that minor to derail it," Alice says. "It actually turned into a very positive conversation."[166]

One of the reasons that magazine writers and editors make great hires in almost any industry is that they have tough skins and are accustomed to near-constant criticism and feedback. When you write a story, it never prints exactly as written. The section editor, copy editor, executive editor, and editor in chief all make changes along the way. These tweaks aren't arbitrary nor are they personal. They are almost always made with one goal in mind: to make the story better, stronger, and clearer for the reader.

EDITOR'S TIP

Set the stage for feedback with clear objectives.

"Journalists are trained never to take feedback personally," says two-time editor in chief Betty Wong Ortiz, who brought this ethos to new roles leading the content departments at Dropbox, Blink Health, and Quip. To make critiques seem less subjective, she recommends communicating clear objectives for each project at the start. "If I clearly outline the goal of a project at the outset, any critical feedback that I give—whether it's a word change or that I don't like the background music in a video—I can justify with a reason that ladders up to the project goal. If you lay that out for everybody, they won't take critiques personally because they understand that its about what's right for the business."[167]

5. REWARD good work.

In some ways, giving positive feedback can be even more important than giving negative feedback. If doing your job well time and again is never noticed, what incentive is there to keep performing at a high level? Of course, we can't all be rewarded and given a pat on the head every time we do something well at work, but over the long haul, leaders must provide positive incentives in order for their superstar employees to keep delivering A+ work.

Before you start doling out rewards, it's important to know what makes your employees happy, which can vary from person to person. For instance,

I have managed employees who love to travel for work, so being given the opportunity to direct photoshoots on location can feel like a great perk. On the other hand, travel can be a burden for other people, as they must arrange for pet sitting or childcare before they can commit to a work trip. Generally speaking, rewards can be divided into a few main categories:

- **Raises, promotions, and bonuses:** These are the best way to reward employees for long-term growth, though by their nature, promotions are generally given much less frequently. Still, smaller salary bumps and bonuses can help keep people happy during the off years.

- **Gifts and perks:** I'll talk more about these in the next chapter, but bestowing a perk—like a gift card or an extra vacation day—can help show appreciation midyear, or when giving a raise isn't possible.

- **New responsibilities:** I often joke that the reward for doing great work is the opportunity to do *more* great work. Letting a junior staff member try their hand at an advanced assignment shows that you are committed to helping them learn and grow. It can also help you gauge if they are ready for a promotion when the time comes. But don't go overboard; doling out too many new tasks without a raise can lead to feelings of underappreciation and burnout.

EDITOR'S TIP

Serve the Sandwich Technique.

Sometimes an employee is doing a great job overall but may have a tiny area that needs improvement. In this case, consider using the Sandwich Technique, wherein a negative critique is sandwiched between two positive ones. This method can be especially helpful for feedback that could be taken personally, such as when a gregarious sales associate is being a bit too chatty during each transaction. In this case, author and leadership coach Jeff Hilderman suggests saying something like: "It's great to see how well you're getting along with everyone. Just please be aware of how much time you're spending with each customer, and limit non-work-related conversation to five minutes. Otherwise, great work!"[168]

THE ART OF CONSTRUCTIVE FEEDBACK

A continual feedback loop is built into the process of making magazines, as top editors and creative directors weigh in at each stage of the writing and design process—but this is not the case in every industry. For many managers, *Step 4: EXPLAIN the results through constructive feedback* is the most difficult part of the STEER process. I have found that there are four keys to delivering constructive feedback that lands with the intended effect.

- **It should be specific, frequent, and given as soon as possible.** Don't wait until the year-end review to tell someone where they are succeeding or falling short. Make it a part of your weekly or monthly process, either through scheduled one-on-one meetings or on-the-fly coaching sessions.

- **Make it a coaching moment—not a scolding moment.** When giving feedback on the more critical end of the spectrum, remind your direct report that coaches and their players are on the same team—meaning you want them to succeed. If you are giving feedback on a poor choice, it can be helpful to talk through what went wrong and offer suggestions— or even ask them for suggestions—on how a similar situation could be handled in the future.

- **Be empathetic.** You have probably received your own fair share of feedback, both positive and negative. How did it feel when someone chewed you out, treating you like an idiot? Compare that with how it felt when a boss treated you like a human being who had made a mistake, as all humans do from time to time. The latter builds a better relationship of trust and collaboration.

- **Be approachable.** Let employees know that you are available if they have questions or need additional feedback along the way. Depending on the number of people you manage, you may not want people bursting in your door all day long with a million questions about their performance. But you should make team members feel comfortable asking your opinion at appropriate times, whether through daily or weekly check-ins, or via a quick email or message that you can respond to at your leisure.

THE TAKEAWAY

Managing people is rarely taught in school or on the job, but it is one of the most important parts of being a business owner or executive. Use this five-step framework to **STEER** your team in the right direction, setting them up for success:

- **STRENGTHS should be leveraged.** Make sure each team member is truly suited for the tasks you assign.

- **TEACH them what success looks like.** Be clear about expectations for the role and your own expectations about how things should run.

- **EMPOWER them to make choices.** Resist the urge to micromanage, while letting employees learn to trust their instincts.

- **EXPLAIN the results through constructive feedback.** Serve as a coach—not just a cheerleader—by offering feedback quickly and often, and reassuring them that you are on their side and care about their success.

- **REWARD good work.** Provide positive feedback both verbally and in more tangible ways when appropriate: rewards, raises, perks, and new responsibilities (that they would actually want).

CHAPTER 14

....

Nurture Your Dream Team

"So I've hired my dream team, trained them, and am providing feedback on a regular basis. That's all I have to worry about, right?" Well, not exactly. While having a boss who cares about you is great, a lot more goes into an employee's decision to stay at a company long-term. Often, it comes down to company culture.

"Company culture is how you do what you do in the workplace," operational consultant Julian Lute explains in an article written for the Great Place to Work Institute, an organization that I'll discuss more later in this chapter. "It's the sum of your formal and informal systems and behaviors and values, all of which create an experience for your employees and customers."

Having worked with top leaders from the *Fortune* "100 Best Companies to Work For" list, Lute says that "company culture is often something you can feel, even as an outsider." He recalls the first time he walked into the lobby of one of the companies on the list. "As I approached the door, employees who were walking in and passing by made eye contact and said 'hello.' The employee behind the desk greeted me warmly, offering me a cup of coffee and a comfortable seat. There was a distinct, positive energy in the building. My first experiences as a guest gave me a taste of how they 'do things around here.'"[169]

During the tech boom, company culture became a hot topic in the business world. For years, the lavish campuses of Silicon Valley were cited as game-changers, offering complimentary meals to their employees, as well as "fun zones" where playing video games or ping-pong was encouraged to get creative juices flowing. These office perks are great—if they contribute to the employee experience. Post-pandemic, many employees may place a higher value on having the flexibility to work from home.

Perks help shape company culture, but the overall employee experience is the true measure of a great workplace. Does the company show it cares by offering perks *in addition to* a competitive benefits package? Is the office an exciting place, where people are positive, smile at each other, and have a bit of fun as well? Do employees feel like the company is interested in them as people, promoting from within and offering opportunities for growth? And finally—and perhaps most importantly—does the company provide employees the opportunity to extract meaning from their jobs?

EDITOR'S TIP
—
When it comes to company culture, think both macro and micro.

If you work for a large company, it may be beyond the scope of your role to overhaul the entire company culture—although as a leader, you may have more sway than you think. Consider joining a committee or offering suggestions to higher-ups who have the power to make more sweeping changes.

Even if you only oversee a small department, you can help facilitate a positive "microculture" in your division. I've worked at publishing companies where happy employees working at a magazine with a charismatic leader were seen collaborating and laughing together throughout the day, while employees at another publication just down the hall hid quietly in their cubicles, avoiding any display that might draw the attention of their icy boss. Not surprisingly, the morale was much higher in the first group.

WHY IT PAYS TO BE 'PERKY'

In the movie *The Devil Wears Prada*, Andy Sachs (played by Anne Hathaway) lands a job that "a million girls would kill for": the assistant to *Runway* magazine editor in chief Miranda Priestly, a steely-eyed and demanding boss portrayed brilliantly by Meryl Streep. The job was not an easy one. It required Andy to answer her boss's calls at odd hours, to stay planted at her desk all day (except when running impossible errands), and to weather Miranda's sharp mood swings and even sharper tongue.

Why would anyone put up with this behavior, you might ask? Well, as other characters point out to Andy, if you can do this job for a year, you can move on to work at any magazine in New York. That is enough of an incentive to get Andy's foot in the door, but part of what keeps her there throughout most of the film—and what keeps many people in jobs that are difficult and not necessarily worth the pay—is the perks.

For Andy, it starts off small—a pair of stilettos from the fashion closet, given to her by the creative director. Soon there are more clothes, many from high-end designers, as well as beauty products, handbags, and even small electronics that were sent to the magazine as gifts from advertisers. Though Andy may be working late, soon she is no longer taking the subway but rather is being chauffeured in a sleek company car. By the end of the film, this 20-something girl in her first job out of college is seen living the high life, dining on an expense account and meeting celebrity designers while accompanying her boss on a business trip to Paris Fashion Week.

While this movie is definitely a work of fiction, *The Devil Wears Prada* is based on a novel of the same name by Lauren Weisberger, who served for a year as assistant to *Vogue* editor in chief Anna Wintour. What I can tell you is this: I have worked for more than 20 years in the industry, including many years in New York City, the hub of publishing. And most of what I saw in the movie—in terms of the perks Andy received—was definitely based in truth. Working on the editorial side of magazine publishing has never been a path to riches (except for a handful of editors at the very top), but it does offer fringe benefits, sometimes in the form of merchandise and travel, other times in the form of cachet or access to prominent people. Editors and art directors who last in the career do so for the love of the work, but depending on which publication and company they work for, the job often comes with a lot of perks. For four reasons, I say offer them whenever you can:

1. Perks create loyalty.

In total, I worked eight years for magazines that regularly covered beauty products, and during that time, I never had to buy a face wash or skin cream. I also spent around the same amount of time working at travel magazines. To write stories, direct photoshoots, or attend conferences, I have been all over the U.S. and to several foreign countries as well. Yes, it was work—and anyone who travels often for their job will tell you that it is not as glamorous as people think. But it can also be a lot of fun, especially when you are traveling to write a story about a hotel or a city, and your only job is to eat, drink, and soak up the local culture. When leaving each of these jobs, I carefully weighed how much I would miss the work and my colleagues—but also, if I am being honest, how much I would miss the perks.

One editor I worked with called beauty products and travel her "golden handcuffs." While many magazine editors and designers move around to different publications frequently to advance their careers, she stayed at the same publication covering the luxury spa industry for almost two decades. And why not? If the pay is decent, and you are getting free beauty products and monthly all-expenses-paid trips to spas and resorts around the world, what incentive is there to leave?

Providing perks *can* help you retain talented employees, creating a sense of loyalty and keeping them around longer, but remember that these fringe benefits can only do so much. If the style of management or company morale is not great, your best employees will eventually leave for another opportunity.

2. When budgets are tight, perks can stand in for pay.

As a manager or business owner, you have probably found that there are times when someone is a great employee and really goes above and beyond in their job. This person might deserve a raise, but perhaps there just isn't enough money to make it happen right away. In this situation, maybe a perk—in the form of a work trip, merchandise, or even a gift card—could help you reward the person. Of course, raises are always preferred, but often verbal recognition paired with a small token of appreciation can be morale-boosting.

Food is often a great perk that doesn't cost a lot. If you manage a bakery, maybe you could let your employees take home the unsold baked goods at the end of the night. If you own a restaurant, consider allowing employees to arrive a half hour before their shift to enjoy a meal on the company dime. Many entrepreneurs could take a page from the Googles of the world: If you provide a free lunch at the office, it becomes a perk for employees—and results in fewer hours away from their desks midday.

3. Perks can help boost sales.

If you have a physical product or service that you are selling, consider offering it to all of your employees, either for free or at a very steep discount. For sales roles, this can be an especially important game-changer.

During college, I held two different retail jobs at the local shopping mall. In the first, I sold bath, body, and skincare products at The Body Shop. Because we were encouraged to try the products and know their ingredients and benefits, it was important that we be allowed to purchase these items at a discount, and to receive free samples during product launches. By knowing the products from personal experience, we were able to "tell and sell," offering customers unique stories about our experience with the items. Similarly, when I worked at the clothing store Guess, we were required to wear the brand's apparel when we were on the clock. By providing a generous discount to all employees, the company made sure that its associates looked the part—driving future sales.

This is especially important if you sell a product that is hard to experience before buying it. Products like the Sleep Number mattress are difficult to demonstrate in person; sure you can lie on the bed, but does that really give you an accurate picture of what it will be like to sleep on that mattress every night for the next decade? By providing one big-ticket item to an employee for free—or at a steep discount—companies can turn their employees into brand evangelists.

4. Perks can make employees happier, healthier, and more productive.

It's great when perks can make employees more loyal or better salespeople, but using them to improve your team's mental and physical health can also be a game-changer. Happy and healthy employees show up to work, and are usually more productive in their jobs. European companies seem to have figured this out better than their American counterparts, and not surprisingly, Europe holds eight of the top 10 spots on the World Happiness Report's list of happiest countries.[170] Taking a page from our friends across the pond, consider ways you can use perks to create a healthy work environment:

- First and foremost, if you are in the C-suite or have a senior role in HR, seriously evaluate the core benefits package. Make health insurance available to all employees, and if possible, have the company shoulder the full cost or a large portion of the premiums.

- In addition to basic health insurance, consider offering paid maternity and paternity leave beyond the required minimums, as well as fertility insurance and other types of care that are considered best-in-class in the U.S. but are standard in many European countries.

- Beyond healthcare, what other wellness-related perks could you offer? A free or subsidized gym membership? Access to nutrition advice? When

I spent one summer working for two magazines based in Stockholm, I was delighted to learn that monthly massages were a perk of the job.

- Remember that taking time away from work is one of the best ways to ensure employees remain fresh and dialed in while on the job. In Europe, many businesses shut down for the entire month of August. Though this may not be feasible in the U.S., you can start by providing ample vacation days beyond the usual two weeks. In fact, some companies have switched to unlimited days, finding that employees still only take what is needed and generally do not abuse the system.

  At Hearst Magazines, we are given four "Summer Fridays" off in addition to our allotment of vacation days. Additionally, in the year following the pandemic, "planned pauses" were scheduled twice throughout the year, allowing employees additional days once we could travel safely again. Because everyone was encouraged to take off at the same time, those "planned pauses" felt a bit like the week between Christmas and New Year's Day. Most people were able to truly disconnect without checking in every few days, as they might have on a typical week-long vacation.

THREE EASY WAYS TO FOSTER EMPLOYEE RETENTION

Perks are just the start of creating a positive company culture. Whether you are running a small department or an entire company, you can utilize these three strategies to create a workplace environment your employees will love.

1. Have fun at work.

On my first day at *Coastal Living* magazine, I wasn't sure exactly what to expect. I had spent the weekend moving into a new apartment (and to a new state), so I was already a bit out of my element. Although I was excited, I was also nervous. Everyone had seemed great during the interview process, but what if the vibe was different during a regular workday?

When I arrived, the entire staff had gathered in a large open area in the office, with smiles on their faces. People I had interviewed with welcomed me warmly, while colleagues I was just meeting introduced themselves. The table contained quite a spread: a beautiful tablecloth, a three-tiered stand covered with layers of tiny breakfast sandwiches, a large bowl of cut fruit, cups for orange juice and coffee, and even a few bottles of prosecco for those who preferred a mimosa at 9 a.m. The spread itself looked ready to be photographed for the magazine. Talk about a warm welcome!

Throughout the years I worked with the fun-loving folks at *Coastal Living*, we literally toasted ourselves at every possible occasion. Stop by the office on any given Friday, and you were likely to be handed a cup of whatever cocktail recipe we were testing for the magazine. If someone had a birthday, cupcakes were baked. For weddings or engagements, happy hours were planned. And around the holidays, I can't begin to tell you about the array of foods that were brought both to the office and to a potluck dinner held at a staff member's house the week before Christmas each year.

To varying degrees, workdays at magazines had always been fun. I can't count the number of lunches—and laughs—I've shared with colleagues over the years. And when you are working long hours (and often late nights) on a fun, creative pursuit, silliness is bound to sneak its way in.

This idea is played out fabulously in an episode of *The Bold Type*, a show about young women working at *Scarlet,* a fictitious *Cosmopolitan*-like magazine in New York City. (The show was executive produced by Joanna Coles, the former editor of *Cosmo* and former chief content officer of Hearst Magazines.) In the penultimate episode of the first season, the staff is trapped in the building for several hours one evening when the entire city block is shut down because the U.S. President is dining in a restaurant nearby.[171]

As the staff goes stir-crazy, the office descends into a bit of an impromptu party at one point; drinks are mixed, fashion accessories are tried on, and dance music is played. Even the editor in chief joins in on the act, pouring scotch for some of her junior staff members.

I just had to smile, knowing that if the same thing had happened at *Coastal Living*, we might have been parading down the halls with cocktails in hand as well. In fact, something similar did happen in 2014 when an unexpected snow storm created impassable roads, trapping many members of the *Coastal Living, Cooking Light,* and *Southern Living* staffs in our office building overnight. An impromptu party for the ages resulted, as the test kitchen directors fired up the stoves and poured out the cocktails, preparing dinner and drinks on the fly for a raucous group of editors and art directors.

If you are going to spend half of your life at work, you might as well enjoy it. But creating a fun place to work doesn't have to be expensive—or involve drinking, as many of the above examples did. Although celebratory happy hours have been common at both *Coastal Living* and VERANDA, we have also taken field trips to art museums and historic buildings. These educational outings offer staffers the opportunity to get to know each other outside of the office, while also providing fodder for future articles.

At *Parenting* magazine, we had an Oreo party to celebrate the 100th anniversary of the cookie, and everyone brought in different flavors and variations for the staff to taste test in the conference room. It was the perfect afternoon treat, taking no more than 20 or 30 minutes out of the day, while giving everyone a chance to kick back and chat for a bit.

That said, you can bring in all the goodies you want, but creating a fun place to work has to be as much about the spirit of the activity as the activity itself. My husband once attended an office "farewell party" that was actually just a weekly staff meeting with a cake in the middle of the table. No one brought plates or forks, the cake was never cut (or even mentioned!), and the recipient didn't particularly like sweets anyway. This "party" could have been a fun way to celebrate and bid farewell to someone who had been at the company for 15 years; instead, it was made awkward by a sad, not even halfhearted attempt.

2. Show you care during tough times.

While having fun at the office is a great way to make the best of the hours spent at work, comedy and tragedy are two sides of the same coin. If we want the laughs we have with our team members to ring true during the good times, we must also be there to support them in bad times. In Chapter 4 on perseverance, I talked about how the best editors show up in times of illness and crisis. While this is true, there are also times when personal events are so impactful that they must take priority over work.

In 2009, when I was living in San Francisco, my father had an emergency surgery and nearly died. I was on the next flight out and barely worked over the course of the next two weeks, which I spent in the hospital. Later that year, he had another surgery that necessitated round-the-clock care during his at-home recovery. For three months, from December 2009 to March 2010, I worked from Kentucky while I helped care for him, thanks to my editor in chief Julie Sinclair, who was extremely gracious and flexible with me (before remote work was common). When Dad passed away in 2011, I had just started working for *Parenting*. Though my vacation days were limited, my boss Jerry told me not to think about work and pitched in to cover for me during the two weeks I was away dealing with my dad's funeral arrangements and estate.

There was another time when I asked a boss for some extra time off to deal with a personal matter, and she agreed, saying trust was a bit like a bank: I had made plenty of "deposits" to the bank by showing a strong work ethic, often arriving early and staying late. When I needed to unexpectedly take a day off—and we weren't shipping an issue to the printer—it was okay to make a "withdrawal" from the bank account.

Sometimes people need support in other ways that aren't time-related. If your team is close and a team member is experiencing some sort of major life change, think about what they might really need and see if the team can help them out. Forming a "meal train" to deliver cooked dinners can be a lifesaver for new parents who are just home from the hospital with an infant, while taking up a collection of money can help soften the blow of a colleague's unexpected financial hardship.

3. Create meaning.

The Great Place to Work Institute has been tracking trends in workplaces long before "company culture" became the buzzword it is today. The organization created its first "Best Workplaces" list in 1984 and currently publishes 20 national lists both for itself and in partnership with other brands; these include *Fortune*'s 100 Best Companies to Work For and *People*'s Companies That Care.

According to its 2023 survey of more than a million employees, the number one thing workers want from employers is purpose—and this is especially true for millennial and Gen Z employees. These days, workers are not just interested in finding jobs with good salaries that also match their skill sets; they are looking for something more. "It's not enough to pay employees well," the results found. "Work must also have meaning."[172]

For some employees, meaning can be all about making a difference. At the package and express mail delivery company DHL Express, which ranked as the No. 2 Best Place to Work in the 2023 survey, 90 percent of employees reported feeling that their work was more than "just a job." This can be partly attributed to the company's dedication to supporting the communities in which it operates, including assisting refugees with job placement and helping reduce environmental impact.

For others, finding meaning can be as simple as feeling as though your voice is heard and that you are valued by the company. The hotel chain Hilton ranked as the top place to work in the 2023 survey, in part because the company prioritizes employee input in decision-making processes that impact them. Across Central and Latin America, Hilton introduced the "My Voice Matters" campaign, spanning eight weeks, during which leaders gathered feedback from more than 5,000 team members. As a result, 84 percent of Hilton employees said that management actively includes them in decisions affecting their roles, surpassing the average of all winning companies by three percentage points.[173]

EDITOR'S TIP

——

How to make work more meaningful for your team

As the editor in chief of *Seventeen* magazine from 2007 to 2014, Ann Shoket is an expert on millennials and particularly millennial women, a group that often prioritizes meaningful work above all else, she says. To attract and retain these team members, Shoket offers sound advice: Set up a mission-driven side project and let your junior employees run it.

"When I was at *Seventeen*, we worked with some local high schools to help struggling students create a school newspaper, and I let some of the younger employees lead that charge," she told CoveyClub founder Lesley Jane Seymour on the *Reinvent Yourself* podcast. "They met with these students once or twice a month ... and it was deeply meaningful to the employees. It was a way for them to have one-on-one human interaction with the people that they were impacting."

Shoket recommends considering how such a project could align closely with your business and your employees' expertise, as helping teens create a publication did for these young editors. If you run a restaurant, for example, a food drive or some other initiative that deals with hunger could be a good fit. Whatever your business, "find some thread of what you do that can be meaningful to your employees," Shoket says. "And then let them lead it."[174]

LIKE ALL LIVING THINGS, EMPLOYEES WILL GROW

After grad school, most of my classmates moved to New York City, eager to dive into exciting careers in the magazine industry. We had dreams of glossy covers, fabulous parties, and lavish offices. However, as newly hired editorial assistants (or, in some cases, interns) on the bottom rung of the corporate ladder, for many of us, the first few years were a lot less glamorous than we had hoped. Opening reader mail, answering telephones for senior editors, and constantly packing and unpacking boxes—of product samples, photo-shoot props, and hot-off-the-press magazine copies—was more common than the martini lunches we had imagined.

To top it off, salaries that were barely above the poverty level meant that, even with master's degrees and gigs at national magazines, living in NYC would require multiple roommates and strict budgets. Sounds like a dream job, right? Still, most of us stayed for years for two reasons: We loved magazines, and we were super ambitious. We couldn't wait to see where our careers would take us.

Maybe you have felt this same ambition in your career, either as a manager or as an entrepreneur. It's easy to want these things for yourself, but as a leader, you have to step back and remember: Your best employees desire that same growth for themselves. They are humans first, and like all living things, they *will* grow. If you try to stop that growth or ignore their need to move forward, you will lose good people and spend a lot of time and money trying to replace them.

FIVE WAYS TO HELP YOUR BEST EMPLOYEES GROW

The best way to retain good employees is to make yourself an active participant in their growth, nurturing them and encouraging them as they progress in their careers. If you do this, it is much more likely that they will remain loyal, putting their energy and passion to work for you and your business. But *how* do you do this?

- **Hiring starts at home.** I mentioned this in Chapter 12, but it bears repeating. When a new position is available, always consider internal applicants *who express interest*. That last part is key: Those who show gumption by asking for the opportunity will feel excited about their new salary and job title, because they feel they earned them. As executive leadership coach Stacy Mayer points out in her book *Promotions Made Easy: A Step-by-Step Guide to the Executive Suite*: "A promotion doesn't *happen* to you. A promotion is something you actively go out and get. It's not handed to you. You have to make it happen."[175]

- **Reviews provide road maps.** Many corporations already have employee review processes in place; ideally, these will be completed at least once annually, with more frequent mini-check-ins throughout the year. While these one-on-one sessions are a great time to provide feedback and set goals, also be sure to ask employees about their job satisfaction and where they see their careers progressing. Some may be genuinely content in their current positions, but for those who have ambition to grow, they will be more likely to stay with your company if you can show them a path for growth, or even lay out a plan together. And if there is not an immediate way that their role can grow, consider the benefits of personal development: Covering the cost of a continuing education class or a workshop that teaches your employee a new skill could be a win-win for both them and the company.

- **Titles are more than words.** Consider a title bump or adding responsibilities to help employees in their career growth. When I worked at *American Spa* magazine, I started as associate art director, reporting to a design director. After two years, I was promoted to art director and allowed to take on more work, including planning, attending, and running more complex photoshoots. Even though the pay raise was minimal, I was thrilled with the new title and responsibilities. When you do promote, try to include some sort of raise or new perk, even if it is small. A 5 percent pay raise or allowing someone to work from home occasionally may do little to impact your bottom line, but it could mean the world to an employee who feels undervalued and is considering leaving the company.

- **Money matters.** Keep an eye on industry-wide salary trends for all of the positions in your company or department, and whenever you are promoting someone from within, try to match what you would have to pay a new employee who was joining you from outside the company. It's an unfortunate fact that candidates promoted from within are often given a lower salary than an outside candidate for the same role might receive. That's a pretty crummy way to encourage loyalty. A mentor once told me that I should try to get at least a 25 percent raise at each new job. Remember that the best employees know this information and are likely to jump ship to a competitor if they see a bleak future of additional work responsibility with only incremental raises at your company.

- **To everything, there is a season.** Sometimes people just need a change. Don't take it personally if someone wants to leave to try their hand at a new role, a new company, or a new industry. Treat the departing employee respectfully, and don't burn bridges. You never know if you will find yourself working with them—or even for them!—again someday.

THE TAKEAWAY

If you have gone to the trouble of recruiting, hiring, and developing your dream team, you should **create a culture** that makes them want to stay.

Workers today want more than just a job; they want to work for a company that **brings purpose and meaning** to their lives and to the lives of others.

You can create a culture that nurtures your team by **having fun** in the workplace and by **showing you care** about them as people, including their personal lives.

Offering perks to your team creates loyalty, can help sell more products, and can help make employees happier and healthier. Perks can also serve as additional compensation when budgets are tight.

Helping team members **grow their skills and their careers** is one of the best ways to keep them engaged long-term. Consider current staff for new job openings, and work to get them raises and title changes when they take on new work.

When an employee resigns, don't take it personally or burn bridges. Be gracious and support the person in their growth, knowing your paths may cross again in the future.

PART FIVE

A is for

AUDIENCE

"The reader is king."

—Felix Dennis, founder of Dennis Publishing (the former publisher of Maxim, Stuff, Blender, The Week, *and other titles)*

In the world of business, thought leaders are quick to dole out crowns. You may have heard the often-repeated phrase, "Content is king." This statement comes from a 1996 article by Bill Gates in which he predicted that the internet would be most successful as a marketplace for content.[176] Other pundits, including many on the business side of publishing, have operated as though the advertiser is king. After all, they reason, who is paying to keep the electricity on so that all of this lovely content can continue to be produced?

But like Felix Dennis, who is quoted above, I have a different take. You can have the most compelling content in the world, winning awards for your editorial vision—but what if nobody reads it? And perhaps you've signed on a slew of luxury advertisers, with slick promotions for their high-end goods—but what if no one sees them? You may call content or advertisers king, but if those fabulous articles and the ads that support them don't find an audience, the kingdom they rule will be pretty small.

You can see why the reader—or consumer—is truly king. Designing a product and creating messaging around it can be exciting, but before you do that, you must first become crystal clear on who your audience of potential customers is—and what pain points they are seeking to remedy. This is an area where editors excel.

"The consumer (aka the reader) is our native language and our North Star," says Laura Kalehoff, founder of Kalehoff Creative and former editor in chief of *Fit Pregnancy* and *Natural Health*. "We've empathized with her, obsessed about her, and found ways to fill her needs since Day 1 of our careers. Most of us hopped roles every couple of years, becoming intimate with a new target audience each time and ever sharper at serving them."[177]

In other words, good editors know that the consumer is really the king, and content is the tool we use to serve them.

SERVING YOUR AUDIENCE LIKE AN EDITOR

Fully understanding your audience *before* you have your final product or messaging is the key to success. In the following chapters, you will learn the two main things you should do to serve your audience like an editor:

- **Know your audience** so that you can **empower them** to improve their lives via your product or service.

- **Build an engaged community** of customers who become evangelists for your brand.

We already know that people are the heart of any good company. While the last section covered the people *inside* the business (your team), this section will focus on the people *outside* the business, who will turn to you, your team, and your products for guidance. Now it's time to meet your customers.

CHAPTER 15

....

Know and Empower
Your Audience

When *Real Simple* published its first issue in the spring of 2000, the media world wasn't blown away; Martha Stewart even referred to the magazine as "real stupid."[178] (In fairness, she may have been bitter that Time Inc. had hired several former *Martha Stewart Living* staffers to launch the competitive brand.)

According to a press release that accompanied the launch, the target audience was "today's overextended, overcommitted, overscheduled woman" in her 30s and 40s—a woman who presumably needed a dose of, well, simplicity in her life. When the magazine hit newsstands, *New York Times* writer Julie V. Iovine sat down with the founding editor, Susan Wyland, to chat about her goals for the magazine and her ideal reader:

> "I see her going into a room by herself, sitting in a comfortable chair with a good view or taking it into the bathtub and shutting the door," said Ms. Wyland, whose premiere issue hits the news racks ... with earnest articles about cleaning the toilet, paying the bills and doing the laundry. That's not exactly bath-time reading for any of the stressed-out women I know. (Their preferred tub-time perusing runs to the gossip glossies, like *Vanity Fair* and *Entertainment Weekly*.)

The article went on to conclude: "*Real Simple* may have the right idea, just the wrong planet."[179]

Of course, hindsight is often 20/20. Although the magazine had a bumpy start, four years and two editors later, *Real Simple* had become a bona fide success. Just 11 months after editor in chief Kristin van Ogtrop took the reins, the magazine had nearly doubled its year-over-year ad revenue, topping the *Adweek* Hot List in March 2004. "*Real Simple* has created a buzz that seems more like a deafening roar," *Adweek*'s executive editor Patricia Orsini wrote. "Media directors tell us it has become the [magazine] to emulate—competitors now talk about how their pages look like *Real Simple*'s." The brand also took home *Adweek*'s award for Best Creative Team for the way its beautiful design resonated with readers, "proving looks and smarts can go together."[180]

It's no surprise that the magazine struck a chord with readers under van Ogtrop's watch; she knew her audience well. As she writes in her book *Did I Say That Out Loud?*: "Unlike every other place I had worked, *Real Simple* spoke to me as a reader—a busy working mother who was just trying to find a manageable level of control in her daily life. The photographs and design were so calming, they were like meditation, or Xanax. Plus, none of the cover lines exhorted you to buy designer shoes or improve your sex life."[181]

Although the magazine had three editors in its first four years, van Ogtrop stayed at *Real Simple* for more than 13 years, growing alongside her readers as they navigated career, health, relationships, parenting—and yes, even toilet cleaning—together. She knew her audience because she *was* her audience.

FOUR STEPS TO KNOW AND EMPOWER YOUR AUDIENCE

Like Kristin van Ogtrop, you may already know your audience well; this is often the case if your business offers a solution to a problem you also had. But what if your ideal customer *isn't* like you? You will need to do some digging to figure out who they are, what their pain points are, and how you can help them conquer those problems and lead better lives. Start with these four steps:

1. Determine your ideal customer and create an avatar for that person—and a persona that will guide them from point A to point B.

In Chapter 7, I talked about my grad school capstone project, where our class was split into four teams to pitch new magazines, ultimately choosing a winner to prototype. Ideally, the magazines we pitched would fill a hole in the marketplace, appealing to an audience that wasn't currently being served.

Although the class eventually landed on *Fuel*, a culture magazine for smart teens, my small group had pitched *SKIRT, the Sex Magazine for Women*. At the time, *Cosmopolitan* was the only mainstream sex magazine for women, and really it was more of a fashion and lifestyle publication that just had sex as one of its main pillars. We pictured something a bit more highbrow, asking: "What if *Architectural Digest* explored the architecture of anatomy, or if *Vanity Fair* took on the culture of the body? What if *Playgirl* ditched its in-your-face porn for the kind of intelligent articles by famous writers that used to make *Playboy* worth reading?" Visually, we pictured a more luxurious publication as well, with thick, glossy paper stock; a large, oversized format; and beautiful, provocative imagery, including the type of black-and-white photography you might find in an artsy coffee-table book.

Next, it was time to define our ideal customer, as well as a personality for our brand. Keeping all of this in mind, we constructed a "Tale of Two Joneses" for our **persona and avatar**:

- First, we decided the **persona** of our magazine would be Samantha Jones, as played by Kim Cattrall in *Sex and the City*: an intelligent woman who owns her own PR firm, dresses fashionably, lives in a gorgeous Manhattan apartment, and—most importantly—has zero hangups about sex, making sure *she* derives pleasure from every encounter. She is smart, cultured, sophisticated, chic, and unapologetically sexy.

Although Cattrall's character was a perfect personification of our magazine concept, she wasn't necessarily our ideal reader. Sure, Samantha would have enjoyed the magazine, but she may have been too busy heading out for another date to have had time to read it. She was already living the promise our brand offered. For our customer, we needed to have another Jones in mind.

- Our **avatar** (which we called the "median reader") was also a character borrowed from pop culture—but the other end of the spectrum: Bridget Jones. She has a walk-up apartment in a less chic neighborhood and is much lower on the ladder at work, where she has a crush on her handsome boss. She is single and loves sex, but isn't always as direct about it as she could be. She is still trying to get her love life in order.

The purpose of the magazine was to sell Bridget Jones on the promise of becoming Samantha Jones by providing her with a stimulating and thought-provoking peek into that world and all its possibilities.

EDITOR'S TIP

Make your avatar as real as possible

For *SKIRT*, we had a short amount of time to brainstorm and present our idea, so making our avatar the protagonist from the popular film *Bridget Jones's Diary* was a great shortcut to show who our ideal customer was. You don't have to rely on an existing or fictional person, though you do need to get super specific. Give your avatar a name and write down as many details as you can about her: Is she single or in a relationship? Does she have children? Where does she work, and how does she spend her free time? What social media apps does she check religiously? What are her favorite TV shows and movies, and where does she shop? All of this information will help you see her as a real person that you are speaking to when you create your marketing messages and other content.

2. Identify their fears, desires, and—perhaps most importantly—their pain points.

Author and self-publishing entrepreneur Chandler Bolt offers sound advice for marketing your product to your audience: Sell them pain pills, not vitamins.

When you go to the vitamin aisle in a store, there are a million different kinds: capsules and tablets, but also chewable vitamins, gummy vitamins, and even vitamins in the shape of cartoon characters. There is a reason for this: We know vitamins are good for us, but the effect is more long-term rather than immediate, so often people put off buying them, or if they buy them, they forget to take them. Thus, these vitamin companies have to work hard to make vitamins exciting—and at times, even candy-like—to entice customers to buy and actually use their product.

Pain pills, on the other hand, are a bit less flashy in their messaging. There's ibuprofen, aspirin, acetaminophen, and a few variations. But they are not sold in fancy packaging or marketed as tasty gummies. They don't need to sell you on taking them. When you wake up in the morning, you may or may not remember to take your vitamins, but if you are in pain, you will immediately reach for the bottle of Advil or Tylenol.

To see what selling pain pills as opposed to vitamins looks like in practice, consider the marketing strategies of many health and fitness companies.

Selling only the physical benefits of workout equipment or nutrition plans doesn't work for most customers. I mean, we all know that exercising and eating a balanced diet will make us healthier, but many of us still don't do it. The best brands in this category go one step further and ask what your *Why* is. This often uncovers the pain point.

In the same way that Toyota employees get to the root of a problem by using the "Five Whys" technique (mentioned in Chapter 2), many of the most successful fitness brands know that the real *Why*—and corresponding pain point—is likely buried a few levels down. For instance, imagine asking a customer: *Why do you want to go to the gym?* To be stronger. *Why?* So that I can play with my children and be there for them as they get older. *Why?* Because my sedentary father passed away when I was a teenager, and I feel like I missed out on so much time with him.

Like therapists, Toyota executives, and fitness marketers, the best editors also won't rest until they get to the real *Why*, which is often a deeply rooted internal pain point.

3. Ask yourself: "How can we help our customers improve their lives and become better people?"

Once you know who your audience is and who they aspire to be, as well as what their pain points are, you are then prepared to lead them across the bridge from avatar to persona.

Circling back to the *Real Simple* example: When the magazine launched, few people in the mainstream media were really talking about home organization—but that was about to change. The Container Store, which already had a handful of locations in Texas and throughout the South, opened its first New York metropolitan area store in 2000, the same year *Real Simple* debuted; within a few years, it had popped up in cities throughout the country.[182] The two brands seemed to blossom alongside each other overnight, sometimes literally. I have distinct memories of visiting The Container Store when I moved to New York City and seeing *Real Simple* as the featured magazine for sale at the checkout counter.

Today, home organization is a $14 billion industry that continues to grow, thanks in part to a new crop of gurus who have blown up in mainstream media: most notably Marie Kondo, who wrote the bestselling book *The Life-Changing Magic of Tidying Up* and starred in the 2019 Netflix series *Tidying Up with Marie Kondo*; as well as Clea Shearer and Joanna Teplin of The Home Edit, whose output includes six books and two seasons of their popular TV series *Get Organized with The Home Edit*, as well as lines of products at The Container Store and Walmart.

These gurus offer you the promise of finally clearing the clutter and creating a home that is organized and calming for you and your family, leaving more physical space for you to live but also more mental space for you to dream. Then they help you go through the steps of getting there, empowering you to make the choice and follow their tips. Along the way, they will provide expert advice (for the price of a book); live experts if you need them (for the price of hiring a consultant); and products that will help you get there (available at a store near you).

So, although they are selling you all of those products and services, what they are *really* selling you is the promise that if you follow their advice, you can take control of the situation, improve your surroundings, and by extension, your own life, allowing you the space and freedom to dream big and then go out and live those dreams.

4. Let them tell you what they want and need.

When I started as design director at *Coastal Living*, the staff was producing a beautiful print edition, as well as a digital edition that was available for purchase on the iPad and other tablets and e-readers. The digital edition had all of the same content but was repackaged to display well on these devices, which all had slightly different sizes and shapes.

It may sound like a minor workflow adjustment to produce these extra versions, but for our small design team, it created a significant amount of additional work. Stories that were fine-tuned and pristine were pulled apart and reimagined for an entirely new—and significantly smaller—format. Lush travel images that were photographed to spread across two pages were cropped to fit a vertical screen; sidebars that offered additional information at just the right moment in the layout were now relegated to the end of the story, so as not to interrupt the flow of the main narrative.

Redesigning each issue for multiple devices may have been worth it if the magazine was selling gangbusters digitally—but it wasn't. Very few readers were turning to these electronic issues. Although magazines like *Popular Science* and *Wired* were industry-leading when it came to the format of their tablet editions,[183] with embedded video, interactive features, and other bells and whistles their tech-savvy audience craved, I always suspected that our quintessential reader just wanted a physical magazine filled with beautiful photography and fascinating coastal stories—something that she could dog-ear while relaxing on the shore.

Eventually, we simplified our digital issue, saving hours of work that we then used to make the print issue better. A few years later, when we conducted a focus group to get feedback on other editorial changes to the magazine, my suspicions were confirmed: Reader after reader told us that they wanted a print copy that they could throw in a tote and carry to the beach, without having to worry about glare from the sun or getting saltwater on their devices.

The lesson to me was that it was vital to know not only *what* your audience wants from you but also *how* they plan to use it. *Teen Vogue* was published in a smaller 6¾-by-9-inch digest format. This was to allow it to fit into a digest-sized slot at checkout stands, but also because its readers wanted a fashion bible that could be taken on the go, easily tucked into a small backpack or purse. A similar philosophy likely went into the design of *Prevention* and *Reader's Digest*, two small but mighty checkout line staples.

What is it about a product that really makes it sing? Focus groups and other forms of market research are one of the best ways to find out this information. Ask end users what they like about using your product, and what they feel could be improved upon. If your product or service has lots of features or variations, it is also important to learn what aspects they don't care about, so you can streamline your idea in future iterations. (Just make sure that the person you hire to conduct this research asks questions that are specific but not leading.)

If market research and focus groups are not feasible, it never hurts to reach out to current or potential customers and ask these questions yourself. If you produce a product that is used in public, you can also settle in for some people watching to observe how it is being used and what people are using it for.

Understanding not just *what* your customer wants from you but also *how* they plan to use it can help you create a product that delivers value—and is a delight to use.

THE TAKEAWAY

It is important to **know your ideal customer** so that you can **empower them** to change their lives.

To help you think of a mass of people (all potential customers) as one person you can speak to, start by identifying who your ideal customer is and creating an **avatar** for that person. The avatar can be based on a person you know, a collection of different characters or traits of your ideal customer, or even someone from pop culture.

Also create a brand **persona** who will guide your avatar from point A to point B, helping them improve their lives and achieve your brand's promise.

While vitamins are great, they are much harder to sell than pain pills. Identify your customers' desires and their fears; then drill down to their **pain points** and build a relationship with them by explaining how your product or service can alleviate those pains.

Sometimes a product does more than meets the eye. By **solving a simple problem,** your product or service can help customers change their lives and become better people.

Being the ideal customer for your product can make knowing your customer even easier, but don't assume that everyone thinks the same as you. Ask potential or existing customers what they like and don't like about your product, and record information about not just *if* they use it but *how* **they use it.**

Visit **LeadLikeAnEditor.com** to download a free workbook that includes **Brand Persona** and **Brand Avatar** templates, as well as other resources.

CHAPTER 16

Build an Engaged Community

n early 2016, Lesley Jane Seymour seemed to be on top of the world. As the editor in chief of *More* magazine, she spoke each month to 1.5 million readers, most of whom were over the age of 40 and felt underserved by the youthful focus of mainstream women's publications. From the outside, the brand appeared to be riding high, having garnered billions of media impressions for a recent issue guest-edited by Michelle Obama—"a first for a First Lady," according to *The New York Times*.[184]

In fact, Seymour and her son were in Washington, DC, attending a Stevie Wonder concert at the White House as guests of the Obamas, when she got a call to meet her boss at 9 a.m. the next day. "When I walked into my boss's office the next morning, I knew the jig was up," she says.[185]

Meredith Corporation, the company that owned *More*, had been largely focused on its mass-market publications like *Better Homes & Gardens*, according to Seymour, and had limited experience selling a smaller, upscale brand like *More* to high-end beauty and fashion advertisers. As the magazine industry shifted, management churned at the company; Seymour had five bosses in eight years and had begun to see the writing on the wall.

Suspecting that *More* may eventually close, Seymour had a backup plan. She had been working on her master's degree in sustainability management at Columbia University, planning to parlay that education and her women's magazine experience into a new career in the beauty industry.

But fans of *More* had a different idea. When the closing was announced, hordes of readers deluged her on social media, begging her to create "something else" for them to replace the magazine they loved. After considering the different topics *More* had covered, Seymour created a 54-question survey, which 627 of these former readers completed. "I made a map of their desires," she says. "And that is how CoveyClub was born."[186]

Named for a small flock of birds called a "covey," the business started as a blog and podcast run out of Seymour's home but has since grown into a full-fledged community of thousands of women (and a few men), many of whom are seeking some sort of reinvention as they navigate the challenges of midlife.

Billed as "a meeting place for lifelong learners," CoveyClub offers virtual and in-person meetups, expert-led classes, and even an app where members can connect and ask each other for advice on topics ranging from health challenges to life disruptions like empty-nest syndrome or losing a partner. As many members navigate beginning "second acts" after corporate downsizing or retirement, CoveyClub also offers content on a variety of business topics, from networking to first-time entrepreneurship.

Members are encouraged to be vulnerable with each other about where they are in their personal or career journeys, prompting other members to offer support and judgment-free advice. Along the way, new connections are forged as members often end up befriending each other, and even buying goods and services from each other. "What makes CoveyClub truly unique is that we deliberately mix business with friendship—because I believe these are the strongest bonds," Seymour says.[187]

HOW MAGAZINES UNITED COMMUNITIES

In today's digital world, it is easier than ever to find your tribe. In fact, for many internet users, that was one of the initial selling points of "going online" in the 1990s. Anyone who lived through this time can still remember the thrill of hearing the pings and whirs of the modem as AOL launched via dial-up, connecting us to a world of information—and to other people. Organized around all manner of topics, the chat rooms and message boards of the early internet allowed users to congregate virtually, planting the seeds for our hyper-connected lives on social media. Today, like-minded strangers can connect even more easily across Facebook Groups and other internet forums.

But this wasn't always the case. In their book *Curating Culture: How Twentieth-Century Magazines Influenced America*, editors Sharon Bloyd-Peshkin (a journalism professor at Columbia College Chicago) and Charles Whitaker (Medill's dean and my former professor) explain how, before the dawn of the internet, consumer magazines helped unite people into communities. For example, during the 1990s—when not everyone had access to the internet—the magazine *Poz* served as a lifeline to HIV-positive people who craved information, connection, and hope that they often could not find at home. It also allowed them to connect in a safe and anonymous space, as many kept their status private in their daily lives for fear of being shunned by their local communities. Similarly, during the meat-centric fast food wars of the 1970s and 1980s, magazines like *Vegetarian Times* linked people who sought vegetable-based recipes—as well as information about how a vegetarian diet was good for both animals and the environment.[188]

The OGs of UGC

Some of the best examples of magazines that create a sense of community are the 15 titles started by Reiman Publications, which founder Roy Reiman sold to the parent company of *Reader's Digest* for $760 million in 2002.[189] Reiman started his first publication in the 1970s after learning that the two biggest farming magazines were eliminating sections geared toward the wives of farmers. Realizing that millions of rural women throughout the country may no longer have a magazine that spoke directly to them, Reiman launched *Farm Wife News*, before eventually changing the name to *Country Woman* to also include suburban and even urban women who were nostalgic for a country lifestyle.[190]

At Reiman Publications, the reader was truly king—or queen. The company succeeded based on two key differentiating factors: First, for more than 30 years, the magazines had no advertisements, meaning editors only had to answer to the readers themselves. Second, and perhaps most important, around 80 percent of each magazine's text was submitted by readers, making Reiman Publications the true pioneers of UGC, or user-generated content.

Knowing that reader-submitted "Letters to Editor" were often the most-read section of many magazines, Reiman used this model to solicit all sorts of content. The magazine invited interactive participation, as the editors asked readers to submit stories, recipes, and photos each month, while also completing polls and entering competitions and contests.

For many years, the format worked. Take user recipes, for example, which made up the entirety of another Reiman publication called *Taste of*

Home. Reiman reasoned that the magazine's salt-of-the-earth readers would prefer time-tested recipes from each other, rather than fancy recipes using exotic ingredients, which often ran in other culinary titles. This bet paid off as, at one point, *Taste of Home* had more readers than *Food & Wine, Bon Appétit,* and *Gourmet* combined, and even today has more subscribers than any other culinary magazine.[191]

At Reiman Publications, "the editorial content nurtured and rewarded reader investment," journalism professor and scholar Sheila Webb writes in *Curating Culture.* "This helped create a devoted following—readers who, by contributing, joined an imagined community and felt they were having a conversation with one another."[192] Reiman himself said his products were not really magazines so much as "conversations."[193] Readers' own estimation of the publications echoed this, as one subscriber likened them to "visiting with people across the country for relaxing conversations among friends."[194]

Originally published by Reiman Publications, these three magazines relied heavily on user-generated content, creating a sense of ownership and community for readers.

FIVE STEPS TO CREATE A BRAND-BASED COMMUNITY

While creating a community is easier than ever with today's digital tools, it's also more competitive, as numerous brands use similar strategies, resulting in consumer overload. Still, a few companies have broken through the noise, building businesses centered on active, engaged communities. So what makes these outliers thrive while other brand-based communities fail to catch on?

Started in 2012 with the goal of bringing "the community and excitement of boutique fitness into the home," Peloton has been widely heralded for the sense of belonging it has created through its online content, instructors, and classes.[195] Even the choice of the word *peloton*—defined as "the main body of riders in a bicycle race"—suggests the company's group-focused mission.[196] Throughout the next five steps, I will explain how companies like Peloton (which has hired several former magazine editors over the years) have successfully harnessed the power of community:

1. Decide if it makes sense for your brand.

For years, working out at home was seen as a convenient option—but also a lonely one. It requires a lot of willpower to keep your energy and spirits up during a tough session, when it would be easier to end early or just skip altogether. For this reason, many exercisers hit the gym to work out surrounded by others, with the most social opting for group fitness classes like spinning.

Peloton combined the convenience of working out at home with the social experience of going to the gym. Through its live classes, the company creates a sense of community that replicates the group fitness experience, including an inspirational instructor and a leaderboard that shows how you stack up against others (a common feature of in-person classes at many studios, like Orangetheory).

In her article "The Peloton Community-Building Playbook," marketing expert and journalist Tiffany Regaudie posits that a large part of the reason Peloton was so successful is because it gets to what is at the heart of close communities: "meaningful interactions between people with shared goals."[197] "A solid workout is hard to accomplish because it requires overcoming physical obstacles," she writes. "When you overcome an obstacle with other people, you create a shared bond—no one else understands what you've experienced better than other people who have also experienced it."

Building a community can take a lot of effort, so before starting, it is important to consider whether it is really right for your brand. Determining if your product creates a "meaningful, sustained experience" among enough people with a common goal is a great place to start.

2. Determine who will be the face of the community.

People make connections with other people, so having someone serve as the face of the community is paramount. Most magazines have mastered this by selecting an editor in chief who embodies the brand, and then putting that person front and center each month.

Conventional wisdom says that the cover is the most important page of any magazine, but I would argue that the Editor's Letter is a strong second. Appearing after the table of contents, this page usually includes a photo of the editor and a personality-driven note, welcoming readers to the issue. Often, the editor will connect one or more of the issue's articles to an experience in her own life—and by extension, to the lives of readers. When readers can relate to the editor, even in an aspirational way, it strengthens their ties to the brand by making them feel connected to an actual person.

When I began working at *Coastal Living,* Antonia van der Meer was editor in chief, and she was the perfect candidate to be the face of the magazine. Like many of our readers, Antonia was married with children. She owned a home in New York City, as well as a beach house in Connecticut that she had grown up in. (Data showed that 82 percent of our readers were homeowners, and many also had a second home.)

Having written more than a dozen books and led several magazines, including Condé Nast's *Modern Bride,* Antonia obviously has writing and editing chops. But more than that, she lives—and loves—the coastal lifestyle. For her, spending time by the sea surrounded by family and friends is not a novelty, or something to be reserved for special occasions. It's her life.

"I was born about 1,000 feet from the water," she writes in *Coastal Living*'s 2015 coffee-table book, *Beach House Happy.* "By the time I was 5, we had moved even closer to the beach, just across the street from the ocean, and my fate was sealed. I was a water baby from the very beginning; the sea was in my blood from the get-go."[198]

In her monthly Editor's Letter, Antonia wrote about very specific topics that were relatable to our readers who—like her—spent as much time as possible at the beach with their loved ones. In one of my favorites, she recounted a Thanksgiving trip to the Caribbean with her family—and how she had packed a frozen turkey in her carry-on bag to make sure the holiday would live up to its full splendor away from home, even if the checked luggage was lost. Who does that?!

When Antonia and I attended a focus group to gather feedback for an upcoming redesign, we sat hidden behind a two-way mirror, listening as readers critiqued our mock-ups. They were excited about some things and less excited about others. But at the end of the session, the moderator surprised them by letting them know Antonia was in the next room over. When she popped in to say hello and thank them for participating, it was as though a celebrity had entered the room. These readers, who were all longtime subscribers, felt as though they knew her. They instantly became much more animated than they had been, asking Antonia about specific stories we had run as well as her own travels, clothing, and home decor—all while eagerly jotting down notes.

Ideally, the face of the brand is someone your readers aspire to be. *Martha Stewart Living* and *O, The Oprah Magazine* used their namesakes extensively on covers and in promotional materials because they knew that their devotees loved them. But even when there isn't a household name attached to the brand, as is more often the case, the best editors embody the magazine, serving as the face of it for their readers. My editor at *Spa* magazine, Julie Sinclair, was not just interested in beauty products or being pampered; she also loved wellness in all its aspects, from energy-healing practices like Reiki to mindful exercise like Bikram yoga. Similarly, Ana Connery, my editor in chief at *Parenting*, was a single working mom with a young child, making her the ideal representative of a brand that promised "Modern Families + Fresh Ideas."

People follow people. It's a simple fact that is true in both social media and traditional media, as well as politics and entertainment. Customers don't always want to interact with a brand; they want to interact with another person. Having a face of the brand that they can relate to humanizes the company and also creates trust.

For companies that are trying to build brand loyalty, having the right person out-front can make all the difference. When Apple redesigned the way computers looked and fit into our lives, first with the iMac and then with the iPod and iPhone, Steve Jobs was there to explain why we needed to "Think Different." Or take TOMS Shoes: When the company launched in 2006, it was based on the story of founder Blake Mycoskie. After meeting a woman who was delivering shoes to disadvantaged children in Argentina, he created TOMS with a "one for one" business model that ensured a pair of shoes would be donated for each one purchased. Mycoskie even traded his CEO designation for the title Chief Shoe Giver, making himself a living embodiment of the company and its mission.[199]

Rather than focus on one person, Peloton has made its instructors the faces of the brand, which makes sense, as they are literally the faces that users see when they log on for classes each day. The instructors are all at various stages of life, with different personalities and teaching styles, offering something for everyone. And like television reporters, by coming into people's homes virtually every day, they have garnered their own fans, becoming celebrities in their own right. More than a dozen Peloton instructors have written books—including a few that landed on *The New York Times* bestseller list.[200]

EDITOR'S TIP

Someone else can be the face of the brand.

At times, it may not be possible for you to be the face of the brand—and that's okay. The important thing is that someone takes on the role. Is there someone else on your team who is gregarious, enjoys connecting with others, and is comfortable on camera? If not, you can also hire someone for this position; depending on what you need, they could take on a diverse range of tasks from speaking publicly about the brand to monitoring a Facebook Group. Just make sure that you have some sort of commitment or contract with this person to guarantee that they will be around for longer than a few months. What you don't want is for the face of the brand to constantly be changing.

If you work in marketing for a larger company, also consider the benefits of using the same face for a long period of time in your ads. For years, Jennifer Aniston served as the face of Aveeno, and Nike's partnership with Michael Jordan set the stage for what the most profitable endorsement deals could look like. But that doesn't mean that you need to have a celebrity-sized budget; by choosing one actor and sticking with her for decades, Progressive Insurance achieves the same effect with Stephanie Courtney, who has served as the face of the company by playing the character "Flo" in its advertisements since 2008.

3. Open the lines of communication by creating a community forum.

Although the popularity of various social media platforms waxes and wanes, Facebook remains one of the best ways to organize groups of people. Facebook Groups are easy to set up, and you can create rules about what is posted and who is allowed to enter. By creating a forum where consumers can post their own reviews and answer each other's questions, you can help build a community. I am currently a member of several Facebook Groups, and the advice and information I've received in them has been extremely valuable. This is low-hanging fruit and easy to do.

While some companies experiment with creating a forum on their own sites, for most brands, having a Facebook Group makes more sense. For starters, you are able to leverage free technology that has already been set up for you. Plus, many people already visit Facebook daily to see what's new with friends and family, making it easy for them to check out the latest from your community as well. In fact, the Facebook algorithm will even serve these updates to them, and if they interact with your group's posts by liking or commenting, they will be shown even more in the future.

Once again, let's look at Peloton as an example. Although they are obviously a high-tech company that streams video content into millions of homes,[201] they have still chosen to go the Facebook route for their community forum. Started in 2015, this closed group (open only to Peloton subscribers) has almost 500,000 members and serves as a place where users can ask questions, share milestones, and offer words of encouragement as well as helpful tips—while also staying up-to-date on the latest company announcements and newly added features.[202]

EDITOR'S TIP

Use Facebook to create a community around a topic related to your business.

You can make a Facebook page for your business, but don't expect a ton of engagement. How many businesses do you actively seek out on social media? Instead, consider making a Facebook Group organized around a topic that is related to your business and important to your customers. For instance, if you sell pet products, you could create a group for pet lovers or for people who volunteer with animals. As we will discuss in the next section on Message, providing content (or in this case, a community) that helps your audience and is related to your business—but doesn't always mention your company in every interaction—is a great way to build trust while positioning your brand as an authority on a topic.

4. Create a challenge to introduce some friendly competition (and self-competition).

Many of the best organic communities are built by groups of people who share a common challenge or goal. Although I definitely would not consider myself a runner, I did complete a half-marathon in my 20s through the Leukemia and Lymphoma Society's Team in Training program. I joined a training group along with several friends from work, and before each of the weekly group "long runs," someone with a direct relationship with the disease got up and spoke about their *Why* for joining. My mom died from lymphoma when I was 22, so funding research for this disease was close to my heart. I personally raised more than $5,000 for the cause by asking friends and family for donations, and on the days I felt like quitting, I was reminded of my *Why*.

For several years, a group of my friends has participated in the Whole Life Challenge, which bills itself as a "six-week health and well-being game." Participants are encouraged to sign up on a team with several friends or family members but can also join another team if they are participating solo. Over a month and a half, members focus on the Seven Daily Habits (nutrition, exercise, mobility, sleep, hydration, well-being, and reflection) by completing tasks that range from stretching to journaling to exercise. By logging progress into the Whole Life Challenge app, which also includes a group chat function, users can achieve badges as well as incentives (like cheat meals) while competing with and supporting their fellow team members.

As previously mentioned, Peloton uses the leaderboard to keep members competitive, as they compare their stats with others taking the class at the same time. But even those who stream classes on demand can feel like part of the community; they are shown the number of riders currently taking the class as well as a ranking of top members who have previously set leaderboard positions for that ride.

While riders can compete with their own stats and those of others, the leaderboard also serves as a way for users to support one another. Peloton users can add hashtags—like #PelotonMoms or #FitFab40s—to their profiles to connect with others who share their demographics or interests. Over time, friendships are forged as riders can follow each other, plan to take classes together, and even send virtual high fives during classes. Peloton even offers a video chat function that allows riders in the same class to check in with each other and provide words of encouragement in real time.

5. Let community members be part of the story.

At *Coastal Living,* we had a pet problem. The problem was not pets themselves—we loved them, as did our readers. The magazine really embraces the relaxing aspects of life lived by the sea, surrounded by family, friends, and four-legged friends. For this reason, advertisers of pet products were a natural fit for our magazine, but they often wanted their ads to appear alongside pet-focused editorial content.

The staff struggled with how to create pet content that was compelling, somewhat easy to produce, and fresh every issue. We tried a lot of ideas over the years, ranging from pet Halloween costumes for an October issue to a flowchart on what breed of dog you should buy based on your beach personality (a French bulldog for the lazy beach bum, a retriever or pointer for the active thrill seeker, etc.).

Eventually our team decided to stop trying to reinvent the wheel every month; instead, why not simply let our readers help us out? We created an online contest called "Our Favorite Beach Dogs" and invited readers to send in photos of their pets at the beach. We hoped that we would get at least a few cute submissions that we could use on the "Coastal Pets" page in an upcoming issue.

Almost as soon as the contest was announced, the reader emails began pouring in. People who have pets are often crazy about them, and it showed. Readers were positively thrilled that their pets could be featured in the magazine.

Not only were the submissions plentiful, but they were also *really* good. As the design director of the magazine, I was the gatekeeper of all photography. It was my job to make sure the pages looked beautiful each month, and although I thought the contest sounded fun, I had secretly dreaded sorting through stacks of bad images in my hunt for ones worthy of publication.

I was pleasantly surprised to find the opposite was true. Some of the shots were so amazing that they looked like they had been professionally photographed. We ended up getting so many great submissions that we decided to run a four-page photo essay of the best ones in our July/August issue, which was typically one of the bestselling issues of the year. Because we had such an influx of images, with new ones coming in every day, we used this feature to kick off a new "Beach Dog of the Month" column, which showed a photo of a pup, along with a bio of the animal and its owner.

Although the resounding success of this experiment was somewhat unexpected, it shouldn't have been. Roy Reiman certainly would not have been surprised. Circling back to the beginning of the chapter, his magazines depended almost entirely on reader submissions.

With the rise of the digital age and social media, the acronym UGC has become a bit of a buzzword in recent years, as internet marketers breathlessly describe how quality user-generated content can be priceless—and data backs this up. According to *Adweek*, 85 percent of consumers say that UGC is more influential than content made by brands directly.[203] It makes sense: People trust other people more than they trust a for-profit corporation, making customer reviews and endorsements all the more important.

Letting customers feel like they have a voice in shaping your brand will drive loyalty. This could be as simple as creating a naming contest for a new product or asking for their tips on innovative uses for a current offering. If your brand produces some sort of written content (and it probably should, as you will learn in Part Six: M is for Message), consider interviewing a few standout customers and including information about their lives, interests, and usage of your product.

Men's Health currently publishes their own MVP Member of the Month each issue (and has done some iteration of this for years), while other fitness magazines have offered updates on a single reader each month over the course of a year-long fitness journey. If your brand has a podcast, consider interviewing some of your most devoted customers. If you have a blog, ask for guest essay submissions. And if your customer has a story about how using your product helped them, let them tell it, then share it widely. Not surprisingly, the community powerhouse Peloton offers more than a hundred of these testimonials in the Member Stories section of its blog, The Output.[204]

For the most devoted of your followers, consider creating a Brand Ambassador designation, as companies like the athletic apparel retailer Lululemon have done. Brand ambassadors receive a discount on products and services, and in exchange, they act as evangelists for your company, spreading the good news through word of mouth, both in person and on social media. In the case of Lululemon, these loyalists also offer the brand a built-in focus group to test and provide feedback on its latest products.

"Everything we do starts with authentic relationships," Lululemon states on the Ambassadors page of its site. "That's why each ambassadorship begins locally, in our stores. When you're an ambassador, you're not just a partner, you're an extension of our brand and an inspiration to our guests."[205]

By feeling like they are a part of your story, loyal customers grow from casual users to your biggest fans. Not only will you keep them as clients for life, but often they will also evangelize you to their friends and family. Returning to the *Coastal Living* example, each time a beach dog appeared in the magazine, its owners let us know that they would rush out to buy several copies and encourage friends and family to do the same. That kind of loyalty is priceless.

EDITOR'S TIP

—

Foster community by introducing a challenge.

CoveyClub founder Lesley Jane Seymour says that challenges have been a way for her to bring her members together around a common cause. "I used to just teach a class on motivation called my '30 Days to Reinvention Plan,'" Seymour tells me, "but we found that working *together* for 30 days was more helpful." Based on bite-sized steps that can be done each day to move you toward a goal, the class was rebranded as the "30-Day Reinvention Challenge," with daily support on the CoveyConnect app, as well as two weekly group check-in calls, where Seymour coaches members through roadblocks they might have along the way.

"One woman wrote a whole poetry book in 30 days, and another woman started cleaning her closets, which led to her writing her will and organizing all of her personal papers. By the end of the month, she was ready to start working on cleaning out her digital photos. I told her, 'Stop, this is going too far. No one does their digital photos,'" Seymour laughs. "Learning together, we can do better than apart—we all know that. But to actually see it in action is fantastic."[206]

THE TAKEAWAY

Long before the digital age, **magazines fostered a sense of community** by connecting readers with common interests, identities, and goals—and then providing them with information, inspiration, and a place to interact with one another.

People follow people. Your customers don't want to interact with a brand; they want to interact with another person. Like a magazine's editor in chief, having a **face of the brand** who people can relate to humanizes your company and also creates trust. This could be you, especially if you are—or at one point were—very similar to the audience you would like to serve. If not, other members of your team could also serve this function.

Open the lines of communication with a forum where customers can post reviews, ask questions, and answer each other's questions. This can be accomplished for free by creating a Facebook Group around a topic related to your brand or around a pain point that your product solves.

Keep your community engaged with **challenges** that allow them to compete with one another—or themselves—over a set period of time.

Stories have the power to unite us. **By letting users be a part of your brand's story,** you can create ties that are much more real. Customers with this type of deep connection are more likely to develop an affinity for your products or services, eventually becoming brand evangelists.

PART SIX

M is for

MESSAGE

"Those who tell the stories rule society."

—Plato

Listen in on any discussion of marketing today, and it's likely that you will hear the word *storytelling* used at some point—but that wasn't always the case. In fact, as recently as 2011, most people associated the word with a campfire activity or a monthly children's program at their local library.

According to LinkedIn, in 2011, only a tiny number of marketers listed *storytelling* as a skill on their profile. Then, as companies like Chipotle and Coca-Cola launched successful (and even award-winning) story-based advertising campaigns, the popularity of using stories in marketing—and talking about it among marketers—grew. Starting in 2012 and into 2013, thought leaders like Seth Godin and Gary Vaynerchuk began extolling the business virtues of this "new" skill, while Jonathan Gottschall's book *The Storytelling Animal: How Stories Make Us Human* provided the science behind *why* we love stories (and was also named a *New York Times* Editor's Choice). By 2012, 25,000 marketers had begun listing *storytelling* as a skill in their LinkedIn profiles; that number quickly ballooned to 200,000 in 2013 and had reached almost 600,000 by the end of 2017.[207] Today, the word is listed on the profiles of more than a million LinkedIn users, myself included.

Of course, we magazine editors initially rolled our eyes when *storytelling* became the latest buzzword in marketing. "Big deal," we grumbled. "Storytelling is what *we* have been doing for decades." But now, as many editors have made the leap into new industries, they have leaned into storytelling, harnessing this skill—or, some would say, art—better than anyone.

CREATE AND REFINE YOUR MESSAGE LIKE AN EDITOR

As simple as storytelling may sound, it must also be intentional. In the following chapters, I will cover the three steps you need to focus on as you craft the message that you will deliver to your potential customers:

- Determine the messaging itself, or **what you say,** by starting with a simple but epic storytelling structure used by the most engaging novels and films.

- Hone the delivery of your messaging, or **how you say it,** by developing your brand voice and deciding the purpose of each message you create.

- Design the look of your messaging, or **how you package it,** by employing a visual language that resonates with your audience, and by curating your words and imagery to show your customers what is important.

As we are bombarded with an avalanche of emails, advertisements, and sales pitches every day, messages that tell a story stand out and pique our interest. And it makes sense: After all, would you rather read a textbook to learn about a new concept, or have the same concept explained to you by way of a story that illustrates the point? If you are ready for a master class in business-based storytelling, turn the page to learn tips and tricks from some of the world's best storytellers: writers and editors.

CHAPTER 17

Determine What You Say

S torytelling may be a hot buzzword, but what does it really mean? To demonstrate what makes an exciting story, let's play a guessing game. I am thinking of the plot of a famous blockbuster movie, and I'll give you a few hints:

- The main character is an unlikely hero who is plucked from their normal life and sent on a harrowing journey by a wise guide.

- Against all odds, this protagonist defeats an evil villain, restoring peace to the land.

- Along the way, the hero grows as a person, discovering who they really are in the process.

Think about these hints for a moment. Do you know which movie I am picturing?

If you guessed *The Wizard of Oz*, you would be right—that's the film I had in mind. But I wouldn't be surprised if, based on these plot points, you guessed something else: perhaps *Star Wars* or *The Lord of the Rings*. There is a reason for this: Many epic stories from film and literature share a similar format known as the Hero's Journey, a concept first written about by mythologist Joseph Campbell in his 1949 book *The Hero with a Thousand Faces*. Campbell suggests that almost all great stories follow a similar narrative, based on centuries of mythology.[208]

This structure is practically in our DNA at this point. It is how humans have told stories for as long as we have been telling them and continues to resonate today because it allows everyday people to imagine themselves as heroes. Once you recognize the key elements and plot points, you start to realize just how many of the most popular literary and cinematic masterpieces utilize the same setup—not only the examples above but also *The Lion King*, *The Hunger Games*, the *Indiana Jones* series, and many more.

But good storytelling isn't just essential for beach reads or blockbuster movies; it is also crucial as you teach customers about your brand. As the author of more than a dozen books, including a *New York Times* bestselling memoir, marketing expert Donald Miller has mastered the art of storytelling. In his book *Building a StoryBrand*, Miller lays out a seven-step framework you can use to explain your business to potential customers clearly, using key elements of the Hero's Journey. He breaks down the story like this:

- Start with a character who wants something

- But then encounters a problem

- And meets a guide

- Who gives them a plan

- And calls them to action

- That helps them avoid failure

- And ends in success.[209]

The first time I saw this structure, it felt familiar to me not just because it followed the plot of many of the most epic movies and books but also because it reminded me of something else I had spent my entire adult life doing: making magazines.

YOUR CUSTOMER IS THE HERO,
AND YOU'RE THE GUIDE

Way back in Chapter 1, we learned about how important it is to play the hero in your own story and not the victim. While this is a key to success in your own life, when you are talking to your customer, you must play a different role: the guide.

A lot of businesses make the mistake of positioning themselves as the hero who can swoop in and save the day, but such thinking puts your customer in the role of the victim or the damsel in distress. Most people don't want to be *saved*, thank you very much. We want to be the heroes of our own stories and *save ourselves*—we might just need a little help along the way.

Good editors instinctively know that their reader is the hero and they are the guide. Part of the popularity of magazines for the past hundred years is the promise that they will provide you with information and guidance that allows you to take action and improve your life in some measurable way.

"Editors know how to take products off a store shelf and put them into a consumer's life in a meaningful way," says Molly Nover-Baker, founder of The Edit Collective, a content agency that builds upon her years as beauty director at *CosmoGIRL!* and *Women's Health*. "We can elicit action from a consumer and provide her with information that is both useful and engaging, thus helping a brand build a loyal customer base, while also creating buzz."[210]

Like the best media brands, guides are marked by two key characteristics: empathy and authority. They understand what it feels like to want something and not know how to get it; they have been there too and have come out the other side a champion. More than any other factors, these two traits often make the difference in whether we instinctively want to do business with someone. As Miller explains: "The one-two punch in communication as a professional is to say *I know what you're struggling with and I can help you get out of it.*"[211]

Research backs this up. Harvard business professor Amy Cuddy has spent decades studying how leaders can make good first impressions. She found that when we meet someone, our brains ask two questions that are the key to making a positive initial impact: "Can I trust this person?" and "Can I respect this person?"[212]

By displaying empathy, we show that we have had similar problems and can relate, making us more trustworthy; and once we explain that we can show the other person how to overcome the same problem and achieve positive results, we earn their respect.

THE PROBLEM

In Chapter 15, I talked about how it is easier to sell pain pills than to sell vitamins. This is especially true in the context of the Hero's Journey. Most heroes start out as everyday folks or perhaps even underdogs who want something important but must solve a problem in order to get it. All good stories have conflict, and for your customer, the conflict is their problem. You can't dance around the problem; rather, it should be one of the first things you talk about in your messaging.

Have you ever seen a commercial for a product you've never heard of and, by the end, you feel like you absolutely need it? This is almost always because the messaging presented a clear problem that you may have already been pondering—or perhaps one you didn't even realize you had. Through cover lines and headlines, media brands always remind readers of the problem, before explaining how to solve it. A recent cover of *Prevention*, for instance, includes the lines "How to Cure a Bad Cough" and "The Best and Worst Foods for Inflammation," tackling two health-related problems a reader may struggle with.[213]

Sometimes you are selling a brand promise based on an external problem, and other times you are selling one based on an internal problem. When I first began working on this book, I joined a self-publishing community that promised to help authors go from a blank page to selling 10,000 copies of their book. In its very effective marketing, the company focused on how they could solve the external problems (How do I write 60,000 to 100,000 words? How do I design my book and cover? How do I publish on Amazon and other platforms?). But perhaps even more importantly, the marketing messages focused on some internal pain points: If I don't finally make the investment to get serious about writing and publishing my first book, what will it feel like to never realize my dream of being a published author?

THE PLAN AND CALL TO ACTION

Once you have positioned your customer as the hero and yourself as the guide that can help them overcome their problem, you must then present a plan for how to do that. If you can give this plan some sort of catchy name, even better.

Once again, magazine editors have been using this approach for decades. Take a sample issue of *Men's Health* (January/February 2024).

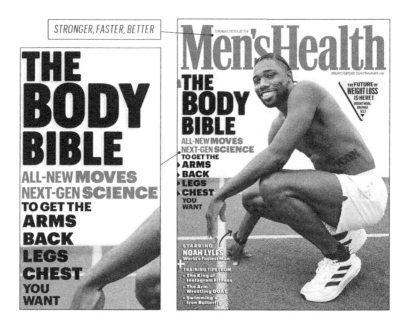

This issue of Men's Health *offers readers a plan ("The Body Bible"), while positioning the magazine as a guide that can help them achieve their fitness goals.*

The small tagline that appears directly above the logo contains the brand promise (**Stronger, Faster, Better**) while the main cover line offers the plan:

THE BODY BIBLE:
All-New Moves [&] Next-Gen Science
to Get the Arms, Back, Legs, Chest You Want

On the table of contents, this plan is touted once again with a page number that serves as a call to action:

THE BODY BIBLE:
Arms. Abs. Chest. Back. Legs. Glutes. If you want to build them, we have the latest science and insider-backed strategy guides. [Turn to page] 64

At this point, you don't need to get too detailed with the plan—that can seem overwhelming to a prospective buyer. Ideally, your plan will have a few simple steps (*StoryBrand* author Donald Miller recommends three to six) that give the hero confidence in your ability to guide them. These steps should be easy to comprehend, offer reassurance that you know what you are doing, and give your customer—the hero—a clear direction of what they should do next.

Let's look at how this message plays out at SelfPublishing.com, the community I joined when I began working on this book. At the time of writing, these are the words that appear on the website at the very top of the homepage:[214]

Become a Bestselling Author Today
We're the **#1 resource** for writing, self-publishing, and marketing books online.

BOOK A FREE CALL

First impressions are everything, and these two simple lines of text immediately set you up as the hero and the company as the guide. Then below that, you get a simplified version of their plan:

Your Path to Publishing Success
Your story has the power to impact lives. We help you get that story into the world with a proven path to author success.

1-1 Book coaching
Time-saving writing tips
Daily group training
Professional cover & formatting
Publishing & launch plan

BOOK A FREE CALL

The most important part of the plan is that it includes a direct call to action. Most of the website is designed in a serene green and navy-blue color palette—except for the BOOK A FREE CALL button. It is in bright orange and appears five times on the home page, and over and over again throughout the site.

There is nothing more frustrating for a potential customer than visiting your website, becoming interested in buying your product or service, and then not knowing how to go about doing that. Always offer a call to action, also known as a CTA. If you have a product that customers can buy online, this could take the form of a BUY NOW button. If your product or service is more nuanced and needs explanation, or if it offers multiple tiers with varying benefits, you may want to have them email you to GET A FREE QUOTE or BOOK A FREE CALL, as SelfPublishing.com does.

SETTING THE STAKES: SHOW WHAT SUCCESS AND FAILURE LOOK LIKE

Leaving the safety and comfort of home to go out and fight battles is not really all that appealing if it only makes life a tiny bit better. Even the most inspiring guide would have trouble convincing a hero to risk life and limb for menial stakes.

We can see how heightened stakes propel the plots of our favorite stories: Will Dorothy triumph over the Wicked Witch of the West and find her way back home? Will Simba defeat his Uncle Scar, bringing peace back to the Pride Lands? After seven books and eight movies, will Harry Potter win the final battle against Voldemort, the dark lord who killed his parents?

Further down on its homepage, SelfPublishing.com accomplishes this by presenting written and video testimonials from first-time authors who found success with the program. Many of them explain how after years of struggling to write a book and making little progress, the program helped them structure a daily writing habit, eventually finishing a first draft that became a bestselling book on Amazon. The message is clear: Do you want to see similar results, or stay stuck in first gear, spinning your wheels but never finishing something you've always dreamed of doing? This message is driven home on the free consultation calls, as staff members ask what it would feel like to join the program and have a book published a year from now versus *not* joining the program and being in the same spot you are today.

By defining how much better life could be if your customer accepts the call to action, while also showing what it would look like if they choose *not* to engage with your business, you create stakes that help people decide to become a hero.

THE TAKEAWAY

Many of the most timeless stories share the same structure, called the **Hero's Journey.** This template can be used to construct a framework for how you relate to your customers.

In these stories, the **hero** is a character who wants something that is out of reach but meets a **guide,** who gives the hero a plan—and a call to action. The guide teaches the hero how to avoid failure and attain an ambitious goal, conquering evil and leading to a happy ending.

In business, **you are the guide** who clearly defines the problem and presents a plan for overcoming it. Sell your customers on your plan with a call to action that allows them to become the heroes of their own stories.

As the guide, you must **set the stakes** to gain buy-in from your customers, showing how sweet success can be if they heed your call to action and follow your plan—and what failure will look like if they don't.

CHAPTER 18

....

Refine How You Say It

n 2018, I received an email from a freelance writer named Lauren Brown West-Rosenthal. A fellow magazine junkie, Lauren spent years on staff at titles like *CosmoGIRL!* and *Us Weekly* before branching out on her own, writing for *Glamour, Parents,* and other big-name outlets, as well as E! and Bravo. She has interviewed A-listers like Anne Hathaway and Ariana Grande, and has even written biographies of Reese Witherspoon and Lindsay Lohan. She reached out to me because she was launching a blog and portfolio site and wanted some help with the design.

Truth be told, I was a bit overextended: I had recently accepted several new projects and also had a list of corporate clients that came with weekly, and often daily, design needs. Though I was on the fence about whether I had time to take on a new client, Lauren shared some of her writing with me, and I fell in love with her voice. She wanted a new logo, website, and blog, all branded with the nickname she had adopted: The Not So It Girl. I was definitely intrigued, but it was her blog's tagline that really sold me: "Lessons in Finding Success Even When Reality Stars Get You Fired, Bankruptcy Is Declared, and You're Faking It Until You Make It."

Look at social media today and you will see that almost everyone is talking about how amazing they are. Honestly, for years, I avoided having a professional presence on social media because it felt so egotistical. "Here are my accomplishments! Here are my fabulous vacation photos! Aren't I cool/smart/glamorous! Follow me!"

Lauren could have constructed her online presence as a highlight reel, as many of us do. But instead, in her blog posts and magazine essays, she writes about her career successes as well as her failures—from getting fired to feeling like an impostor in her job. Lauren's writing style is funny, friendly, and matter-of-fact—like a no-bullshit conversation with a close friend.

Though she has moved on from her Not So It Girl moniker (I guess we can't be boys and girls forever!), Lauren continues to write with humor and wit about her financial, parenting, and weight-loss ups and downs. By owning her mistakes and showing her human side, she has developed a voice that resonates with her audience—and continues to get her writing assignments—because it is both relatable and vulnerable.

DEVELOPING A BRAND VOICE

Trying to explain what makes a brand voice successful brings to mind the famous quote from Supreme Court Justice Potter Stewart. When asked to describe his test for obscenity, he wrote that although he couldn't *define* what makes something obscene, "I know it when I see it."[215]

Good editors realize that it's not just what you say but how you say it that truly resonates with readers. In the world of magazine publishing, editors often move around to different magazines, and each new role requires new ideas—but also a way to present familiar concepts through a new lens and brand voice. Even within the same category, subtleties in brand voice can and should exist. One brand may speak to you like a sassy best friend, while another may take a more earnest or even serious tone. A story about breast health, for instance, would have a different tone in *Cosmopolitan* than it would in *Prevention*.

Developing a voice for yourself or your brand can be tough, and there is definitely some trial and error involved. But once you find it, and start using it on a daily basis in the way you think and talk about your brand, you will find that it becomes a part of its DNA. Here are some tips for finding the right voice for your brand:

1. Start by going back to the basics.

If you have spent some time carefully crafting your vision, mission, and pillars or brand values, these can serve as a great starting point when developing your brand voice. For instance, let's recall the Chapter 9 examples from Marriott, the world's largest hospitality company that is the parent of 30-plus hotel brands. Although there were clear differences between the ultra-luxurious St. Regis and the fun-yet-budget-friendly Moxy Hotels, you can even see subtle differences between brands within the overarching luxury category.

For instance, on the Marriott page that lists all of its brands,[216] St. Regis falls under a heading of *Classic Luxury*, along with the JW Marriott and Ritz-Carlton brands. The language describing these brands evokes what we traditionally think of as the hallmarks of luxury; phrases like *impeccable service*, *modern indulgence*, and *refined taste* are used. But then, just below these three chains, there is a heading called *Distinctive Luxury*. Brands in this category offer luxury with a twist, and that twist is what helps each of them create a unique brand voice.

At W Hotels, for instance, you will find "an iconic lifestyle brand that boldly colors outside the lines of luxury."[217] Click through to its homepage, and you will see pictures of interiors with nightclub-inspired mood lighting, as well as blog posts that include interviews with house-music DJs and reviews of the latest albums and fashion. This distinct visual branding is echoed in the brand's playful voice, which can be easily seen in its naming conventions. The brand's most lavish rooms are called WOW Suites, while its pools and gyms are known as WET and SWEAT. According to the brand style guide, hotel programming should use similar naming, as seen in YUM packages that focus on enhanced dining experiences, as well as SIP—or Social Interactive Playtime—events, located in the hotels' swanky cocktail lounges. Like Moxy Hotels, this brand might appeal to a young and trendy crowd—but one who wants a more luxurious experience and is willing to pay for it.[218]

Also in the *Distinctive Luxury* category is a brand called The Luxury Collection: "a curated ensemble of the world's most iconic hotels that truly define their destinations."[219] With an emphasis on place, each property is "intrinsically connected to its locale." Click through to the brand's homepage and you will see aerial photos of Greek islands next to images of camels traversing the desert. For these hotels, the focus is less on the overarching brand than on the individual properties, appealing to travelers who seek immersion in the local culture. For several years, I designed marketing pieces for a Luxury Collection hotel in Chicago and learned the subtleties of the brand's tone firsthand. Its brand values included words like *indigenous, rare,* and *captivating,* while communications were used to "transport the guest through evocative storytelling, vivid descriptions, and engaging narratives." Unlike the playful voice of W Hotels, the Luxury Collection utilizes more refined language to engage "the seasoned traveler who craves the authentic."[220]

2. Next, revisit your persona and avatar.

In Chapter 15, I talked about how you should have a persona for your brand and also an avatar for your customer. Think of your brand and your customer as two people having a conversation. Your customer is the hero, and your brand is the guide—but guides can take on many forms. Do you speak to your customer like a cool, in-the-know friend? Or like an older, wiser mentor?

For years, *Parenting* magazine spoke in an earnest tone—like parenting advice from your doctor or perhaps your own mom. When editor in chief Ana Connery took the reins, she strived to make the content more conversational. The new tagline ("Modern Families + Fresh Ideas") helped inform this, as did the new avatar: a young mom in her 20s who watched reality television, came of age online, and was fluent in social media. An updated—and more fun—brand voice reflected this pivot, as did the covers, which began featuring celeb moms like Jessica Alba, Kourtney Kardashian, and Bethenny Frankel.

As you work on your brand voice, consider what other forms of media your target audience may be consuming. Although the nuances of voice vary, generally speaking, your brand should talk *to* your audience, not *at* them; it should sound familiar and resonate with your customers. As we learned in the last chapter, then best guides display equal parts of authority and empathy.

EDITOR'S TIP

Take risks when exploring your brand identity.

As founder of the brand consultancy Monologue and former VP of global editorial and publishing at Netflix, Michelle Lee knows what makes a world-class brand tick. While it may be tempting to copy a successful competitor, she recommends looking for "white space" in the market by focusing on what *isn't* currently being said and done. "Brand identity should be something that feels really authentic to you, but it also needs to feel original," she says. To achieve this, Lee told me that leaders must temper data about what is working in the marketplace with their own gut instincts—a lesson she learned during her six years as editor in chief of Condé Nast's beauty bible, *Allure*.

"I was brought on to be a transformational editor, so I had to take a risk sometimes and do something that no one else was doing," she says. In 2017, Lee put a hijab-wearing model on the cover—a first for a major U.S. magazine—and also banned the term "anti-aging" from *Allure*'s lexicon, sparking global conversation about how we speak about aging. "Everything has to come back to the people that you're trying to reach and what it is that they're looking for. If you only follow the data, you're actually never doing something new," she explains. "Because it's the risk that's the new thing, and there's no data that's going to show you whether or not that's going to work. Sometimes, you have to trust your gut."[221]

3. Then create a brand voice chart.

If a winning brand voice falls into the "I know it when I see it" realm, then sometimes the easiest way to nail down your voice is to write examples of what it is and isn't. If you Google "Brand Voice Chart," you can find lots of examples online. (You can also visit LeadLikeAnEditor.com to download a free workbook that includes a template.) Most follow a similar format:

- First, choose three words that describe your brand voice (you can add more later if you'd like).

- Then, write a description of what each characteristic means and examples of what it looks like in action—as well as what it doesn't look like.

THE TWO TYPES OF MESSAGING

Now that you have your brand voice nailed down, how exactly do you use it? Essentially, almost all of the messages that you communicate will be designed with one of two purposes in mind: either to make a sale or to build a relationship. Let's take a closer look at these two types of content.

CONTENT TYPE 1: Content That Converts

I've used *Men's Health* as an example twice now, both for its spot-on mission statement and enticing cover lines. I admire the brand and think it does a lot of things really well. But on December 10, 2009 (eight years before Hearst purchased *Men's Health*), the media world was abuzz about the magazine's most recent cover—and not for a positive reason.

That day, the now-defunct website Gawker.com published an article with the headline "*Men's Health* Loved This Cover So Much They Used It Twice." The article showed the December 2009 cover alongside the cover of the October 2007 issue. Gawker noted that, aside from showing a different actor, much of the new cover was very similar or, in some cases, exactly the same:

> The entire left side of cover lines has virtually identical copy and layout: the six pack abs, the poster, the results in nine days, the "gain muscle, lose weight," the ultimate nutrition plan, and the eat better and think smart. The 1,293 is the same even though apparently then it was what women want in bed and now it is tips to get money, fitness, sex, and nutrition. Is there something about the number 1,293 that focus groups really well? Or maybe a numerological thing?[222]

From left: the December 2009 and October 2007 covers of Men's Health

The following day, David Zinczenko, *Men's Health*'s editor in chief at the time, told the *New York Post* that it wasn't a mistake, but that the similar headlines only made it onto the newsstand copies; subscribers got something different. "It was only newsstand copies, it was not inadvertent, and it was part of overall branding strategies that we wouldn't share for magazines, books, international editions, mobile applications, or anything else," said Zinczenko.[223] Later that day, he elaborated in an interview with the website Mediaite: "Twenty years of *Men's Health* has certainly produced several lines that have proven themselves effective at the newsstand, which makes up about 20 percent of our print run. We plan to keep using the most effective marketing tools to reach the largest market we possibly can."[224]

For years, it has been a joke that health and fitness magazines recycle cover lines. Just take a look at the newsstand anytime during the month of January and count how many variations you see on the theme of reinvention. The cover line "New Year, New You!" has become such a cliché that some magazines have even bucked the trend with covers proclaiming "New Year, SAME YOU!" Although people in the media industry may have had a brief chuckle at *Men's Health*'s expense, no one was really surprised. The editors of that magazine—and many others—don't recycle cover lines because they are lazy. They do it because it works.

EDITOR'S TIP

Get help from the professionals.

Writing seems deceptively easy. Technically, everyone can do it—but that doesn't mean everyone is good at it. Hiring a pro to write sales copy can have a measurable return on investment; in fact, sometimes even the pros hire pros! Although *Entrepreneur* editor in chief Jason Feifer felt comfortable writing magazine articles, he always wondered why editors also wrote the cover lines, which are technically marketing copy used to sell issues. Since he wasn't trained as a marketer, Feifer hired a marketing agency to help him rethink cover lines and gained invaluable insight that resulted in a successful overhauling of the brand's covers. Strong sales followed, he reports, and "I realized ... how much value can come from seeing things in a new context."[225]

If you are considering hiring someone with writing and editing chops to lead your content strategy, I would recommend reaching out to Chandra Turner, founder of The Talent Fairy recruiting agency. As I mentioned in the introduction, she has made it her mission to connect leaders in a wide array of industries with her expansive network of talented professionals, most of whom were longtime magazine editors as well. Visit TheTalentFairy.com for more info.

Three Rules for Writing Content That Converts

In the last chapter, we learned that the key to winning over a potential customer is to find a pain point they have and show how your brand can serve as a guide that gives them a plan to solve that problem, making them a hero. While most great marketing, like most great stories, follows this structure, there are a few more points to keep in mind as you craft the actual messages your customer will encounter.

1. Be specific.

The more specific the problem you solve, the better and clearer your messaging can be. Good copywriting walks the line between being so general that no one really relates and so specific that only a small group will relate. You can't be all things to all people, so when in doubt, it is usually better to err on the side of specificity. Former *Cosmopolitan* editor Kate White explains that "thin-slicing" a concept can sometimes make it even stronger. A great cover line, she says, deals with a universal issue but hooks you by addressing a specific aspect of it. For example, compare the cover line *9 Stress-Busting Tips* to the more precise *What to Do When Stress Keeps You Up at Night.* "The second is just grabbier," she explains. "You can't help but wonder: How do they *know*?"[226]

Relatable subjects conveyed with a spot-on voice helped *Cosmo*'s cover lines earn a sterling reputation even *outside* of the publishing industry, says Chandra Turner, a former editor and founder of the boutique recruiting agency The Talent Fairy. Preparing for a move from magazines to the business world, Turner signed up for a content marketing course and discovered on the first day that she may have known more about the subject than she realized. "I got out my notepad, eager to write down all the secrets to this mysterious 'other side' of content creation. But I ended up not writing anything down," she recalls. "I remember clearly one lesson was all about writing snappy [email] subject lines. Their example for mastering copy like that? Look at *Cosmo*'s cover lines. That's when I relaxed. After all, I was an editor at both *Cosmopolitan* and *CosmoGIRL!* where I wrote lots and lots of cover lines. *I can do this!*"[227]

2. Don't be afraid to repeat yourself.

If you are working on a product or service that solves a specific problem, you may spend most of your workday thinking about it. But for your customer, the problem is likely one of many pain points in their lives. Although they might identify with the solution that you offer, it may take some time for that realization to kick in.

Often attributed to Benjamin Franklin, the phrase, "If you fail to plan, you plan to fail," informs the philosophy behind many of the offerings at SelfPublishing.com. The company doesn't need to convince people to write a book; most customers who come to their site already have the desire and are well aware of the pain point of wanting to write a book, perhaps even having tried to write a book, and never finishing.

What their customers need is a guide with a *plan* to help them *succeed.* And that is the main thing the company sells them. It's no accident that its homepage uses the word *plan* 12 times and the words *succeed* or *success* nine times. For instance, they want you to call so that they can "help you create a personalized publishing **plan** that sets you up for **success** from the start." They call their five-step process the "Author **Success Plan**."[228]

Don't be afraid of repeating your key points in your sales copy or in your conversations with customers. People learn through repetition and don't always pick up on something the first or even second time. To avoid sounding like a robot, try making the same point but in a different way each time. In his bestselling book *The Ultimate Sales Letter*, marketing expert Dan S. Kennedy offers examples of ways you can tell a customer the same thing:[229]

- In a straight-forward statement

- In an example

- In a brief story, sometimes called a "slice of life"

- In testimonials

- In a quote from a customer, expert, or other spokesperson

- In a numbered summary

We can see this played out on the SelfPublishing.com homepage. Yes, the word *plan* is used a dozen times, but sometimes it is used in larger headlines, while at other times it appears in a direct statement, a numbered list, and even in a quote from a satisfied customer.

3. Test your idea.

Great marketers know that the only way to fine-tune their sales presentations is to test them over and over again. Although that 2009 *Men's Health* cover may have looked like a lazy recycling of cover lines, each of those phrases had been tested on covers before and had proven to sell. In fact, Gawker later revealed that some of the lines had not been used twice, as originally thought, but several times over the years.[230]

When I worked at Time Inc., we were encouraged to do A/B cover testing often. Sometimes we would send a cover to the printer two different ways: version A would be the control, and version B would have a variation. This could be a slightly different blurb or maybe a different color that was used, or perhaps one of the cover lines would be inside a circle or button. By doing this over and over and seeing which version sold better on the newsstand, we were able to hone our messaging so that we could use the words, colors, and design elements that readers preferred. It would often take months for the final sales results to be tallied, but there may be quicker ways to test sales copy in your business. If you sell online, it can be relatively easy to set up a test site with two slightly different landing pages to see which converts better. The results may surprise you.

EDITOR'S TIP
—
Test one thing at a time.

If you think back to high school science class, you may recall that when you are testing a hypothesis, you must control all other aspects *except* for the one variable you are testing. The same is true in marketing. Choose one thing to focus on for each test, be it a particular image, the wording of a main headline, or perhaps the placement or color of a BUY NOW button. If you create two landing pages with different copy, different images, and different layouts, you'll never know whether it was the text or design that customers preferred.

CONTENT TYPE 2: Content That Builds Relationships

In his book *Build for Tomorrow,* author and editor in chief of *Entrepreneur* Jason Feifer talks about how he travels around the country giving keynote speeches on his signature topic: finding opportunity in change. When you are facing a change in your life or in your work, one of the practices he advocates is asking yourself: "What is this for?" In the case of media companies, Feifer believes that in order for them to survive, they must ask themselves: "What is *content* for?" The answer, he says, may prove that they need to expand beyond the content business.

"Today, content is for building relationships," he says. "People trust a media outlet because of its content, even if they don't regularly read it." Drilling down, if content is for building relationships, then what are relationships for? "Relationships are an opportunity," he continues. "An opportunity to provide products and services that people will pay for, because of the trust that has been built by the content."[231]

Traditional media has certainly shifted, but it isn't dead. In fact, decades of content production—and the level of authority and trust that content fostered—have enabled many brands to pivot into other streams of revenue. In the introduction to this book, I talked about how *Good Housekeeping* still produces a print magazine but also earns money from membership programs, books, in-person events and expos, branded products, and e-commerce. Similarly, Feifer's own brand *Entrepreneur* has expanded from just writing about entrepreneurs to offering books, events, online webinars, e-commerce, memberships, and even virtual business consulting.

EDITOR'S TIP

—

In relationship-building content, don't try to sell.

While content that converts should include a clear CTA early on, content that builds relationships may not mention the product at all. (As an example, check out the exercise and nutrition plans on Peloton's blog.) For this type of content, companies often hire former magazine editors to write in a voice that resonates with consumers and strengthens ties to the brand—without overtly selling to them.

As a former editorial director at Nike, Sarah Z. Wexler oversaw the launch of the Nike Training Club App's first paid subscription program, which included more than a hundred articles and video scripts. For this level of content creation—a first for Nike—Wexler leaned on her experience having written for dozens of magazines, ultimately developing a brand voice that fell somewhere between the enthusiasm of a fitness publication and the "cool guy" vibe of *Esquire*, where she worked early in her career. "People already trusted Nike and its celebrity trainers, who were our experts," she told me. "Our goal was to keep the brand cool and *not* make the content feel cheesy, like we were selling something. It had to feel really authentic."

By providing service rather than selling, the app resonated with consumers, who logged on for exercise content but often turned to Nike for merchandise as well—a result of their positive (and sales-free) customer experience.[232]

Five Types of Relationship-Building Content and How to Use Them

The best relationship-building content offers a story, a chance to connect, or helpful information to your customer, bringing value to their lives and credibility to your brand. This can be done in several different ways:

- **Personal Stories:** Telling stories about real people helps build emotional connections and fosters empathy. You can share narratives that resonate with your audience via personal anecdotes, profiles, and case studies.

- **User-Generated Content (UGC):** Keep in mind that the best stories are often told by the people who lived them. Encouraging your audience to contribute their own images, reviews, or testimonials not only fosters a sense of community but also demonstrates social proof and authenticity.

- **Interactive Content:** Boost audience engagement with interactive content pieces such as quizzes, polls, surveys, and contests. This type of content invites two-way communication and strengthens relationships by involving the audience in a way that feels fun and even game-like for them.

- **Service Content:** By providing valuable educational resources—or service content, in magazine-speak—you can empower your audience to improve their lives. Sharing your expertise via how-to guides, tutorials, or industry insights helps position your brand as a trusted guide.

- **Community Content:** Creating opportunities for your audience to connect with each other can foster a sense of community that brings them back to your brand week after week. Consider hosting online forums, Facebook Groups, or live events where your audience can share their experiences, ideas, and advice with each other.

Five Rules for Relationship-Building Content

If you are going to the trouble of creating unique content to build relationships with your customers, it is imperative that you make the most of the endeavor by having clear goals and monitoring customer response to your content. With that in mind, here are a few best practices:

- **Make it personal.** Tailor your content to specific segments of your audience based on their interests, preferences, and behaviors. Personalized content resonates more deeply with individuals, making them feel understood and valued.

- **Respond to feedback.** On social media, don't "post and ghost." Actively listen to your audience's comments and inquiries, responding promptly and thoughtfully to demonstrate that you value their input.

- **Keep communication consistent.** Instead of pursuing short-term transactions, nurture ongoing engagement with your audience via email newsletters, social media updates, blog posts, and podcasts. Consistent communication strengthens the relationship over time, helping keep your brand top of mind while also demonstrating your commitment to their success. And don't worry about a bit of repetition across platforms; no one sees every piece of content you create.

- **Offer empathy and support.** Keep relationship-building content positive by offering empathy about your audience's challenges. By providing support, encouragement, and solutions to help them overcome obstacles and achieve success, you will again position your brand as a trusted guide.

- **Make the most of your effort.** While this type of content doesn't need to sell directly, you should have some clear goals for it. At the very least, it should offer an opportunity for potential customers to continue an ongoing relationship with your brand. This could mean having a CTA button at the end, or if that feels too salesy, a spot to sign up for your email newsletter to receive a free lead magnet.

EDITOR'S TIP

Build your email list with a lead magnet.

Any marketer will tell you that a good email list is like gold. One of the best ways to get customers' email addresses, placing them into your sales funnel for current and future promotions, is to offer a free lead magnet. This is usually a downloadable digital file that delivers high-value content to the consumer, in exchange for entering their email address. It can be a guide, an action plan, a checklist, or some other useful tool that provides immediate value, so that a customer won't feel duped once they download it. To grow the email list for VERANDA's free "Trade Secrets" newsletter, which is targeted to interior designers, we offer new subscribers "Our Exclusive Guide to the Perfect Pitch" with editors' tips they can use when submitting their latest decorating projects for publication.

Similarly, ThePointsGuy.com—a site that explains how to maximize credit card points for travel—offers new subscribers a chart that shows how much Chase, Citibank, and American Express points are worth if you transfer them to various airlines or hotels. Even better, the chart is followed by a step-by-step guide for how to make these transfers. I signed up for their email list just to get this PDF and reference it often. I have even recommended this freebie to friends.

Technically, new followers who sign up *only* to get your lead magnet could unsubscribe after receiving the free download, but if the content in your lead magnet is truly high-value, people will likely stay on your list to see what other useful nuggets you will provide.

THE TAKEAWAY

Develop an authentic **brand voice** that resonates with your ideal customer by revisiting your vision, mission, and pillars (or brand values).

To make sure your messaging stays on brand, create a list of characteristics that describe your voice and organize them into a **brand voice chart**, adding examples of what your brand does and doesn't sound like.

There are two types of content: content that converts and content that builds relationships. It is important to know *why* you are creating a piece of content before you begin working on it.

When creating **content that converts,** be specific, use repetition to drive home your point, and test relentlessly to see what is working.

Content that builds relationships doesn't need to sell customers on your brand. Rather, it should be personal and offer immense value, guidance, empathy, and the opportunity for connection. While you aren't selling, you *should* provide a way for the customer to continue receiving communication from you, fostering a long-term relationship.

Visit **LeadLikeAnEditor.com** to download a free workbook that includes a **Brand Voice Chart** template, as well as other guides and resources.

CHAPTER 19

Polish How You Package It

n 2007, when I was just a few years into my career, I met Carla Frank, the founding design director of *O, The Oprah Magazine,* which was one of the hottest titles on the newsstand and had been called the most successful magazine launch in recent history.[233] We met at a Society of Publication Designers "Pub Crawl"—short for Publication Crawl—that offered a group of junior and student designers the chance to visit several magazine offices throughout Manhattan and meet with the top person on each creative team. There was a snowstorm that day, so I was one of the only people who showed up for the tour, giving me a one-on-one audience with Carla, as well as the design directors at *Entertainment Weekly*—a testament to the power of showing up no matter what.

At that meeting, Carla shared two of her insights about magazines, which could also be applied to other brands. When I questioned why the design of one section appeared a bit different than others, she said that magazines are like people—sometimes they have a few unexpected idiosyncrasies. Then as we were looking at images from a recent fashion photoshoot, she explained how every minute detail worked together to create the overall effect. "You can have the perfect set, the perfect model, and the perfect outfit," she said, "but the wrong shoe can ruin the whole thing."

THE BRAND IS IN THE DETAILS

Flash forward six years, and I was now running the creative team at a national magazine. For the 2013 redesign of *Coastal Living*, the editor in chief Antonia and I decided we wanted a cover that really made a splash—something the magazine had never done before. Although we had photographed all sorts of subjects for our covers in the past—beaches, interiors, and even food—we had never put a celebrity on the cover.

For years, lifestyle and fashion magazines had often shown models on their covers, but in the late 1990s, as the era of the supermodel waned and celebrity obsession began to reach a peak, editors began to wise up and realize that celebrities came with a built-in fan base and selling power.[234] But at *Coastal Living*, we had a delicate line to toe because our readers consistently said they turned to the magazine to get *away* from the media onslaught of their everyday lives. We knew we had to find a celebrity who was both aspirational *and* relatable, stylish but also with an interior design background. And above all else, the person had to be inherently, authentically coastal.

In the end, we chose India Hicks, who is tall and blond, with a beachy laid-back glamour. She came by her design roots honestly, as India's father, the acclaimed British interior designer David Hicks, was known for creating fabulously chic rooms in the 1960s and 1970s. The family are cousins of British royalty, and India was a bridesmaid in Prince Charles and Princess Diana's 1981 wedding. Though they had spent much of their time in the U.K., the family also owned properties in the Bahamas; India, in particular, had taken the coastal lifestyle and run with it, making Harbour Island her main home, and launching island-inspired jewelry and home decor lines. Adding to her appeal, she was also a recognizable face to design enthusiasts, as she had hosted the second season of the Bravo reality series *Top Design*.

With a crew of almost ten in tow, we took off to Windermere Island in the Bahamas to shoot India at her late father's home, which she had renovated to its original glory after a hurricane ravaged the island. This wasn't the first time a big photoshoot had taken place there; the mid-century modern home had been the backdrop for iconic portraits of the Hicks family, taken in 1980 by the legendary photographer Slim Aarons. (A fun sidenote: With few hotels nearby, my editor Antonia and I spent the shoot bunking at the family's cottage across the road from the main house, where Charles and Diana had slept when they visited!)

For the shoot, we brought along a hair and makeup team, as well as a fashion stylist who flew in from New York with gorgeous gowns, chic jumpsuits, and an entire case of Christian Louboutin heels. As we shot India all over the house in various ensembles, I remember her saying to her daughter Domino: "Look at mommy's beautiful shoes—your Uncle Christian designed these!" The woman was connected.

But something about the whole thing didn't feel right; we knew it, and so did India. *Coastal Living* readers love the authentic "beach lifestyle," which India Hicks certainly lives. But they also know that island life is all about being laid-back. Our readers wanted to see well-designed but comfy sofas that you might flop on in a wet bathing suit, as well as chic rugs that you still felt comfortable padding across with sandy feet.

For our final shots, we photographed India with toned down hair and makeup, in a strapless sundress, barefoot. And after we had gotten lots of great shots in the living room, we took her right out to the porch—and then down to the beach—with kids and dogs in tow.

The cover was a success, and at a party held to celebrate the launch of the redesign, India thanked our editor in chief for skipping the Louboutins and running the shot of her barefoot in a sundress. It made sense for our brand and for hers.

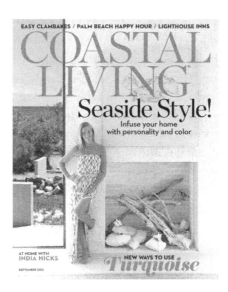

India Hicks on the September 2013 cover of Coastal Living

CURATE YOUR MESSAGE

Have you ever visited a boutique that made you feel like you needed every-thing there, as if it had somehow all been hand-selected for you? This usually means that the shop has been carefully curated—and the ideal customer that the shop owner had in mind is probably very similar to you.

Just like at an art gallery or museum, careful curation is also the back-bone of successful magazines. The internet has made it easy to call up info in a second, which certainly has its advantages when you are looking for the answer to a very specific question. But the problem with using a blind web search to get all of your information is that there is too much choice, and often it's hard to know the accuracy of facts sourced from a random site.

For the last century, people have relied on magazines for info about all sorts of things, from the top holiday gifts to the best cleaning supplies to the hottest vacation destinations. Sometimes we don't want or need all of the information in the world at our fingertips; what we really need is someone to curate it for us. Although anyone can post an article online, and any website can post hundreds of articles a day if they have the manpower (or access to AI), sometimes less can be more.

With a finite number of pages, magazine editors make tough choices each issue—and really, each day—about what stories are important enough to print. For years, *Entertainment Weekly* published the "The Must List," which let readers know in a single spread what 10 movies, albums, TV shows, and books were hot that week. I love it when people do the work for me.

Many studies have documented what researchers call the Paradox of Choice, and most seem to come to the same conclusion: As humans, we think we want lots of choices, but oftentimes, this can lead to confusion and become debilitating.[235] We are usually happier with a few good choices.

Curating for your customer is a powerful strategy from the editor's playbook that can improve the messages you communicate, the design of those messages, and even the products those messages are intended to sell. For instance, if you are opening a new restaurant, start by curating the menu for your guests. A beautifully designed and printed menu with clear sections for appetizers, entrees, and side dishes is much easier to read than the digital "running list" menus that we accessed by QR code during the pandemic—and sadly, that remain in many establishments. But while the design of a menu is important, so is the content it shows. Smaller, more curated menus have been trending at upscale restaurants for several years because they allow chefs to do a few things well—and because most people would rather choose from a dozen entree options, rather than 100.

Along those lines, if you sell consumer packaged goods, consider how many variations you really need to produce. I recently read a glowing review of Colgate's Optic White toothpaste on GoodHousekeeping.com and was excited to try it. But in the aisle at CVS, my excitement waned and confusion set in. There were 15 variations of Optic White toothpaste, not to mention another 15 non-Optic-White Colgate varieties. How different are people's teeth that we need 30 toothpaste options from a single brand?

Although these examples veer more into the product realm, which we will talk about in the next section, the marketing that each of these products requires overcomplicates the messages the company must send to differentiate between its various options. When it comes to messaging, it's good to leave your customer with a KISS: "Keep it short and simple," or the more spirited version, "Keep it simple, stupid."

When designing a landing page for your product or the homepage of your website, it can be tempting to include as much information as possible. But remember: People usually scan websites, rather than reading every word. If you have thousands of words on your homepage, visitors could easily miss the main point because it got buried in the word soup.

As the world's most visited website, Google has just five words in buttons on the center of its homepage: "Google Search" and "I'm Feeling Lucky." Those two phrases accomplish a lot. The call to action is clear in the first button, and the second button displays some of the cheeky personality the company has become known for.

EDITOR'S TIP

Ensure your website passes the grunt test.

Author and marketing expert Donald Miller asks new consulting clients whether their websites can pass the grunt test, and I pose the same question to you. In other words, are your offering and purpose so clear that a caveman could look at your site for five seconds and grunt out the answers to three key questions:

1. What do you offer?

2. How will it make my life better?

3. What do I need to do to buy it?[236]

The most effective websites deliver this info in a few sentences set in large, easy-to-read type at the top of the homepage, immediately followed by a CTA button with a short phrase like *Buy Now* or *Get a Quote*. "If those three questions cannot be answered within five seconds of looking at your website, you're losing money," Miller writes in his book *Business Made Simple*.[237]

Magazines have followed this intrinsically for years in their carefully curated cover lines. The website grunt test more or less began as the grocery store grunt test: In the seconds between putting their items on the checkout conveyor belt and paying, could supermarket shoppers see what your magazine offered and how it could improve their lives by helping them stress less, make easier weeknight meals, or lose weight without giving up carbs?

People need to be convinced that your product will help them improve their lives *before* they learn about the history of your family-owned business or that you received an award from your local chamber of commerce. It's fine to include that information elsewhere on the site in an "About" section, for those who want to do a deep dive or need more convincing. But on the homepage, make sure you have clearly answered their three main questions first.

HOW TO DESIGN YOUR MESSAGE

Over the course of my career, I've spent tens of thousands of hours focused on information design. This has largely been in the world of publishing, but I have also designed marketing materials for a variety of other ventures, ranging from TV shows and retailers to cruise lines and hotels. Though a full exploration of graphic design is beyond the scope of this book, most of what I have learned can be boiled down to this: People *do* judge a book by its cover. In other words, what we say matters, but the way we present it is often just as important. Here are some of my rules for packaging your message in a way that your audience will love:

1. Don't skimp on design.

Whether it's an ad, website, or product packaging, make sure you hire a professional designer, or at least consult with one. Design can be fun, and the people who package modern computer software would have you believe that anyone can be a designer. (Now there's some effective messaging!) But too many times I have seen people shell out for expensive design programs and then open them with confused looks on their faces. Alas, you can't expect to press a button and have Adobe Photoshop spit out a gorgeous ad any more than you can expect to become the next Picasso overnight just because you bought a paintbrush.

It has taken years of experience for you to gain *your* specialized knowledge and skills; similarly, graphic design is learned over time. If you are interested in learning design, you can certainly take a class or teach yourself using online tools—but it is unlikely that your initial results will be suitable for a world-class brand.

The good news is that there are great designers at all price points and in all styles. Ask another business owner who they use, or look online at sites like 99designs.com. You might be surprised to find that having something professionally designed makes you fall in love with the end product even more—and gives you more confidence when you share it with the world.

EDITOR'S TIP
—
Choose the right designer for your brand.

Whether you seek out a new designer online or talk to someone who was recommended, make sure their aesthetic fits your brand. Ask what types of projects they have worked on before, and don't hire anyone without taking a peek at their portfolio. While there are lots of great designers out there, not everyone shares the same skills and taste. And remember: Sometimes even the pros hire pros. When we revamped the *Coastal Living* logo in 2013, I hired a typography designer who specialized in creating and modifying fonts. Technically, I *could* have done the work myself, but for such an important project, going with an expert was worth it.

2. Create a look your audience will love.

Good design doesn't have to be complicated—it just has to resonate with your audience. And of course, it helps if you know who your audience is (see Chapter 15). For years, teen magazines were known for their collage-style layouts, which resonated with girls who pieced together similar collages in scrapbooks or on the walls of their bedrooms. These publications also used bright colors in their type and graphics to create a fun and youthful vibe.

Contrast this with most high-fashion magazines, which barely use color at all. *Vogue, Elle, Harper's Bazaar, Town & Country*—pick up a copy and you will see they only use black type, with perhaps an occasional pop of red. This simplified color palette allows the photography to shine, while serving as a visual shorthand for luxury.

I love the branding for JLo Beauty, the skincare line launched by Jennifer Lopez in 2021. In addition to close-up shots of the star's flawless skin, the branding and packaging uses soft beiges and pinks, mixed with a signature copper color. From the buttons on the website to the bottles of cleanser, this shimmering metallic shade telegraphs a sense of richness and luxury, while also hinting at the glowing bronze complexion that has become Lopez's hallmark—or as her messaging phrases it, "That JLo Glow."

3. Show what's important.

Open a magazine and take a moment to notice everything *except* the words in the articles. There are photos and illustrations, of course, and these often help depict what the text describes. To explain a more complex concept, a layout may also include an infographic, which is another word for a chart or graph. These can be especially helpful when you are trying to illustrate a key point involving numbers.

Once you've made it past these more visual elements, I want you to also look at the display copy, which is editor-speak for all of the other text that *isn't* the running text of the story. There are headlines, subheads, captions, and often large quotes pulled out from the text. All of these help readers see what the story is about at a glance. They create a visual hierarchy by highlighting what is important so that readers can get the gist and decide if they want to dive in further. They also provide entry points into longer articles; one reader may be drawn in by the headline while another person's eye may land on a caption or pull quote first.

Finally, look at the white space. When you are creating a layout for a marketing piece, it can be tempting to fill the page with text and images, but sometimes what *isn't* on the page can help what *is* on the page stand out. Often, when I have created a layout for a magazine feature, I will step away and come back the next day to look at it with fresh eyes. Many times, this results in my adjusting all of the elements slightly so there is a bit more negative space on the page. For a master class in using white space, check out *Real Simple* magazine. Its brand promise—practical solutions to everyday problems, presented in a simple, relaxing format—results in articles that even *look* light and airy, without text and images crowding every inch of the page.

4. Surprise and delight your customer.

If you have created a brand that people immediately recognize, congrats—that is really an accomplishment. But don't forget to surprise and delight your customers along the way. For a VERANDA article about new skyscrapers returning to classic design styles, we deviated from our usual imagery of beautiful homes to show a "skyline" we created using the photos of the buildings mentioned in the story. Another time, at *Parenting*, we analyzed the details of a kiddo's back-to-school outfit in greater detail by printing the vertical image sideways across a spread, requiring readers to turn the magazine 90 degrees to read it.

Spread designs that mixed things up a bit in the pages of VERANDA *and* Parenting

Delight can be funny too. Dollar Shave Club launched in 2011 with a fun logo and compelling name, but it was the irreverent YouTube video featuring its founder Michael Dubin sarcastically lampooning other overpriced razor companies that helped the business achieve buzzworthy status. The viral video brought in 12,000 orders in the 48 hours after it was released and has been viewed more than 28 million times. The popular commercial cut through the noise, continually drawing in new customers and allowing Dubin and his partner to sell the brand to Unilever for $1 billion just a few years later.[238]

THE TAKEAWAY

Branding is in the details, and that includes the visual details. How your message is packaged is just as important as the message itself.

Curate your messages to be short and to the point. Remember the KISS principle: "Keep it short and simple," or if you prefer, "Keep it simple, stupid."

Don't skimp on design: Whether we like it or not, people *do* judge a book by its cover.

Create a look your audience will love by choosing a design aesthetic that is appropriate to your brand and your customer.

Show what's important by creating a **visual hierarchy** of information in your messaging. On your website, this means answering three questions at the top of the page: What do you offer? How will it make my life better? What do I need to do to buy it?

While your core branding should be simple and clear, don't forget to **surprise and delight** your customers from time to time. This could be done via an unexpected design element, something that requires them to interact with the product in a different way, or even using humor in your messaging.

PART SEVEN

P is for

PRODUCT

> ### "Don't find customers for your products; find products for your customers."
>
> *—Seth Godin, bestselling author and entrepreneur*

My freshman year of college, I began working part-time as a sales associate at The Body Shop. Founded in 1976 by Anita Roddick, the company had a backstory that I loved. Throughout her 20s, Roddick had traveled the globe, and in each new place she visited, she noticed how beautiful the local women were and asked what products they used on their skin. The answers surprised her: cocoa butter in Tahiti, rice scrubs in Japan, oil from the Brazil nut in South America, and so on. When she returned home to Brighton, England, Roddick experimented with making products based on these ingredients, selling them out of a small shop to help support her and her family. The products were an instant hit, and Roddick opened a second store the following year in 1977.[239] Almost 50 years later, The Body Shop operates around 3,000 stores in more than 70 countries.[240]

When I started in 1998, employees were offered extensive training in the stories behind the products. For each offering, we were required to learn:

- three *ingredients* in the product,

- three *benefits* it provided,

- and three *other products* that complemented it.

In addition, every product had a tester bottle, which we used to fill sample vials for ourselves and for curious customers who may not be ready to buy. Because I had learned about and tried every product, while also learning the *Why* behind the company's support of humanitarian and animal-rights charities, selling The Body Shop's wares came naturally to me and even gave me a sense of purpose as a salesperson.

Although I worked on and off with the company for four years, there was a brief period during my junior year when I worked as a sales associate at the clothing store Guess. On paper, this job wasn't much different: Both were retail gigs in the same mall, paying a similar wage. But at Guess, selling didn't come easily to me. A bit embarrassed by my performance, I told our district manager how I had excelled at The Body Shop, where I could explain the benefits of each item. I asked if he had any tips. "You're not selling benefits," he reminded me. "You're selling style."

Now, it could be argued that the benefits were less direct; perhaps I could talk about how a top flattered someone's shape, even if I wasn't educated on the fabric it was made from. But I am not a fashionista at heart, and for me personally, style without substance made for a difficult sell. I lasted less than a year at the job before making the move back to The Body Shop.

When you have a product or service with substance, one that allows you to bring immense value to your customers and helps them solve a problem, the messaging that we talked about in the last section almost seems to fall into place. If you have a product that *really* delivers the goods, asking people to buy it isn't self-serving; quite the opposite, it would be selfish *not* to share your amazing creation with the world.

BUILD LIKE AN EDITOR: CREATING A PRODUCT PEOPLE WILL LOVE

There are two parts to creating a product or service that flies off the shelves. The following chapters will teach you to:

- **Create a product** that your customers need and that will improve their lives, addressing a pain point they may have.

- **Deliver that product** seamlessly in the way they want to receive it.

If you are starting a business, this section will teach you how to hone your products or services to serve your customer best. And if you are a leader at a company that already has a well-defined offering, you will learn how your lineup can be improved, expanded, or sold in new ways. The most important thing to remember is this: When your product has real substance and is delivered in a convenient way that helps make people's lives better, you are no longer *selling* but rather *serving*. Are you ready to start?

....

CHAPTER 20

Create the Product Your Customers Need

When Abe Peck—the grad school professor who I mentioned in Chapter 4—spent a full day teaching about B2B publishing, some of my classmates' eyes glazed over. The problem wasn't Abe's teaching style—trust me, he's hilarious—but rather the subject.

Most of us had come to grad school with dreams of working for the biggest magazines in the industry. Newshounds fantasized about bylines in *Time* or *Newsweek*, while the more stylish among us had their sights set on *Harper's Bazaar* and *Vogue*. Working at *Drug Store News* and covering the latest Walgreens financial report wasn't on anyone's vision board. But something Abe said that day caught my attention: He recommended that we consider at least *starting* our careers at B2B publications. Entry salaries were often higher, he told us, and from day one we would play an integral part of a small staff.

This stuck with me, and a few weeks later, when Abe invited the class to happy hour with a few alumni who were in town from New York City—and who all worked at small trade publications—I was one of only two students who attended. Over drinks, I chatted with an editor who worked for *Home Channel News,* a trade publication covering the channel of distribution for products in the home improvement industry. Although it wasn't exactly one of the gorgeous interior design titles I had dreamed of working for, I took her business card, kept in touch throughout the year, and contacted her just before graduating. I was in luck, she said: The magazine had an immediate opening for someone who knew layout programs *and* could also copy edit.

A few weeks later, I had moved to New York City and landed a job as the publication's sole designer and copy editor. While many of my classmates competed for entry-level editorial assistant positions at major magazines, almost overnight I went from being a student to having responsibility for the layout, imagery, and accuracy of every article in a national, biweekly publication. What I had needed was a job; what I got was a crash course in creating a top-notch product for a niche audience.

THERE ARE RICHES IN THE NICHES

When I started at *Home Channel News*, its parent company—Lebhar-Friedman, Inc.—was the world's largest independent trade publisher for the retail and food service industries. It launched in 1925 with *Chain Store Age*, which its founders created to serve an emerging wave of multi-location retailers and their suppliers. As the industries it covered blossomed throughout the 20th century, Lebhar-Friedman grew with them. Along the way, its roster expanded to include titles like *Nation's Restaurant News* and *Drug Store News*, as well as a range of directories, newsletters, and websites, and even a few trade shows and conferences.

Did the company publish sexy newsstand titles like *Vogue* or *Vanity Fair*? Certainly not. But in a crowded marketplace, those brands face fierce competition—not only for single-copy sales and subscriptions but also for the dollars of luxury goods advertisers, who have no shortage of ways to reach high-end consumers.

For the industries that Lebhar-Friedman covered, the competition was much less stiff, and from the beginning, the company dominated many of the categories it covered. If you were an executive at Walgreens, *Drug Store News* was mandatory reading for industry insights. Similarly, if you had a product or service you wanted those Walgreens executives to see, you advertised in *Drug Store News*—end of story. The company may not have been on the same scale as Condé Nast or Hearst, but when I started in 2004, it employed several hundred people, had yearly sales of almost $100 million, and occupied two floors of a Park Avenue high rise.[241] Not bad for a privately held company that most people had never heard of.

When you are defining your target customer, building a product to serve them, and crafting the message that tells them about the product, it can be tempting to try to be all things to all people. It's easy to look at businesses like Disney or Apple and conclude that the secret to global domination is offering something for everyone. But like Lebhar-Friedman, both of these mega-companies started with products that catered to a specialized—and often underserved—market.

Before it owned billion-dollar theme parks and cruise lines; major entertainment franchises like Star Wars and Marvel; and channels of distribution as varied as ESPN, ABC, and Hulu, Disney launched more than a century ago as a studio for full-length animated films—a category that may seem broad by today's standards but at the time was so small that it didn't even exist yet! Similarly, though they are now known for innovating best-in-class smartphones, watches, and tablets, Apple started by making easy-to-use desktop computers specifically for individuals. Though that market has grown immeasurably in the past four decades, when Steve Jobs introduced the first Apple Macintosh in 1984, selling computers for people to use at home was considered quite specialized; most of the nascent computing industry was focused on providing technology solutions for large companies.

FIVE REASONS TO NICHE DOWN

If you try to have your product mean something to everyone when you start, you can end up having it meaning nothing to anyone. What I would recommend instead is to drill down as far as you can on your ideal customer and offering. This will help you in five key ways:

1. It's easier to know your audience.

When I started my first business, I had some legal and tax-related questions that were somewhat specific to my own situation. I searched Amazon for a book that might have the answers, but I found that many of the most popular business titles were long, comprehensive tomes that seemed a bit intimidating to a first-time entrepreneur.

Eventually I came across two books that did catch my eye. The first, by Bernard B. Kamoroff, was titled *Small Time Operator: How to Start Your Own Business, Keep Your Books, Pay Your Taxes, and Stay Out of Trouble.* Designed specifically for small businesses, the book and its cheeky subtitle covered many of the pain points I was already facing.

Even more on topic was the second book I bought, June Walker's *The Confident Indie: A Simple Guide to Deductions, Income and Taxes for the Creatively Self-Employed.* This book offered sound advice for artists, performers, and entrepreneurs in creative industries, using examples common to those trades.

At just over 200 pages each, neither of these books were as comprehensive as some of the 500-page business bibles I saw on Amazon. But both authors knew their audience well—and as a member of their target demographic, I felt like they were speaking directly to me.

Often, this feeling of having a product made just for you can lead to higher customer engagement. In the case of magazines, consumers tend to spend longer engaging with issues of more niche brands. According to 2023 data, VERANDA readers spent an average of 48 minutes with each issue—the highest rate in our competitive set and third-highest rate at Hearst—despite the fact that we are one of the company's smallest editorial brands.

2. It's easier to hone your brand voice.

Once you know your audience and avatar, it is a snap to hone your voice because you know exactly who you are speaking to. Editors are true masters at this craft; throughout their careers, many moved around from publication to publication, learning the specifics of each magazine's avatar. For this reason, an article about something as commonplace as planning a trip will sound different in *Travel + Leisure* than it will in *Real Simple* or *Cosmopolitan*. Knowing your very specific customer will make it easier to speak to them using examples and language that resonate. If you are also a member of this demographic and have chosen to be the face of the brand, customers will likely respond to the authenticity of your brand voice and support you because they feel like they know you and find you relatable.

In fact, your brand probably *shouldn't* resonate with everyone. The branding company Worstofall Design (a play on co-owner Steve Wasterval's last name) intentionally wants people who *don't* align with its edgy "badass brand" values to steer clear. "Badass brands require guts, because being loved by some means being misunderstood, and even disliked, by others. They stand against something as much as they stand for something," the agency's homepage explains. "Badass brands are brave, sometimes irreverent, and always unapologetic and for it they gain a kind of loyal following that can't be bought, only earned."[242]

3. You can create products to meet a specialized need.

When Alli Webb founded the hair styling salon Drybar, she didn't cater to every man, woman, and child who needed a haircut. She didn't even focus on women and their myriad haircare needs, from cuts and coloring to extensions. Instead of being just another salon, Drybar set itself apart with what it was—and what it wasn't. The motto of Drybar is "No cuts. No color. Just blowouts."

By drilling down on a specific niche in the haircare market, Drybar soon became a salon brand women everywhere associated with hair *styling*. In New York City and Los Angeles, trips to Drybar became weekly and sometimes even daily occurrences for women in high-powered roles—including many top magazine editors—where a carefully coiffed image was paramount.[243]

4. Qualified leads and referrals are easier to come by.

When you have a product or service that caters to a very specific avatar, getting new customers becomes much easier. If you asked me to recommend "a good lawyer," I wouldn't know who to name. Are you being sued? Contemplating a divorce? Ready to write a will? Or buy a house? A general practice attorney I know may technically be able to help with any of those things, but that doesn't necessarily make them the first person that comes to mind.

But if you said, "I am a creative entrepreneur with a new business idea that I think is groundbreaking and am looking for someone to help me think through whether I should trademark the idea before starting to work on it"—well, then I know just who to tell you to call. When you cater to a specific person with a specific problem, it stands to reason that your ideal customer may know other people who are facing the same issue. If you invite them into your story and serve as a guide, helping to solve their problem, they will be more likely to recommend you the next time a friend mentions having a similar problem.

5. It allows you to consider a B2B model.

If you have an existing B2C business with a strong product and message that caters to consumers, great! But if you are starting a new business or creating a new product offering, I would encourage you at least to consider a B2B model.

When I left the publishing industry and launched my own branding and design business, I started without a strong idea of who my ideal customer was. My clients ranged from moms who wanted birthday party invitations to solopreneurs who needed logos to major companies—like buybuy BABY, Carnival, and Marriott—that already had strong, established brands but needed design work for specific projects.

As time went on, I discovered that although it was sometimes fun working with the first-time solopreneurs and party-planning moms, those one-off projects weren't moving the needle. I often spent more time explaining the process of working with a designer and making multiple rounds of changes because these clients weren't sure what they wanted exactly.

With the larger companies, the process was more streamlined—for me and for them. Their brands were established, so instead of reinventing the wheel, I usually worked on individual projects that had a specific objective, while using established brand guidelines that made getting final approval much easier. And when it came time for payment, the invoicing process was much more consistent. I recall that buybuy BABY had a specific file-naming system that all vendors followed and a specific timeline for payment. Once a month, I submitted an invoice PDF with a particular file name, and a few weeks later, the direct deposit hit my bank account—making it almost as reliable as an employee paycheck.

And the best part—in my opinion—about selling a B2B product or service? You may not need to maintain as robust a brand presence on social media, other than perhaps LinkedIn.

EDITOR'S TIP

Can you be too niche?

When launching a new magazine, publishers talk about what the potential "universe" is, meaning how many people fit the ideal demographic (and if they are using a direct mail or email campaign to reach them, how many names and addresses are available on a list that they could access). If you were launching a magazine targeted at French bulldog owners, for instance, the universe would be much smaller than that of a magazine for all dog owners, and positively tiny compared with the universe of a magazine for all pet owners. That said, in 2022 French bulldogs passed Labrador retrievers and golden retrievers as the most popular breed in the U.S.,[244] so maybe their growing fan base *would* be more likely to buy products specifically related to their precious fur babies.

When you niche down, just make sure that there are enough people in your target audience to support your business, considering that only a fraction of any available universe will actually buy. In his memoir *The Ride of a Lifetime*, Disney CEO Bob Iger offers advice he learned from a former boss: "Avoid getting into the business of manufacturing trombone oil. You may become the greatest trombone-oil manufacturer in the world, but in the end, the world only consumes a few quarts of trombone oil a year!"[245]

THREE KEYS TO CREATING THE PERFECT PRODUCT

1. Alleviate a pain point.

In the last section, I talked about how crucial it is to make sure your marketing messages address your customer's pain point. While this is important in the marketing stage, it is absolutely essential in the product creation stage.

We all have our favorite brands in any product category. Some of these we may love and constantly recommend to our friends. But other products we may use just because we always have, and not necessarily feel like a brand evangelist. I bought Bounty paper towels for years because my parents had always used them, and I especially liked their "Select a Size" format. But when I discovered that Costco paper towels were similar and cheaper, I didn't lose sleep over making the switch. Nor did I evangelize either brand to friends and family.

But then there are the products that I buy religiously and go out of my way to recommend. Almost all of these products solve a specific pain point, whether it is Supergoop! Unseen Sunscreen that goes on clear and doesn't burn your eyes, or Anson Belts, which allow for micro-adjustments, banishing that "too tight or too loose" feeling when your weight fluctuates a bit. I have recommended both of these products to friends and family multiple times because they each eliminate an annoyance with a beautiful and elegant solution.

Think about some of the annoyances in your life, remembering that if something is a pain point for you, it likely is for someone else as well. What is the current solution—if any—and how could it be improved upon? Sara Blakely famously came up with the idea for Spanx by cutting the legs off a pair of pantyhose. She knew her ideal customer—essentially herself— wanted a control-top undergarment that didn't require their legs to be covered with hosiery, especially during hot and humid summer days. It was a simple idea that later made her a billionaire.[246]

When searching for a pain point you can eliminate, keep in mind that we all want our lives to be easier, and ask yourself how your product or service might remove the friction from an annoying task. As James Clear points out in his bestselling book *Atomic Habits: An Easy & Proven Way to Build Good Habits & Break Bad Ones*: "If you look at the most habit-forming products, you'll notice that one of the things these goods and services do best is remove little bits of friction from your life." He cites meal delivery services, dating apps, ride-sharing services, and even text messaging as innovations that caught on because of the friction they eliminated.[247]

2. Design a solution with style and substance.

When The Home Depot opened its first Manhattan store in 2004, it was a big deal. The company took out a giant billboard in Times Square, and the news was featured in all of the major outlets, including *The New York Times*. Because I was working at *Home Channel News*, a trade magazine that covered the building supply industry, I attended the opening night event; Home Depot's CEO Bob Nardelli and Mayor Michael Bloomberg were both on hand to christen the new store. Editors at *Vanity Fair* may have hobnobbed with celebrities at the Oscars, but they had nothing on me!

While Home Depot's first urban outpost was big news, it was the design of the store that everyone buzzed about that night. In each conversation, the sentiment was the same: "This place is gorgeous!" Venture into a Home Depot almost anywhere else in the country, and *gorgeous* is probably not the first word that comes to mind. Sure, this big box retailer has tons of useful items and even some pretty ones; however, the store itself is really just a giant warehouse, built more for function than style.

But the Manhattan location was different. It was built inside two existing limestone buildings on 23rd Street, and much of the historic facade was preserved. The sleek interior featured loft-style architecture, Greek-inspired columns, and a glass-enclosed atrium filled with apartment-friendly plants. Instead of row after row of cardboard boxes holding extra stock—a common sight in many warehouse stores—this Home Depot was merchandised as well as the designer clothing boutiques lining Fifth Avenue, just a few blocks away. Yes, you could find the usual hardware and building supplies, but also entire kitchens and baths that had been constructed to show how the merchandise would look in a home, bringing design to the forefront.

I remember thinking that these useful products, presented in an elevated way, would be a hit with the local clientele. "The customers in New York are more sophisticated and demanding, so we had to take it up a notch," Christine McVeigh, the project director of Home Depot's Manhattan development team, told *The New York Times*.[248]

Like the team behind Home Depot's first Manhattan store, magazine editors have always known that style and substance *must* go hand in hand. Monthly print titles can rarely break the latest news, so instead, they have to make their stories insightful, thought-provoking, and beautiful. Magazines have always led the way visually, spending millions of dollars on photoshoots and illustrations each year. It has never been enough just to present our readers with useful information; we also have to gift wrap that info in a package that is easy—and hopefully fun—to read.

As magazines began feeling the pinch in the late 2000s and budgets were slashed, the need for good design became even greater. Now we are competing not just with each other but also with increasingly high-definition television, computer, and smartphone screens. News magazines need images that convey a sense of immediacy and action as well as a video can and portraits of people that rival those hanging in museums.

With the democratization of design—anyone can launch a beautiful Squarespace site or buy elegant business cards from Moo.com's templates—it is even more crucial that your product stands out as being beautiful. Design is a big part of the reason Target is more fun to shop in than Walmart, or that Anthropologie has developed a cult following for its whimsical catalog and in-store merchandising. Even commodities like dish soap are not immune; witness the proliferation of Method and Mrs. Meyer's products, which are pretty enough to leave out on the counter, while you might prefer to stow the unsightly Palmolive bottle under the sink.

3. Find a unique position.

If you've picked up an issue of *New York* magazine anytime in the last two decades, you've likely seen its iconic "Approval Matrix," the last page of every issue. The infographic that is central to this popular department resembles a piece of graph paper that has been divided into four sections by a horizontal X-axis (representing a range from Despicable to Brilliant) and a vertical Y-axis (representing a range from Lowbrow to Highbrow). What results is a grid with four quadrants running clockwise from the top left: Highbrow/Despicable, Highbrow/Brilliant, Lowbrow/Brilliant, and Lowbrow/Despicable.

Subtitled "Our deliberately oversimplified guide to who falls where on our taste hierarchies," the page serves as a visual way to cover diverse high- and low-culture topics in the zeitgeist—from politicians and opera openings to reality stars and rat infestations. In magazines, standard departments like this often come and go with redesigns and changing tastes among readers. The fact that the Approval Matrix has held on for more than 20 years and counting—while also becoming a plot point in the popular TV series *Younger* and even spawning its own short-lived talk show—is a testament to its brilliance.

The first time I saw the Approval Matrix was not the first time I'd seen a chart like this. Known as a positioning map, this type of four-quadrant diagram is used in business to compare a product or brand to the competition. Each competitor is charted based on two benefits that are important to consumers, making it easier to identify a gap—and potential opportunity—in

The Approval Matrix from the September 20, 2024, issue of New York *magazine*

the marketplace. Although positioning maps may be common in business classes, as a journalism major, I had never encountered one until the first week of my grad school capstone project.

As I've mentioned, our class was divided into four groups, each tasked with developing and presenting an idea for a new magazine. We would then vote and the winning idea would be chosen to become the prototype, which we would work on throughout the final quarter of grad school. My group—composed of three 20-something women and myself—started the assignment by discussing our favorite magazines and what we liked and disliked about them. This was 2003, during the height of HBO's *Sex and the City*. The show was groundbreaking for the way it depicted women owning and celebrating their sexuality, while also being smart, hilarious, and extremely stylish. Some of the members in my small group lamented the fact that most women's magazines had yet to catch up.

And just like that, we had our concept: *SKIRT, the Sex Magazine for Women*. Instead of showing a waifish model on the cover, each issue of *SKIRT* would showcase a hot cover guy. For the debut issue, our plan was to feature Hollywood bad-boy Colin Farrell—in a kilt, no less. (Remember: It was 2003 and the magazine was called *SKIRT*.) As part of the presentation, we were also asked to create a four-quadrant chart to show our competition, including existing magazines in the space. We decided to plot *SKIRT* on a positioning map of other women's publications, representing a range from Quick Reads to Deep Reads and from Sex-focused to Fashion-&-Lifestyle-focused.

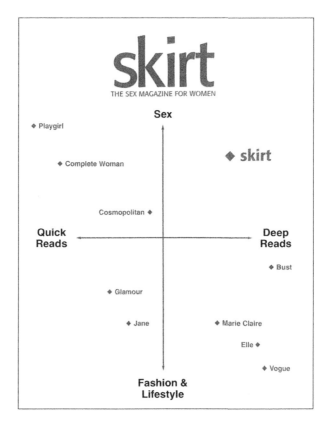

Positioning map for my grad school group's 2003 new magazine concept, SKIRT

Whether you are creating a huge global brand or small local business, positioning maps are a great way to think about your competition and how you fit into the mix. No one wants to be an "I do that too" brand if you can be an "I do that differently" brand. Unless your idea is truly original, such as a new invention, someone already offers a product or service similar to yours. What makes your brand stand out? Other than the back page of *New York* magazine, positioning maps are rarely shown to customers, but they can be an invaluable behind-the-scenes tool. Plotting out where you fall in comparison to other brands can help you determine what makes your brand better, while also helping you create talking points that you can use with potential customers who may wonder how you stack up against the competition.

THE TAKEAWAY

There are riches in the niches. Drilling down into a niche audience can help you know your customer more clearly, making it easier to hone your brand voice and cater to a specific need.

When you become known as the expert in a niche, **referrals come more easily.**

When starting a new business, consider the **advantages of a B2B** rather than B2C model. It can be easier to deal with a few high-paying professional B2B clients rather than a more scattered (and often lower-spending) audience of consumers.

The best products have three things in common: They alleviate a pain point, offer style and substance, and occupy a unique position in the marketplace.

Create a **positioning map** to help you figure out what makes your brand different from others on the market, informing the products you create, which customers you target, and how you engage with them.

Visit **LeadLikeAnEditor.com** to download a free workbook that includes a **Positioning Map** template, as well as other guides and resources.

CHAPTER 21

....

Deliver the Product Efficiently

R eclined on a low-slung sofa, with a caipirinha in hand and a light-weight wool blanket draped casually around my shoulders, I turn to my friends Cristina and Phillip to see that, just like me, they are content—practically purring—and melting into their seats. After a weekend filled with the boisterous storytelling and infectious laughter that often come when old friends travel together, we are at last silent, contemplative, listening to the waves crash. We take in the open-air splendor that is Parador La Huella, a culinary mecca for sandy-footed seafood lovers built right on the beach in the tiny Uruguayan town of José Ignacio. The breeze is gentle, but the drinks are strong, and we are all thinking the same thought: How had we overlooked this glorious spot before, and why in the world are we leaving tomorrow? I break the silence. "What if we stayed just a few more days?"[249]

Sounds delightful, doesn't it? This was the opening paragraph of an article I wrote for *Coastal Living* during my final days as design director, and to this day, it remains as one of my favorite stories that I have written. But it didn't start that way.

EMBRACE THE FIRST DRAFT

I began my career as a journalist, but as I veered more into design and creative direction, my writing took a back seat. Although I penned articles from time to time, I often went months writing nothing longer than a quick email. Like any body part that isn't used regularly, my writing muscle had gotten weak.

The Uruguayan travel essay was the first writing assignment I had taken on in a while, and as I wrote, I did lots of meandering on the page. There were unnecessary details about a day that it rained, and I had started with the boring logistics of how we had planned a trip to Buenos Aires, but then decided to go to Uruguay first for two nights, almost as an afterthought.

When I finished the first draft and turned it in to Tracey Minkin, the brilliant travel editor at *Coastal Living*, it was almost twice as long as the space allowed, and there was plenty of fat to trim. Not surprisingly, the story came back to me covered in red ink. It took a few rounds of rewrites, but eventually the piece was reworked, rewritten, and polished like a precious stone, transforming from a bloated, meandering mess to something I was proud of.

Magazine writers and editors know that all good writing is really just thoughtful rewriting. But you can't self-edit as you go along, making sure one sentence is perfect before you move on to the next. The best thing to do is get it down on paper and figure out how to make it beautiful later. As a *New York Times* bestselling author of more than 40 books for children and teens, Shannon Hale puts it another way: "When writing a first draft, I have to remind myself constantly that I'm only shoveling sand into a box so later I can build castles."[250]

In many ways, the same thing goes for business. I wonder how many great ideas throughout history never saw the light of day because their owners wanted them to be perfect before releasing them. The unfortunate thing about perfection is that it almost never really comes.

KNOWING WHEN TO USE 'TK'

Reporters love using the abbreviation TK, which is shorthand for *to come*. When you are writing an article, there may be a statistic that you need to check or a fact that you need to confirm, but stopping to look it up online would slow down your flow. Or it may be something that requires a phone call to someone or visiting a library to track down the information. In this case, writers insert the abbreviation "TK" and move on. (Given the scarcity of English words containing the letter combination TK, this abbreviation proves to be more easily searchable than TC when it is time to add the fact later.) For example, you may write: "Opened in the year TK, White Horse Tavern is the oldest restaurant in the country." Or perhaps: "According to a new report, first-time homebuyers were responsible for TK percent of all residential real estate purchases last year."

If the information is particularly hard to come by, the piece may even progress on to an editor or copy editor with the TK still included. This is usually more efficient than having the writer hold on to the story until the fact can be confirmed. The editor can still get the gist of the story and edit it for content and clarity, even if one or two facts can't be nailed down; then the missing information can be added later in the process.

Do you have a service that clients are clamoring for, but you just can't figure out all the bells and whistles of your website? Put up a simple landing page with your contact info and a way to preorder or get on the waiting list for the product, and let the rest be TK. Have you invented an amazing app but there is one feature that is a little buggy? Maybe it's time to get a beta version into the hands of potential clients and let the bug fix be TK.

The first personal computers certainly had glitches (even the latest models do now). That didn't stop Bill Gates from moving forward with the creation of Microsoft and improving the product as he went along. Or if you prefer Apple devices, look at the iPhone. Every year, Apple releases an updated iOS system for users to download. Often, the new operating system brings as many bugs as it does useful features, but this doesn't stop the company from innovating. They get the product into the hands of their customers, take notes on what they can improve, and fix the bugs later.

Allowing for a few TKs lets you get a minimum viable product (or MVP) out into the world to meet the initial needs of customers and gather feedback for future enhancements. Such insights can be more cost-effective than spending time and money to create a "perfect" product with extensive features—only to find out your customer doesn't need them and actually wants something different.

DONE IS BETTER THAN PERFECT

Working at a magazine can feel a lot like the movie *Groundhog Day*: Every issue, you brainstorm ideas, and the best ones get added to a lineup; then they are assigned to writers who will create the text, to photographers and illustrators who create the visuals, and to editors and designers who will meld the two to tell a story.

As editors and designers, there are times when we can get deep into the minutiae of, well, everything. The correct word choice, the perfect image, the best font. At times, I have printed out 20 versions of the same cover with slight tweaks to the size or font of the individual cover lines, so that we can pin them to the wall and see which pops the best. Each issue, we agonize over which photo or turn of phrase is most compelling, all with an impending deadline looming. Along the way, each of us is trying our best to make the end product a little bit better until it is just right. And then … we let it go.

Throughout my career, I have worked with two kinds of editors in chief. The first would weigh in heavily at the beginning and throughout the process, and once the copy was edited and the pages were designed, would tweak and fine-tune a bit—and then happily let it go, confident that we had done our best to create a compelling issue. The second kind of editor would actually be less critical at the start, and as the stories came together, would seem happy with the product and process. Then, a day or two before the issue went to press, she would grow bored with her own vision and want to tear each story apart and rethink how it was written or presented. These editors burned the midnight oil and expected others to do so as well, spreading panic and anxiety as they revised the pages down to the last possible second before we released them to the printer. I'll let you guess which kind of editor I prefer.

There is no perfect way to tell any story, and no perfect way to design any page. Similarly, there is no one way to sell a product or a service. This is why setting deadlines (see Chapter 10) is so important. It is our job to do the best we can in the time allowed—and then let it go.

Sometimes we are so concerned with presenting a perfect version of ourselves—or our product or business—that we become paralyzed. But working at magazines taught me that there isn't one perfect way. If you don't like how you did something, the good news is you get to do it all over again tomorrow.

CONSIDER YOUR DISTRIBUTION MODEL

I have a strange confession: Sometimes I purposefully arrive at a doctor's appointment as much as a half hour early, just to make sure I have a few minutes to peruse whatever magazines they have in the waiting room. I realize this is the sign of a true junkie, and I should probably look into some sort of 12-step program.

In 2017, I started visiting a new barber; on my second visit, she was running behind by almost 30 minutes. Some people would have been angry or annoyed, but as I settled into a comfy leather sofa, I was actually thrilled. A pile of glossy magazines covered the coffee table, and on top was the crown jewel: the latest issue of *Departures*. In case you aren't familiar, *Departures* was a beautiful travel and style magazine that published bimonthly for almost 20 years. If you *do* remember this magazine and fondly recall reading it in the past, there is a pretty good chance that you also own an American Express Platinum Card, as that was the only way to get it.

For years, I assumed that there were really just two ways to get any magazine: buy a copy on the newsstand or pay for a subscription. But in grad school, I learned that although most of the big-name magazines used that model, others had a different distribution model. Closed circulation magazines, for instance, were only available to you if you met certain criteria; in the case of *Departures*, this meant owning an American Express Platinum Card. For decades, luxury advertisers clamored to be in the publication, as it went to many of the highest earners (and biggest spenders) in the country. Before user data was as prevalent as it is in today's digital landscape, *Departures* stood out to these advertisers because the magazine could actually quantify how much its readers spent on luxury goods—not by asking them in surveys, as other publications might, but because its parent company had full access to its readers' American Express credit card statements. At its peak, the magazine—which you couldn't buy, even if you wanted to—brought in up to $50 million a year in revenue.[251]

As in the case of *Departures,* it can sometimes pay to think outside the box when it comes to distribution. Prior to the rise of the internet, most consumer products were distributed through a conventional distribution model with three levels: the producer, the wholesaler, and the retailer. While many of the products we buy in stores still follow that model, some producers have decided to cut out the middleman, striking deals directly with retailers. Others have cut out both the wholesaler *and* retailer by selling directly to the consumer through pop-up shops, brick-and-mortar locations, and the internet.

Of course, no single model is right for every product, but there are three things you should ask yourself when choosing a distribution method:

- **Where are my customers shopping for items like this?** For certain products, especially ones that require demonstration, selling online with photos and videos can be a great way to show consumers what the product looks like *and* how to use it. For this type of product, targeted social media ads can also lure people in with a photo or video, before directing them back to your site.

- **How can I make my first sale?** You may have a product that you would love to see on the shelves of drug stores like Walgreens and CVS, or perhaps big-box retailers like Target and Walmart. While that may be possible (and even advisable) in the long run, is there another place you can test the product first? Perhaps on your own website, or by selling on a third-party site like Amazon? For crafty items, would trying to sell on Etsy or at a craft fair provide proof of concept before approaching the buyers at Michaels and Hobby Lobby? While sites like Amazon and Etsy may take a cut of your profit, the exposure you get from listing your product there could prove to be invaluable. Unlike internet search engines, such as Google, these sites are actually internet *sales* engines; customers visit them when they are ready to buy, and often their billing and shipping information is already stored, reducing the friction required to purchase your product.

- **What will be my means of fulfillment?** Do you have a warehouse or employees who can help facilitate delivery? If you are starting small, it may be okay to store products in a spare room or in your garage, but you will need to allow time for making daily trips to the post office. If you plan to sell on Amazon, signing up for their FBA (Fulfillment by Amazon) program allows you to store products at their warehouses, while also using their employees to pack and ship the items, all at a fraction of the cost of opening your own distribution center and hiring your own team.

EDITOR'S TIP

Subscriptions aren't just for magazines.

First pioneered by magazines and newspapers, the subscription model is now used by many businesses, ranging from streaming services to delivery boxes that contain beauty products, ready-to-cook meals, clothing, and more. If you offer your product or service via subscription, you can create a roster of repeat customers that will provide a recurring revenue stream. This steady cash flow—and list of loyal clients—could prove invaluable if you decide to expand your business into new markets or product lines.

USING YOUR MAIN PRODUCT AS A GATEWAY

We had one hour left in Lisbon, and I was starving. My husband and I were on a transatlantic cruise from Barcelona to New York, and this stop proved to be one of my favorites. Having never been to Lisbon before, I was instantly entranced with the city's beautiful architecture and charming cobblestone streets. It reminded me of San Francisco, where I lived for several years; there was a vibrant street life, a bustling waterfront, and *so* many hills. We had spent the day wandering them all, and although we had seen a number of cute cafés along the way, we kept delaying lunch as we pushed forward on our death march.

Now we had an hour before we were due back at the ship, and I definitely needed a snack. My only requirements were that it be authentic, delicious, and something I wouldn't find anywhere else. Easy enough, right? But as we neared the port and I grew more hangry, the establishments became increasingly touristy, making me nervous that my one meal in Portugal would be a bad one.

And then I saw it: Like an oasis, there was a giant food hall bearing the *Time Out* logo. A global magazine with editions based in several cities around the world, *Time Out* has always been synonymous with the pulse of a city. My first experience with the brand was in 1996, when, as a sophomore in high school, I went to the U.K. for a class trip, and a teacher recommended I pick up a copy of *Time Out London* to see what would be going on while we were there. Years later, when I lived in Manhattan, I often scanned the entertainment section of *Time Out New York* for buzzy off-Broadway plays and cabaret shows, as well as exhibits at smaller museums that may not make it into the *New York Times.*

Starting as a concept hatched in 2014 by the team at *Time Out Portugal,* the Time Out Market is now one of the most popular attractions in Lisbon. We were there on a weekday at 2 p.m.—when the lunch crowd should have been winding down—and the place was positively packed. And it was easy to see why.

As a tourist, trying an unvetted eatery can be a big commitment. What if the food is terrible? What if there is a better restaurant just around the corner? Harnessing the authority and trust of a globally recognized editorial brand, the Time Out Market addresses this pain point by housing satellite locations of more than 30 of Lisbon's best bars and restaurants—including two chefs with three Michelin stars—all under one roof.[252]

Everything in a Time Out Market is chosen, tasted, and tested by *Time Out*'s journalists and critics, who operate under a simple rule: "If it's good, it goes in the magazine. If it's great, it goes on to the Market."[253] A decade after the first market opened in Lisbon, hungry customers—including both tourists and locals—can visit Time Out Markets in New York, Chicago, Boston, Montreal, Barcelona, Dubai, and Cape Town, with more locations on the horizon.[254]

As I've mentioned in previous chapters, for years, magazines have built reputations as trustworthy sources and discerning curators of culture. It makes sense that products and experiences bearing their names would be great as well.

Time Inc. excelled at leveraging our authority to branch into other lines of business. At *Coastal Living,* we had our own line of furniture, licensed through a partnership with Stanley Furniture, and eventually went on to add a stationery line through FineStationery.com and other home products through Bed Bath & Beyond. The creation of a Bed Bath & Beyond collection was partly inspired by our sister magazine, *Real Simple,* which sold an array of home organization products through this once-ubiquitous retailer. *Southern Living* sold (and continues to sell) house plans that you can buy and take to a builder, while *Cooking Light* created a line of low-calorie frozen meals to compete with the Healthy Choice and Lean Cuisine brands.

Of course, leveraging a customer relationship built on trust to launch a new product is not just the domain of media companies. Once you have built a strong and loyal following, think about how you can use the authority you have built with your customers to alleviate a *different* pain point they might have. This could result in a variation on the product you already sell. Or, as in the case of *Time Out,* it could propel you into an entirely new direction, offering exciting—and lucrative—opportunities for growth.

THE TAKEAWAY

The best products are created over time with trial and error. By embracing two editorial concepts—**the first draft** and **the "TK"**—you can get a minimum viable product out into the world much more quickly. This allows you to meet the initial needs of customers and gather feedback for future product enhancements.

There is no one way to sell a product or a service. Waiting until something is perfect to release it can lead to paralysis, as perfection never comes. **Done is better than perfect**—and you can always make improvements in the next iteration.

Consider which **distribution model** is best for your product, knowing this can change over time as your brand grows. When choosing a method, ask yourself where customers already shop for similar items, how you can make your first sale, and how you will fulfill orders.

Subscription products and services offer more value to your customer while also bringing recurring revenue each month, providing valuable capital for you to grow your business.

Once you are delivering a solid product to a loyal customer base, consider how you could alleviate another pain point your clients may have, using your **main product as a gateway** to new offerings.

CONCLUSION

recently attended a webinar designed to teach magazine editors about how AI could be used as a tool in their everyday work. Not surprisingly, the virtual room was filled with plenty of skeptics. After a decade of hearing about how print was dead and digital was the way of the future, many of these editors had more recently been subjected to arguments that their jobs would be (or at least could be) replaced altogether by artificial intelligence.

Over the next 45 minutes, these editors learned about what AI is, how it works, and how they could use it to their advantage when writing and reporting stories. Along the way, they asked insightful questions, debated ideas that were presented, and genuinely smiled at the instructor when they learned something new about AI that could be useful to them. For the last 15 minutes, they broke off into small groups to experiment with Hearst's own version of ChatGPT and explore how it could help in the research and outlining of a story—not the writing itself.

By the end of the session, most of these editors left in an upbeat mood, eager to experiment further with AI for their next article. I was reminded of how writer and entrepreneur Shane Snow says that the best leaders—and most journalists—tend to be "Skeptical Optimists," who question all information and assumptions that are presented to them, while still assuming that the best is possible.

For this book, I have contacted travel advisors, book agents, interior designers, life coaches, university deans, and executives at a wide array of organizations, ranging from Google and Citibank to nonprofits. Despite the varied fields they represent, all of these high achievers have two things in common: They weren't afraid to face change head-on, and, after having done so, they were thriving using the skills that they had learned as editors.

It was no surprise to me. At the end of the day, editors are hired to make things better, whether that is a magazine article, a book like the one you are reading, an advertisement, or even an entire corporate marketing plan. But their editing skills don't stop with the written word; just as they have the ability to see what is superfluous and what is essential in text, the best editors are able to apply these skills to the business world, ensuring that the departments and companies they run do so in the most efficient way possible.

Like these editors, you can achieve success by moving forward with optimism, curiosity, passion, and perseverance, facing changes and challenges as they arise. Along the way, embrace the truth to make informed decisions, using your own integrity as an internal barometer. Set aside the time to plan out your vision and mission, as well as your yearly and daily schedule, and don't forget that keeping your team happy and motivated shouldn't be an afterthought but rather an effective way to protect what may be your company's most valuable asset. And finally, when it comes to your sales, remember that if you create a product that is truly valuable, and connect with your customers authentically, empowering them to improve their lives, you are no longer *selling* but rather *serving*.

As you move forward as a leader, revisit the MY STAMP method as a guide, owning the fact that *you* are the hero in your story and the editor of your own life. If you have the courage to lead like an editor, you are only bound by the limits of your vision, meaning you can shape your business, your career, and your life into whatever you want it to be.

ACKNOWLEDGMENTS

have to start by thanking all of the editors—including my colleagues at many publications—who have shaped my life over the past two decades. A special thanks to Ana Connery and Antonia van der Meer, two of my former editors in chief, who I am happy to still see from time to time for lunch and laughter (though not often enough!). And an extra special thanks goes to my current team at VERANDA, including our fearless leader Steele Thomas Marcoux. You are not only the most talented people I know but also the kindest and most supportive. I still can't believe I get paid to make something beautiful with you every day!

Along those same lines, there have been a handful of teachers—who, in many cases, were also writers and editors—who have shaped me as a journalist and as a human being: Rebecca Reisert, Glennda Tingle, Sarah Watson, Rick Knoop, Tracy VanMeter, Abe Peck, Marcel Pacatte, Kathi Kern, Kate Black, Dana Smith, and Lisa Bannon are standouts among many, many others.

One educator who deserves a special thanks is Linda C. Winkler, my high school journalism teacher, who I am pleased to call a friend almost—gasp!—30 years later. (How is that possible?) When I was just a teen, you opened my eyes to the sense of personal and professional fulfillment that comes with leading the staff of a monthly publication, and I was forever changed. Thank you for always reminding me that, although design is my passion, words are my first love. I still remember when I started working as an art director, you asked: "But you will keep writing … right?"

Like any good journalist, I recognize that I don't have all the answers—so I found the people who do. I must extend a huge thank-you to the generous professionals who took time from their busy schedules to chat with me, either about being an editor or writing a book (or both): Lindsay Bierman, Michael Clinton, Heather Chadduck Hillegas, Michelle Lee, Margaret Magnarelli, Steele Thomas Marcoux, Stacy Mayer, Susan Moynihan, Meaghan B Murphy, Betty Wong Ortiz, Lesley Jane Seymour, Kristin van Ogtrop, Lauren Brown West-Rosenthal, Sarah Z. Wexler, and Charles Whitaker. Your stories were inspiring, and your insights were invaluable.

An extra big thanks goes to *Entrepreneur* editor in chief Jason Feifer (and to our amazing mutual friend Lauren Eggert for the introduction). Jason generously gave me his one hour of free time on a Friday afternoon for a walk through Brooklyn's Prospect Park, while discussing how the worlds of editors and entrepreneurs intersect. Thank you also for writing one of my favorite books and for making change seem a lot less scary—and even exciting!

On behalf of hundreds of other magazine editors, a special thanks also goes to Chandra Turner not only for speaking with me but also for starting the website Ed2010.com, which gave editors a chance to congregate and network together for more than two decades; and then for continuing that conversation with her Talent Fairy consultancy and "After Magazines" Facebook Group, two lifelines at a time when many of us nervously shifted away from publishing and into countless other industries. You truly are a fairy godmother to so many editors.

Another fairy godparent is Chandler Bolt, the founder of SelfPublishing .com. I have wanted to write a book for as long as I can remember but never stuck with it. Without the guidance of Chandler and his team, there is no way that you would be reading this today. This man and his company change lives, and if you have ever considered writing a book but don't know where to start, they can help you too. Visit **Refer.LeadLikeAnEditor.com** to get a free copy of Chandler's book *Published.* and learn how *you* can write and publish your first book.

As I mentioned in Chapter 7, Chandler often says that reading a book is like getting a "$15 mentor," which means I've had a lot of mentors over the years who I've never even met. Thanks to Kate White, Hank Gilman, Martha Stewart, and countless others whose books I have filled with sticky notes and highlighter marks. And a special thanks goes to the brilliant and inspiring Donald Miller for not only writing several excellent books for small business owners but also for taking time to chat with me about why writers often make the best leaders. I may take you up on your offer to visit your writing cabin in Nashville when I start working on my next book!

And finally, there are several people in my personal life who I must thank. First and foremost, my parents, who supported me unwaveringly throughout their all-too-brief time on earth. Although you are gone, I carry you with me every day.

While my parents can never be replaced, their support has been carried on by a few parental figures in my life—Janice Mingus, Martha Frisch, and Cristina De Oliveira Sr.—and by my family by marriage, who've always welcomed me as one of their own: the Feldmans, Camhis, Bergmans, Negrins, and Tassones.

For only children, friends often take the place of siblings—and if that is the case, I've got some amazing brothers and sisters. To Phillip Barker, Matt Crowle, Joe Farace, Deena Goldblatt Campbell, Sarah Greaves-Gabbadon, Angela Grovey, Chris Hartman, Jeninne Lee-St. John, Danielle McGurran, Emily and Ross Moore, Laura Oglethorpe, Christine O'Neill, Chris Parente, Veronica Sooley Pugh, Lynn Serra, John Tompkins, Cameron Wyatt, and so many others (you know who you are!): Thank you for being a friend. We've traveled down a road and back again. Your heart is true; you're a pal and a confidant. ;-)

And, of course, a special thank you goes to the BFFs:

To my brother-from-another-mother Matt DiPasquale, thanks for all those late-night sessions of "girl talk" on topics ranging from the best Broadway shows to the music of our favorite pop divas.

To my ride-or-die girl Jill Smith Muth, thanks for always being my partner in crime and *never* the voice of reason when someone asks if we'd like just one more dirty martini.

And, of course, to my two favorite editors, Cristina De Oliveira and Alice Oglethorpe, thanks for being early readers of this manuscript and providing words of wisdom, as always. Journalism brought us together as grad school classmates, but love has kept us together, as we've weathered heartbreaks, celebrated triumphs, and gasped for breath during too many "cases" of uncontrollable laughter to count.

And last but *definitely* not least, thank you to Craig Feldman, who puts up with me (and my never-ending piles of magazines) every day. There is no one else I'd rather share a veggie pizza, a *Playbill* collection, and a life with. I surely love you!

RESOURCES

Good journalists know that synthesizing the insights of industry experts is often the key to creating a well-researched story. Throughout this book, I have shared words of wisdom from some of my favorite business, leadership, and self-improvement authors. If you would like to dive deeper, these are my top 25 picks. Happy reading!

1. *Atomic Habits: An Easy & Proven Way to Build Good Habits & Break Bad Ones* by James Clear

2. *Build for Tomorrow: An Action Plan for Embracing Change, Adapting Fast, and Future-Proofing Your Career* by Jason Feifer

3. *Building a StoryBrand: Clarify Your Message So Customers Will Listen* by Donald Miller

4. *Business Made Simple: 60 Days to Master Leadership, Sales, Marketing, Execution, Management, Personal Productivity and More* by Donald Miller

5. *Clone Yourself: Build a Team that Understands Your Vision, Shares Your Passion, and Runs Your Business for You* by Jeff Hilderman

6. *Deep Work: Rules for Focused Success in a Distracted World* by Cal Newport

7. *Fire Your Hiring Habits: Building an Environment that Attracts Top Talent in Today's Workforce* by John W. Mitchell

8. *Grit: The Power of Passion and Perseverance* by Angela Duckworth

9. *I Shouldn't Be Telling You This: Success Secrets Every Gutsy Girl Should Know* by Kate White

10. *Integrity: The Courage to Meet the Demands of Reality* by Henry Cloud

11. *Intentional Integrity: How Smart Companies Can Lead an Ethical Revolution* by Robert Chesnut with Joan O'C. Hamilton

12. *Leaders Eat Last: Why Some Teams Pull Together and Others Don't* by Simon Sinek

13. *Promotions Made Easy: A Step-by-Step Guide to the Executive Suite* by Stacy Mayer

14. *Rich Dad Poor Dad: What the Rich Teach Their Kids About Money That the Poor and Middle Class Do Not!* by Robert T. Kiyosaki

15. *ROAR: into the Second Half of Your Life (Before It's Too Late)* by Michael Clinton

16. *Start With Why: How Great Leaders Inspire Everyone to Take Action* by Simon Sinek

17. *The Best Advice I Ever Got: Lessons from Extraordinary Lives* by Katie Couric

18. *The Martha Rules: 10 Essentials for Achieving Success as You Start, Build, or Manage a Business* by Martha Stewart

19. *The One Thing: The Surprisingly Simple Truth Behind Extraordinary Results* by Gary Keller and Jay Papasan

20. *The Ride of a Lifetime: Lessons Learned from 15 Years as CEO of the Walt Disney Company* by Robert Iger

21. *The War of Art: Break Through the Blocks and Win Your Inner Creative Battles* by Steven Pressfield

22. *What Makes Great Managers Great: How to Raise Engagement, Give Feedback, and Answer the Questions No One's Asking* by Curtiss Murphy

23. *Who Moved My Cheese?: An A-Mazing Way to Deal with Change in Your Work and in Your Life* by Spencer Johnson

24. *You Can't Fire Everyone: And Other Lessons from an Accidental Manager* by Hank Gilman

25. *Your Fully Charged Life: A Radically Simple Approach to Having Endless Energy and Filling Every Day with Yay* by Meaghan B Murphy with Beth Janes O'Keefe

NOTES

1   2024 Edelman Trust Barometer, January 2024. https://www.edelman.com/trust/trust-barometer.

2   Richard Edelman, "Trust at Work." Edelman Insights, January 21, 2019. https://www.edelman.com/insights/trust-at-work.

3   "Good Housekeeping," Hearst Magazines Advertising, accessed October 13, 2024, https://advertising.hearstmagazines.com/brands/good-housekeeping.

4   "*Good Housekeeping* 2024 Media Kit." (*Good Housekeeping*, 2024).

5   "Product Reviews & Ratings from the Good Housekeeping Institute," accessed October 13, 2024, https://www.goodhousekeeping.com/product-reviews.

6   "*Good Housekeeping* 2024 Media Kit." (*Good Housekeeping*, 2024).

7   "*Good Housekeeping* 2023 Media Kit." (*Good Housekeeping*, 2023).

8   Emily Petsko, "Reports of Mark Twain's Quote about His Own Death Are Greatly Exaggerated," *Mental Floss*, May 15, 2023, https://www.mentalfloss.com/article/562400/reports-mark-twains-quote-about-mark-twains-death-are-greatly-exaggerated.

9   Chandra Turner, "2024 Editorial Hiring Report," The Talent Fairy, powered by Ed2010, January 10, 2024, https://ed2010.com/uncategorized/our-2024-survey-results-are-in/.

10   "*Highlights* (Magazine)," Wikipedia, February 26, 2024, https://en.wikipedia.org/wiki/Highlights_(magazine).

11   Nicole Serena Silver, "Accessing the Power of Your Mind: Placebo Effect and Mindset," *Forbes,* February 17, 2022, https://www.forbes.com/sites/nicolesilver/2022/02/17/accessing-the-power-of-your-mind-placebo-effect-and-law-of-attraction.

12   Mia Primeau, "Your Powerful, Changeable Mindset," *Stanford Report*, Stanford University, September 16, 2021, https://news.stanford.edu/report/2021/09/15/mindsets-clearing-lens-life.

13   Philip Brickman, Dan Coates, and Ronnie Janoff-Bulman. "Lottery winners and accident victims: Is happiness relative?," in *Journal of Personality and Social Psychology* (1978), 36(8), 917–927. https://doi.org/10.1037/0022-3514.36.8.917.

14   Meaghan B Murphy with Beth Janes O'Keefe, *Your Fully Charged Life: A Radically Simple Approach to Having Endless Energy and Filling Every Day with Yay* (TarcherPerigee, 2021), xiii.

15   Murphy, xvii.

16 Martin E. P. Seligman, *Learned Optimism: How to Change Your Mind and Your Life* (Vintage, 2006), iii-iv.

17 Seligman, 96.

18 Carol S. Dweck, *Mindset: The New Psychology of Success* (Ballantine Books, 2006; trade paperback ed., 2016).

19 Dweck, 20.

20 Dweck, 112.

21 Dweck, 125.

22 Donald Miller, *Business Made Simple: 60 Days to Master Leadership, Sales, Marketing, Execution, Management, Personal Productivity and More* (HarperCollins Leadership, 2021), 8.

23 Paul Harris, "You Go, Girl," *The Guardian,* November 19, 2005, https://www .theguardian.com/media/2005/nov/20/television.usa.

24 Nicole Sands, "Months before Interviewing Michael Jackson Accusers, Oprah Winfrey Opened up about Her Own Abuse," *People,* March 5, 2019, https://people.com/tv/oprah-winfrey-details-own-abuse-months-before -interviewing-michael-jackson-accusers.

25 Michael Clinton, *ROAR: into the Second Half of Your Life (Before It's Too Late)* (Beyond Words, 2021).

26 Clinton, 33–34.

27 Miller, *Business Made Simple,* 11.

28 Brooks Barnes, "Bob Iger, Acknowledging 'Challenging Times,' Meets with Disney Employees," *The New York Times,* November 28, 2022, https://www .nytimes.com/2022/11/28/business/media/disney-bob-iger.html.

29 Barnes, "Bob Iger, Acknowledging 'Challenging Times,' Meets with Disney Employees."

30 Robert Iger, *The Ride of a Lifetime: Lessons Learned from 15 Years as CEO of the Walt Disney Company* (Random House, 2019), xxii.

31 Iger, 86–87.

32 Miller, *Business Made Simple,* 25.

33 Murphy, *Your Fully Charged Life,* 87–88.

34 Murphy, 168–170.

35 Liz Krieger, "In Defense of Dabbling." Medium, June 21, 2019. https://forge .medium.com/in-defense-of-dabbling-e7f734fcf3e5.

36 David J. Epstein, *Range: How Generalists Triumph in a Specialized World* (Macmillan, 2019).

37 Krieger, "In Defense of Dabbling."

38 Francesca Gino, "The Business Case for Curiosity," *Harvard Business Review,* September–October 2018. https://hbr.org/2018/09/the-business-case -for-curiosity.

39   Gino, "The Business Case for Curiosity."

40   Charles Whitaker, personal interview, October 30, 2023.

41   Gino, "The Business Case for Curiosity."

42   Gino, "The Business Case for Curiosity."

43   Shane Snow, "How to Use Skepticism to Lead More Innovatively (without Being a Jerk)," *Forbes,* May 21, 2020, https://www.forbes.com/sites/shane snow/2020/05/21/how-to-use-skepticism-to-lead-more-innovatively-without -being-a-jerk.

44   Gino, "The Business Case for Curiosity."

45   Emma Bazilian, "The Ultimate Guide to Grandmillennial Style," September 4, 2019, https://www.housebeautiful.com/lifestyle/a28594040/grandmillennial -design/.

46   Elizabeth Mayhew, "The 'Grandmillennial' Style Brings Tradition and Peaceful Decor into the Home," *The Washington Post,* May 7, 2020, https:// www.washingtonpost.com/lifestyle/home/the-grandmillennial-style-brings -tradition-and-peaceful-decor-into-the-home/2020/05/26/b4e8f6e8-99ed -11ea-a282-386f56d579e6_story.html.

47   Mayhew, "The 'Grandmillennial' Style …"

48   Dana Brown, *Dilettante: True Tales of Excess, Triumph, and Disaster* (Ballantine Books, 2022), 108.

49   Lindsay Blake, "This Old-Timey Merry-Go-Round in Griffith Park Inspired Walt Disney to Create Disneyland," *Los Angeles* magazine, September 3, 2015, https://lamag.com/film/this-old-timey-merry-go-round-in-griffith-park- inspired-walt-disney-to-create-disneyland.

50   Cal Newport, *Deep Work: Rules for Focused Success in a Distracted World* (Grand Central Publishing, 2016), 86.

51   Newport, 14.

52   Newport, 115.

53   Angela Duckworth, *Grit: The Power of Passion and Perseverance,* (Scribner, 2016; first trade paperback ed., 2018), 280.

54   Susan Moynihan, personal interview, September 6, 2018.

55   Sergey Faldin, "What Woody Allen's 'showing up' Quote Really Means," Medium, July 13, 2020, https://sfaldin.medium.com/what-woody-allens -showing-up-quote-really-means-ee743f0adbbb.

56   Duckworth, *Grit.*

57   Duckworth, 49.

58   Steven Pressfield, *The War of Art: Break Through the Blocks and Win Your Inner Creative Battles,* (Black Irish Entertainment, 2002; first trade paperback ed., 2012), 69.

59   Steven Pressfield, *Turning Pro: Tap Your Inner Power and Create Your Life's Work* (Black Irish Entertainment, 2012), 122.

60   "From the Editors," *New York* magazine, November 3, 2012, https://nymag .com/nymag/letters/hurricane-sandy-editors-letter-2012-11.

61   Heather Chadduck Hillegas, personal interview, October 19, 2023.

62   Duckworth, 6.

63   Katie Couric, *The Best Advice I Ever Got: Lessons from Extraordinary Lives* (Random House Trade Paperbacks, 2012), 56.

64   Richard Farson and Ralph Keyes, "The Failure-Tolerant Leader," *Harvard Business Review,* August 2002, https://hbr.org/2002/08/the-failure-tolerant-leader.

65   Miller, *Business Made Simple,* 25–26.

66   Couric, *The Best Advice I Ever Got,* 68.

67   Couric, 51–52.

68   Couric, 132–134.

69   Couric, 19–20.

70   Jason Feifer, *Build for Tomorrow: An Action Plan for Embracing Change, Adapting Fast, and Future-Proofing Your Career* (Harmony Books, 2022), 141.

71   Feifer, 141–142.

72   Martha Stewart, *The Martha Rules: 10 Essentials for Achieving Success as You Start, Build, or Manage a Business* (Rodale, 2005).

73   Stewart, 151–152.

74   Stewart, 155.

75   Stewart, 155.

76   Stewart, 156.

77   Stewart, 157.

78   Martha Stewart (@marthastewart48), "I am so thrilled to be on the cover of the @SI_Swimsuit issue!" Instagram, May 15, 2023. https://www.instagram .com/p/CsRowziOTdO.

79   Spencer Johnson, *Who Moved My Cheese?: An A-Mazing Way to Deal with Change in Your Work and in Your Life,* (G.P. Putnam's Sons, 1998; 2002 ed.), 74.

80   Feifer, *Build for Tomorrow,* 1–2.

81   Feifer, 249.

82   Kate White, *I Shouldn't Be Telling You This: Success Secrets Every Gutsy Girl Should Know* (HarperBusiness, 2012).

83   Robert Chesnut with Joan O'C. Hamilton, *Intentional Integrity: How Smart Companies Can Lead an Ethical Revolution* (St. Martin's Press, 2020), 13.

84   Jessica Long, Chris Roark, and Bill Theofilou, "The Bottom Line on Trust," Accenture, October 30, 2018, https://www.accenture.com/content/dam /accenture/final/a-com-migration/manual/pdf/careers/pdf-43/Accenture -Enterprise-Agility-Web.pdf.

85   Chesnut, *Intentional Integrity,* 45.

86   *Merriam-Webster.com Dictionary,* s.v. "integrity," https://www.merriam-webster .com/dictionary/integrity.

87   Henry Cloud, *Integrity: The Courage to Meet the Demands of Reality* (HarperBusiness, 2006; first paperback ed., 2009), 9.

88   Cloud, 9.

89   Cloud, 95.

90   Cloud, 126.

91   Steele Thomas Marcoux, personal interview. November 30, 2023.

92   "Top 25 Supermarket Operators by Sales," *Supermarket News,* July 7, 2021, https://www.supermarketnews.com/retail-financial/top-25-supermarket -operators-sales.

93   Fiona Soltes, "2023 Top 100 Retailers," National Retail Federation, July 5, 2023, https://nrf.com/blog/2023-top-100-retailers.

94   Jim Collins, *Good to Great: Why Some Companies Make the Leap ... and Others Don't* (Harper Business, 2001), 65–70.

95   Collins, 68.

96   Collins, 69.

97   Collins, 70.

98   White, *I Shouldn't Be Telling You This,* 77–78

99   White, 78–79.

100 Iger, *The Ride of a Lifetime,* 125.

101 Anna Davies, "Do You Know When to Go With Your Gut?," *Cosmopolitan,* April 2012.

102 Feifer, *Build for Tomorrow,* 93–94.

103 Feifer, 94–95.

104 Annie Duke, *How to Decide: Simple Tools for Making Better Choices* (Portfolio/ Penguin, 2020), 68–69.

105 Suzy Welch, *10-10-10: 10 Minutes, 10 Months, 10 Years: A Life-Transforming Idea* (Scribner, 2009).

106 Suzy Welch, "The Rule of 10-10-10," *O, The Oprah Magazine,* September 2006, https://www.oprah.com/spirit/suzy-welchs-rule-of-10-10-10-decision -making-guide/all.

107 Welch, "The Rule of 10-10-10."

108 Welch, "The Rule of 10-10-10."

109 Welch, "The Rule of 10-10-10."

110 Hank Gilman, *You Can't Fire Everyone: And Other Lessons from an Accidental Manager,* (Portfolio/Penguin, 2011; paperback ed., 2012), vii.

111 Chesnut, *Intentional Integrity,* 42–44.

112 Chesnut, 44.

113 Chesnut, 44.

114 Michelle Lee, personal interview, October 25, 2024.

115 Lindsay Bierman, "Lindsay Bierman Profile," LinkedIn, n.d., https://www
.linkedin.com/in/lindsaybierman.

116 Lindsay Bierman, "Installation Address," University of North Carolina School
of the Arts, (lecture, September 25, 2015), https://www.uncsa.edu/chancellor
/speeches/20150925-installation-address.aspx.

117 Lindsay Bierman, personal interview, October 23, 2023.

118 Bierman, personal interview.

119 Bierman, personal interview.

120 "About." *Harper's Magazine*, July 21, 2020. https://harpers.org/about.

121 Henry J. (Henry Jarvis) Raymond, "A Word at the Start," *Harper's Magazine*,
June 1850, https://harpers.org/archive/1850/06/a-word-at-the-start.

122 Grant Cardone, *The 10X Rule: The Only Difference Between Success and Failure*
(John Wiley & Sons, 2011).

123 Britt Skrabanek, "Difference between Mission and Vision Statements: 25
Examples," ClearVoice, February 23, 2024, https://www.clearvoice.com
/resources/difference-between-mission-vision-statement-examples/.

124 Simon Sinek, *Leaders Eat Last: Why Some Teams Pull Together and Others
Don't*, (Portfolio/Penguin, 2014; paperback ed., 2017), 52.

125 Skrabanek, "Difference between Mission and Vision Statements."

126 Patrick Hull, "Be Visionary. Think Big.," *Forbes*, December 10, 2021, https://
www.forbes.com/sites/patrickhull/2012/12/19/be-visionary-think-big/.

127 Whitaker, personal interview.

128 Patrick Hull, "Answer 4 Questions to Get a Great Mission Statement," *Forbes*,
January 10, 2013, https://www.forbes.com/sites/patrickhull/2013/01/10
/answer-4-questions-to-get-a-great-mission-statement.

129 "*Men's Health* 2024 Media Kit" (*Men's Health*, 2024).

130 "*The Atlantic* Magazine's Mission Statement," Shapes of Digital Media,
July 4, 2014, https://editorofthenextvanityfair.wordpress.com/2014/07/04
/the-atlantic-magazines-mission-statement.

131 "*The Atlantic* 2023 Media Kit" (*The Atlantic*, 2023).

132 "*The Atlantic* 2024 Media Kit" (*The Atlantic*, 2024).

133 "*Reader's Digest* 2024 Media Kit" (*Reader's Digest*, 2024).

134 "Core Values & Heritage," Marriott, https://www.marriott.com/culture-and
-values/core-values.mi.

135 "A Hotel Brand for Every Type of Journey," Marriott, accessed March 20, 2024,
https://www.marriott.com/marriott-brands/explore-our-brands.mi.

136 "A Hotel Brand for Every Type of Journey," Marriott.

137 Moxy Hotels, https://moxy-hotels.marriott.com.

138 Bierman, personal interview.

139 *The Devil Wears Prada* (United States: 20th Century Fox, 2006).

140 David Moin, "How Nordstrom's Anniversary Sale Became a Retail Phenomenon," *Footwear News* via Yahoo!Life, September 13, 2021, https://www.yahoo.com /lifestyle/nordstrom-anniversary-sale-became-retail-043041982.html.

141 Emily DeLetter, "Why Are There Multiple Amazon Prime Days in 2023? Here's What to Know," *USA Today*, October 11, 2023, https://www.usatoday .com/story/money/shopping/2023/10/10/amazon-prime-days-2023-why -multiple-deal-events/71127666007.

142 Cydney Henderson, "Sports Illustrated Swimsuit Issue, Created to Combat Winter, Became a Cultural Phenomenon," *USA Today*, January 19, 2024, https://www.usatoday.com/story/sports/media/2024/01/19/sports-illustrated -swimsuit-issue-history-models-athletes/72286647007.

143 Moin, "How Nordstrom's Anniversary Sale Became a Retail Phenomenon."

144 C. Northcote Parkinson, "Parkinson's Law," *The Economist,* November 19, 1955, https://www.economist.com/news/1955/11/19/parkinsons-law.

145 Jason Feifer, personal interview, October 13, 2023.

146 Margaret Magnarelli, personal interview, November 10, 2017.

147 Jeff Hilderman, *Clone Yourself: Build a Team That Understands Your Vision, Shares Your Passion, and Runs Your Business for You* (Jeff Hilderman, 2017), 32–33.

148 Kristin van Ogtrop, personal interview, October 4, 2023.

149 Magnarelli, personal interview.

150 Gilman, *You Can't Fire Everyone*, 194–195.

151 Anthony J. Bradley and Mark P. McDonald, "People Are Not Your Greatest Asset," *Harvard Business Review*, December 6, 2011, https://hbr.org/2011/12 /people-are-not-your-greatest-a.

152 Chuck Blakeman, "It's Time to Debunk the Myth That People Are Your Greatest Asset," *Inc.*, July 14, 2015, https://www.inc.com/chuck-blakeman /it-s-time-to-debunk-the-myth-that-people-are-your-greatest-asset.html.

153 Lauren Weber, "CEOs No Longer Say 'People Are Our Greatest Asset,' According to New Report," *The Wall Street Journal,* November 17, 2016, https://www.wsj.com/articles/ceos-no-longer-say-people-are-our-greatest -asset-according-to-new-report-1479412130.

154 Simon Sinek, *Start with Why: How Great Leaders Inspire Everyone to Take Action,* (Portfolio/Penguin, 2009; paperback ed., 2011), 105.

155 Gary Keller and Jay Papasan, *The One Thing: The Surprisingly Simple Truth behind Extraordinary Results* (Bard Press, 2013).

156 John W. Mitchell, *Fire Your Hiring Habits: Building an Environment That Attracts Top Talent in Today's Workforce* (Forbes Books, 2023), 55.

157 Elaine Welteroth, *More Than Enough: Claiming Space for Who You Are (No Matter What They Say)*, (Viking, 2019; Penguin, first paperback ed., 2020), 222.

158 Welteroth, 186.

159 Greg McKeown, "Hire Slow, Fire Fast," *Harvard Business Review,* March 3, 2014, https://hbr.org/2014/03/hire-slow-fire-fast.

160 Rocio Lorenzo and Martin Reeves, "How and Where Diversity Drives Financial Performance," *Harvard Business Review,* January 30, 2018, https://hbr.org/2018/01/how-and-where-diversity-drives-financial-performance.

161 Gilman, *You Can't Fire Everyone,* 5.

162 Gilman, vii.

163 Sarah Clarke, "Playing to Strengths — Do Your People Do What They Love, Every Single Day?," LinkedIn, May 17, 2018, https://www.linkedin.com/pulse /playing-strengths-do-your-people-what-love-every-single-clarke.

164 Curtiss Murphy, *What Makes Great Managers Great: How to Raise Engagement, Give Feedback, and Answer the Questions No One's Asking* (Houndstooth, 2023).

165 Betty Wong Ortiz, personal interview, November 3, 2023.

166 Alice Oglethorpe, personal interview, September 17, 2024.

167 Wong Ortiz, personal interview.

168 Hilderman, *Clone Yourself,* 157.

169 Julian Lute, "Company Culture—Meaning, Benefits and Strategies," Great Place To Work, August 27, 2021, https://www.greatplacetowork.com/resources/blog /company-culture-meaning-benefits-and-strategies.

170 "Happiest Countries in the World 2024," World Population Review, accessed March 5, 2024, https://worldpopulationreview.com/country-rankings/happiest -countries-in-the-world.

171 Lynn Sternberger, "Before Tequila Sunrise" episode, *The Bold Type,* August 29, 2017.

172 "The Best Companies to Work For in the US ," Great Place To Work, 2023, https://www.greatplacetowork.com/best-companies-in-the-us.

173 Ted Kitterman, "World's Best Workplaces Make Strong Case for Building Trust with Workers," Great Place To Work, November 16, 2023, https://www.great placetowork.com/resources/blog/worlds-best-workplaces-make-strong-case -for-building-trust-with-workers.

174 Lesley Jane Seymour and Ann Shoket, "How to motivate a millennial, and what to do if you work for one," *Reinvent Yourself* podcast (CoveyClub, June 28, 2017).

175 Stacy Mayer, *Promotions Made Easy: A Step-by-Step Guide to the Executive Suite* (Houndstooth, 2021), 26.

176 Div Acharya, "What Does Content Is King Actually Mean? A Beginner's Guide," LinkedIn, August 20, 2022, https://www.linkedin.com/pulse/what-does -content-king-actually-mean-a-beginners-guide-acharya.

177 The Talent Fairy (@thetalentfairy), "Why do editors make the best hires? Laura Kalehoff of Kalehoff Creative knows editors are great audience whisperers!" Instagram, October 8, 2019. https://www.instagram.com/p/B3XHPZen8KI.

178 Jon Fine, "The Amazing Success of 'Real Simple,'" *Advertising Age*, August 13, 2001, https://adage.com/article/media/amazing-success-real-simple/32253.

179 Julie V. Iovine, "Is Simplicity a Grand Illusion or Grand Plan?," *The New York Times*, March 23, 2000, https://www.nytimes.com/2000/03/23/garden/at -home-with-susan-wyland-is-simplicity-a-grand-illusion-or-grand-plan.html.

180 Patricia Orsini, "Magazine Hot List 2004: Highlights," *Adweek*, March 20, 2009, https://www.adweek.com/performance-marketing/magazine-hot-list-2004 -highlights-111715.

181 Kristin van Ogtrop, *Did I Say That Out Loud?: Midlife Indignities and How to Survive Them*, (Little, Brown Spark, 2021; first paperback ed., 2022), 103.

182 "The Container Store," Wikipedia, https://en.wikipedia.org/wiki/The _Container_Store.

183 John C Abell, "Wired iPad App Sells 24,000 Copies in First 24 Hours," *Wired*, May 27, 2010, https://www.wired.com/2010/05/wired-ipad-app-sells-24000 -copies-in-first-24-hours.

184 Sydney Ember, "Michelle Obama Guest-Edits Issue of *More* Magazine," *The New York Times*, June 11, 2015, https://www.nytimes.com/2015/06/12 /business/media/michelle-obama-guest-edits-issue-of-more-magazine.html.

185 Lesley Jane Seymour, "When Life Forced Me to Reinvent," CoveyClub Email Newsletter, October 6, 2023.

186 Seymour, October 6, 2023.

187 Seymour, October 6, 2023.

188 Sharon Bloyd-Peshkin and Charles Whitaker, eds., *Curating Culture: How Twentieth-Century Magazines Influenced America* (Rowman & Littlefield, 2021).

189 Susan Hodara, "Reader's Digest Acquires Reiman and Its Readers," *The New York Times*, May 26, 2002, https://www.nytimes.com/2002/05/26/nyregion /in-business-reader-s-digest-acquires-reiman-and-its-readers.html.

190 Roy Reiman, *'I Could Write a Book…'* (Grandhaven Group, 2005).

191 Sheila Webb, "Reaffirming the Pastoral Life: Reiman Publications 1970–2007," essay, in *Curating Culture: How Twentieth-Century Magazines Influenced America*, ed. Sharon Bloyd-Peshkin and Charles Whitaker (Rowman & Littlefield, 2021), 73–82.

192 Webb, 75.

193 Webb, 79.

194 Webb, 75.

195 "About Us," Peloton, https://www.onepeloton.com/company.

196 *Merriam-Webster.com Dictionary*, s.v. "peloton," https://www.merriam-webster .com/dictionary/peloton.

197 Tiffany Regaudie, "The Peloton Community Building Playbook," Banknotes, April 27, 2021, https://hashtagpaid.com/banknotes/the-peloton-community -building-playbook.

198 Antonia van der Meer, *Beach House Happy: The Joy of Living by the Water* (Oxmoor House, 2015), 9.

199 Blake Mycoskie, *Start Something That Matters,* (Spiegel & Grau, 2011; trade paperback ed., 2012).

200 Chris Lewis, "Books by Peloton Instructors & Other Peloton Books," Pelo Buddy, December 18, 2023, https://www.pelobuddy.com/peloton-books/.

201 Brian Dean, "Peloton Subscriber and Revenue Statistics (2024)," Backlinko, February 8, 2024, https://backlinko.com/peloton-users.

202 "Official Peloton Member Page," Facebook, https://www.facebook.com/groups /pelotonmembers/.

203 Kimberlee Morrison, "Why Consumers Share User Generated Content (Infographic)," *Adweek,* May 17, 2016, https.//www.adweek.com/performance -marketing/why-consumers-share-user-generated-content-infographic/.

204 "Member Stories," Peloton, accessed September 15, 2024. https://www.one peloton.com/blog/topic/connect/member-stories.

205 "About the Program," lululemon, accessed March 8, 2024, https://shop .lululemon.com/ambassadors/about-the-program.

206 Lesley Jane Seymour, personal interview, October 9, 2023.

207 Jason Miller, "The Rise of Storytelling in Marketing—as Told by LinkedIn Data," LinkedIn, December 4, 2017, https://www.linkedin.com/business/marketing /blog/content-marketing/the-rise-of-storytelling-in-marketing-as-told-by -linkedin-data.

208 Joseph Campbell, *The Hero with a Thousand Faces,* (New World Library, 1949; third ed., 2008).

209 Donald Miller, *Building a StoryBrand: Clarify Your Message so Customers Will Listen* (HarperCollins Leadership, 2017).

210 The Talent Fairy (@thetalentfairy), "No one knows the consumer like an editor." Instagram, February 25, 2020. https://www.instagram.com/p/B9AAXwnHPIb.

211 Miller, *Business Made Simple,* 101.

212 Amy Cuddy, *Presence: Bringing Your Boldest Self to Your Biggest Challenges* (Little, Brown and Company, 2015), 71–72.

213 *Prevention*, January 2024.

214 SelfPublishing.com, accessed March 9, 2024, https://selfpublishing.com.

215 "I Know It When I See It," Wikipedia, https://en.wikipedia.org/wiki/I_know _it_when_I_see_it.

216 "A Hotel Brand for Every Type of Journey," Marriott, accessed March 20, 2024, https://www.marriott.com/marriott-brands/explore-our-brands.mi.

217 "Marriott Luxury Brands," Marriott, accessed November 1, 2024, https://www. hotel-development.marriott.com/brands/luxury-brands

218 "W Hotels Worldwide: A (Style) Guide to Worldwide Travel," Naoto Ono Creative, accessed October 13, 2024, https://www.naotoono.com/work/w -hotels-worldwide-identity.

219 "Marriott Luxury Brands," Marriott.

220 The Luxury Collection Visual Brand Identity Guidelines, January 2019.

221 Lee, personal interview.

222 Brian Moylan, "*Men's Health* Loved This Cover so Much They Used It Twice," Gawker, December 10, 2009, https://www.gawkerarchives.com/5423710 /mens-health-loved-this-cover-so-much-they-used-it-twice.

223 Keith J. Kelly, "*NY Times* Prepares to Cut Two Dozen Positions," *New York Post*, December 11, 2009, https://nypost.com/2009/12/11/ny-times -prepares-to-cut-two-dozen-positions.

224 Robert Quigley, "Further Clarification from *Men's Health*: More on Repeated Cover Lines," Mediaite, December 11, 2009, https://www.mediaite.com/print /mens-health-repeated-covers-clarification.

225 Feifer, *Build for Tomorrow,* 164–168.

226 White, *I Shouldn't Be Telling You This,* 142–143.

227 Chandra Turner, "Not-so-Secret Advice from Editors Who Pivoted to Content Marketing and Branded Content," The Talent Fairy powered by Ed2010, March 30, 2022, https://ed2010.com/generic/unsolicited-advice/advice-from-editors -who-left-editorial-for-content-marketing-and-branded-content.

228 SelfPublishing.com homepage, accessed March 9, 2024, https://selfpublishing .com.

229 Dan S. Kennedy, *The Ultimate Sales Letter: Attract New Customers, Boost Your Sales* (Adams Media, 2011), 109.

230 John Cook, "Update: *Men's Health* Stopped Writing New Cover Lines Years Ago," Gawker, December 11, 2009, https://www.gawkerarchives.com/5424291 /update-mens-health-stopped-writing-new-cover-lines-years-ago.

231 Feifer, *Build for Tomorrow,* 181.

232 Sarah Z. Wexler, personal interview, December 5, 2023.

233 "Oprah Winfrey's Official Biography," Oprah.com, May 17, 2011, https://www .oprah.com/pressroom/oprah-winfreys-official-biography/3.

234 Alex Kuczynski, "Trading on Hollywood Magic; Celebrities Push Models off Women's Magazine Covers," *The New York Times*, January 30, 1999, https:// www.nytimes.com/1999/01/30/business/trading-on-hollywood-magic -celebrities-push-models-off-women-s-magazine-covers.html.

235 Alina Tugend, "Too Many Choices: A Problem That Can Paralyze," *The New York Times,* February 26, 2010, http://www.nytimes.com/2010/02/27/your -money/27shortcuts.html.

236 Miller, *Business Made Simple*, 118.

237 Miller, 118.

238 Ben Sherry, "He Built Dollar Shave Club and Sold It for $1 Billion…," *Inc.*, October 21, 2022, https://www.inc.com/ben-sherry/michael-dubin-dollar -shave-club.html.

239 Anita Roddick, *Body and Soul: Profits with Principles, The Amazing Success Story of Anita Roddick & The Body Shop* (Crown, 1991).

240 "About Us," The Body Shop, accessed September 15, 2024, https://careers .thebodyshop.com/content/About-Us-The-Body-Shop/?locale=en_US.

241 "International Directory of Company Histories," Encyclopedia.com, accessed July 16, 2024, https://www.encyclopedia.com/books/politics-and -business-magazines/lebhar-friedman-inc.

242 Worstofall Design homepage, accessed March 9, 2024, https://worstofalldesign .com.

243 Alli Webb, *The Messy Truth: How I Sold My Business for Millions but Almost Lost Myself* (Harper Horizon, 2023).

244 Melanie Haid, "Most Popular Dog Breeds of 2022," American Kennel Club, May 23, 2023, https://www.akc.org/expert-advice/dog-breeds/most-popular -dog-breeds-2022.

245 Iger, *The Ride of a Lifetime*, 61.

246 "Sara Blakely," *Forbes*, accessed September 19, 2024, https://www.forbes.com /profile/sara-blakely.

247 James Clear, *Atomic Habits: An Easy & Proven Way to Build Good Habits & Break Bad Ones* (Avery, 2018), 154–155.

248 Glenn Collins, "Decks and the City," *The New York Times*, September 8, 2004, https://www.nytimes.com/2004/09/08/nyregion/decks-and-the-city.html.

249 Victor Maze, "Unexpectedly, Uruguay," *Coastal Living*, November 2015, 42.

250 Shannon Hale (@haleshannon), "When writing a first draft, I have to remind myself constantly that I'm only shoveling sand into a box so later I can build castles." Twitter, August 27, 2015, https://twitter.com/haleshannon/status /636907891379736576?lang=en.

251 Keith J. Kelly, "Meredith/AMEX Slashes Staff, Ends Print of Departures and Centurion Mags," *New York Post*, March 25, 2021, https://nypost.com/2021 /03/25/meredith-slashes-staff-ends-print-of-departures-and-centurion-mags/.

252 "Time Out Markets," Time Out for Business, https://business.timeout.group /united-states/product/markets/.

253 "The Best of Lisbon," Time Out Market, https://www.timeoutmarket.com /lisboa/en/concept/.

254 "Time Out Market," *Time Out*, https://www.timeout.com/about/market.

Thanks for reading!
What did you think?

I love to hear success stories and would appreciate your input to make the next edition of this book even better!

Please take one minute to leave a helpful review on Amazon, letting me know what you thought of the book.

To leave your review, scan this code or visit
Review.LeadLikeAnEditor.com

Thanks so much!

Victor Maze

Extra credit: If you use the GoodReads website or app, you can leave a review there as well!

Made in United States
Orlando, FL
18 January 2025

57422600R10163